The European Union and National Civil Procedure

Editors:
Anna Nylund and
Bart Krans

The European Union and National Civil Procedure

intersentia

METRO

Ius Commune Europaeum

Intersentia Ltd
Sheraton House | Castle Park
Cambridge | CB3 0AX | United Kingdom
Tel.: +44 1223 370 170 | Fax: +44 1223 370 169
Email: mail@intersentia.co.uk
www.intersentia.com | www.intersentia.co.uk

Distribution for the UK and Ireland:
NBN International
Airport Business Centre, 10 Thornbury Road
Plymouth, PL6 7 PP
United Kingdom
Tel.: +44 1752 202 301 | Fax: +44 1752 202 331
Email: orders@nbninternational.com

Distribution for Europe and all other countries:
Intersentia Publishing nv
Groenstraat 31
2640 Mortsel
Belgium
Tel.: +32 3 680 15 50 | Fax: +32 3 658 71 21
Email: mail@intersentia.be

Distribution for the USA and Canada:
International Specialized Book Services
920 NE 58th Ave. Suite 300
Portland, OR 97213
USA
Tel.: +1 800 944 6190 (toll free) | Fax: +1 503 280 8832
Email: info@isbs.com

The European Union and National Civil Procedure

ISBN 978-1-78068-380-5
D/2016/7849/91
NUR 822

British Library Cataloguing in Publication Data. A catalogue record for this book is available from the British Library.

CONTENTS

ABOUT THE AUTHORS

Neil Andrews is professor of Civil Justice and Private Law, University of Cambridge. His works include *Andrews on Civil Processes* (2 volumes, Intersentia, Cambridge, 2013; *Contract Law* (2nd edn, Cambridge University Press, 2015). Nha1000@cam.ac.uk

Isabelle Després is a full professor at the University of Nantes. She studied in Saarbrücken and Strasbourg, where she defended her thesis on French pre-trial discovery. She specializes in civil procedure and edited the French civil procedure code commentaries for Dalloz for 10 years. Isabelle.despres@univ-nantes.fr

Aleš Galič is a professor of civil procedure, private international law and arbitration at the University of Ljubljana, Faculty of Law, Slovenia. He is also a senior legal advisor to the Slovenian Constitutional Court. Ales.galic@pf.uni-lj.si

Viktória Harsági is professor and Head of Department at Pázmány Péter Catholic University Faculty of Law, Department of Civil Procedure Law in Budapest, and lecturer at the Andrássy Gyula German Speaking University in Budapest. Harsagi.viktoria@jak.ppke.hu

Wolfgang Hau, Dr., is a full professor at the University of Passau (chair for private law, civil procedure, and private international law) and part-time judge at the Higher Regional Court of Munich. hau@uni-passau.de

Bart Krans is a full professor at the University of Leiden (chair for Private Law and Civil Procedure Law). Among his publications are books on the influence of EU law on Dutch civil procedure law, on the law of evidence and on the law of obligations. He is a member of several editorial boards in his fields. Previously he was a full professor at the University of Groningen. h.b.krans@law.leidenuniv.nl

Anna Nylund is professor at University of Tromsø – the Arctic University of Norway. Her teaching and research includes issues in national and comparative civil procedure, and issues in alternative dispute resolution, with emphasis on mediation. She studied law at the University of Helsinki and defended her doctoral thesis on access to second courts there. She is a member of several international scholarly associations in her fields. Anna.nylund@uit.no

Clement Salung Petersen (PH.D., LL.M.) is an Associate Professor at the University of Copenhagen, Faculty of Law. His main areas of research are civil procedure and enforcement of intellectual property rights. Clement.petersen@jur.ku.dk

Anna Piszcz Dr. Hab., is professor at the University of Białystok (Poland), Faculty of Law, Temporary on Duty of Chairman of the Department of Public Economic Law; member of the Advisory Board to the President of the Office for Competition and Consumer Protection. piszcz@uwb.edu.pl

Piet Taelman is a senior full professor at Ghent University Law School (Belgium). He teaches courses on Civil Procedure and has written on a wide variety of topics on civil procedural law in national and international journals and book chapters. He has been admitted to the Ghent Bar in 1982 and has practised as a lawyer and arbitrator during almost the whole of his academic career. Piet Taelman served as dean of the Ghent Law School from October 2008 till September 2014. Piet.taelman@ugent.be

Anna Wallerman received her LL.D. degree in 2015 from the University of Gothenburg, where she is currently an associate senior lecturer. She has previously been a visiting scholar at the universities of Oxford and Zürich. Her research interests are civil procedure and EU law. Anna.wallerman@law.gu.se

LIST OF ABBREVIATIONS

ADR	Alternative Dispute Resolution
APC	Polish Act on the Pursuit of Claims in Group Proceedings
BGBl	Bundesgesetzblatt
CJEU	Court of Justice of the European Union
CJP	Code of Judicial Procedure (Sweden)
CJQ	Civil Justice Quarterly
CMLR	Common Market Law Review
CPA	Civil Procedure Act (Slovenia)
CPC	Civil Procedure Code (Netherlands), (Poland)
DG	Directorate General
EC	European Community
EC-Treaty	Treaty Establishing the European Community
ECHR	European Convention on Human Rights
ECJ	European Court of Justice
ECtHR	European Court of Human Rights
ECR	European Court Reports
EEA	European Economic Area
EEC	European Economic Community
EFTA	European Free Trade Association
ERPL	European Review of Private Law
ERT	Europarättslig tidskrift
EU	European Union
EUCFR	European Union Charter of Fundamental Rights
EuZW	Europäische Zeitschrift für Wirtschaftsrecht
GPR	GPR – Zeitschrift für das Privatrecht der Europäischen Union
HCCP	Hungaria Code of Civil Procedure
IIC	International Review of Intellectual Property and Competition Law
IP	Intellectual Property
IPrax	Praxis des Internationalen Privat- und Verfahrensrechts
JT	Juridisk tidskrift
JZ	JuristenZeitung
LGDJ	Librairie générale de droit et de jurisprudence
NIR	Nordiskt immateriellt rättsskydd

NJA	Nytt juridiskt arkiv
NJW	Neue Juristische Wochenschrift
ODR	Online Dispute Resolution
OJ	Official Journal
OSP	Orzecznictwo Sadów Polskich
PIL	Private International Law
Rt.	Retstidende
RÅ	Regeringsrättens årsbok
TFEU	Treaty on the Functioning of the European Union
TRIPS	The Agreement on Trade-Related Aspects of Intellectual Property Rights
WTO	World Trade Organisation
ZEuP	Zeitschrift für Europäisches Privatrecht
ZPO	Zivilprozessordnung (German Code of Civil Procedure)
ZZP	Zeitschrift für Zivilprozess

Anna Nylund and
Bart Krans*

THE EUROPEAN UNION AND NATIONAL CIVIL PROCEDURE – A ROCKY ROAD OR A SMOOTH PROCESS?

Europe is in a period of increasing Europeanisation of civil procedure. The European Union (EU) relies on national systems to apply and enforce EU law and it leaves procedural issues to the Member States. Therefore, many procedural elements of EU law are based on decentralised enforcement. According to the Rewe/Comet-doctrine, Member States have 'procedural autonomy' as long as the national civil procedure complies with the principles of equivalent and efficient enforcement.[1] In the course of the years, the EU court has ruled many times on topics that can be referred to as some form of European procedural law.

The Amsterdam Treaty of 1997 gave the EU increased competencies in civil justice. Article 81 of the Treaty of the Functioning of the European Union (TFEU)[2], which gives the EU the power to develop judicial cooperation in civil matters with cross-border implications, and article 114 on the adopting measures to establish and improve the functioning of the internal market, give EU competence to issue secondary law in the field of civil justice. Thus, EU has gained significantly more influence on national civil procedure for both cross-border and purely national cases. Further, the EU Fundamental Rights Charter[3], in particular article 47 giving a right to an effective remedy and to a fair trial, contributes to the expansion of powers within the field of civil justice.

According to Bart Krans, Europeanisation of civil procedure consists of three pillars. The *first pillar* consists of influences from the European Convention on Human Rights and the Charter of Fundamental Rights. The *second pillar* consists of the growing number of European secondary law concerning the crossroads of civil procedure law and private international law, especially cross-border proceedings and judicial cooperation, such as the Brussels I Regulation[4], the Regulation on European

* Anna Nylund is Professor of Law at the Faculty of Law, University of Tromsø - The Arctic University of Norway. Bart Krans is Full Professor of Private Law and Civil Procedure Law, Leiden University, the Netherlands.

1 Case 33–76 *Rewe-Zentralfinanz eG et Rewe-Zentral AG v Landwirtschaftskammer für das Saarland* [1976] ECLI:EU:C:1976:188.

2 Consolidated Version [2012] OJ C326/47.

3 Charter of Fundamental Rights of the European Union [2012]OJ C326/391,.

4 Regulation (EU) 1215/2012 on jurisdiction and the recognition and enforcement of judgments in civil and commercial matters [2012] OJ L351/1.

Enforcement Orders[5] and the Small Claims Regulation.[6] The *third pillar* can be characterised as 'invisible' as it consists of a number of issues that are not regulated in a coherent way. Partly it emanates from case law from the European Court limiting procedural autonomy to promote equivalent and efficient application of EU law. Partly it emanates from procedural rules in Directives. Many Directives of a mainly substantive nature include procedural (or quasi-procedural) rules that influence national civil procedure. Examples of the third pillar are *inter alia* rules on costs and the free choice of a lawyer; *ex officio* application of EU (consumer and competition) law;, and rules on disclosure of evidence in intellectual property right cases and anti-trust law.[7]

Some of the EU instruments, especially in the third or second pillar, may lead to *spontaneous – or spillover – harmonisation*. Some of the secondary law in the second pillar, such as the European Small Claims Regulation and the Mediation Directive[8], function as a model for national legislation. Several Member States have introduced court-connected mediation for all cases rather than only cross-border cases to avoid discrimination between purely national and cross-border cases or difference in rules. In the third pillar, spillover harmonisation occurs when rules for a narrow set of specific cases are extended to other types of cases or even all cases to avoid internal fragmentation. For instance, rules on disclosure of evidence in anti-trust cases can lead to the introduction of (more) general rules on disclosure, or the introduction of collective redress for limited types of claims to more general rules on collective redress.

The supremacy of EU law and, *inter alia*, the requirements of effectiveness and equivalence may be relevant for several topics of national civil procedural law, for example *ex officio* application of EU law, enforcement, insolvency proceedings, evidence, etc. Both EU legislation and doctrinal changes in EU case law (stressing the direct enforceability of EU law or otherwise) may very well touch upon various topics of the procedural law of the Member States. This leads to several questions. Has EU law affected the court system, and if so how? Has EU law led to changes in legal culture? Which doctrines, which pieces of legislation or features in legislation pose problems for national civil procedure? Are some legal systems or topics more prone to integrate European rules, and are others more resistant to changes?

This book focuses on national law and the impact of EU legislation, case law and policies on national law, not EU law as such.[9] The contributions in this book explore

5 Regulation (EC) 805/2004 creating a European Enforcement Order for uncontested claims [2004] OJ L143/15.

6 Regulation (EC) 861/2007 establishing a European Small Claims Procedure [2007] OJ L1999/1.

7 For a more detailed discussion, see Bart Krans, 'EU Law and National Civil Procedure Law: An Invisible Pillar' 23 European Review of Private Law 567.

8 Directive (EC) 52/2008 on certain aspects of mediation in civil and commercial matters [2008] OJ L136/3.

9 For an overview of EU law related to the civil justice area, see inter alia Eva Storskrubb, *Civil procedure and EU law: a policy area uncovered* (Oxford University Press 2008), Viktoria Harsagi and Miklos Kengyel (eds.), *Der Einfluss des Europäischen Zivilverfahrensrechts auf die nationalen Rechtsordnungen* (Nomos 2009), Burkhard Hess, *Europäisches Zivilprozessrecht: ein Lehrbuch* (Hüthig Jehle Rehm 2010) and Burkhard Hess, Maria Bergström and Eva Storskrubb (eds), *EU Civil Justice. Current Issues and Future Outlook* (Hart 2016).

Europeanisation of national civil procedure law. The book aims to uncover, understand and compare how the national civil procedure in different countries react to Europeanisation, and therefore to reveal and understand similarities and divergences between different countries.

The countries included in the study consist of large and small states; old Member States and new Member States, even a non-Member State; countries representing civil law, common law, former socialist systems and Scandinavian legal cultures. With a view to accessibility the papers are ranged in alphabetical order: Belgium (Piet Taelman), Denmark (Clement Salung Petersen), England (Neil Andrews), France (Isabelle Després), Germany (Wolfgang Hau), Hungary (Viktória Harsági), the Netherlands (Bart Krans), Norway (Anny Nylund), Poland (Anna Piszcz), Slovenia (Aleš Galič), and Sweden (Anna Wallerman).

All the authors have taken their national system as a starting point. A central topic is how the civil procedure systems of the various Member States have reacted to EU law. The authors were asked to go into the question whether EU legislation or EU case law was cause for reforms of parts of national civil procedure law. This focus also means that the aim of this book is not to go into the consequences of EU Regulations for several types of cross border issues (small claims etc.). However, if this type of Regulations has led to noticeable changes in the national system – spontaneous harmonisation – those changes are disseminated. From the range of possible topics, the authors were asked to go into the changes they consider most relevant or interesting for their country.

By comparing and analyzing the findings in the several Member States, we hope to provide, in addition to the aforementioned central question, the reader some insight on several topics. Are there differences in the impact of EU Law on national civil procdure law of the Member States, and if so, what are they? Are there any general trends in the way the procedural systems of national Member States react to EU law? Are there differences in the way Member States react to the EU? If so, can a specific factor be determined that explain these differences? In the concluding chapter we will come back on these questions.

It is beyond the scope of this study to offer a comprehensive analysis of the level, depth or method of Europeanisation of EU Member States or particular countries. The goal is rather to offer a first sketch of some similarities and differences. It may be difficult to attribute similarities and differences to particular attributes of each country, as this is a general study on the impact of EU law, not just focusing on national cases or on cross border cases. The texts are not comprehensive analyses of Europeanisation of the civil procedure of the particular country. However, we believe the contributions offer an initial understanding of the main topic and relevant information for practitioners, academics and policy makers throughout Europe.

The papers were (in draft) presented and discussed during a seminar at the university in Tromsø in November 2015. That was, at least for us, an inspiring meeting. Subsequently the papers were altered.

We would like to express our gratitude to the University of Tromsø – the Arctic University of Norway and the Fridtjof Nansen Fund for their financial contribution. It made both the seminar and the publication of the book possible. Emma Tamba, student in Tromsø, has provided very valuable assistance while preparing the submitted papers for publication. Of course we are also grateful to all the authors for their participation and timely delivery of the papers. For us, it made the collaboration a joyful experience.

Piet Taelman*

SOME EUROPEAN CHALLENGES FOR BELGIAN CIVIL PROCEDURE

1. The Invisible Pillar Raises Serious Compatibility Issues between EU (Case) Law and Belgian Civil Procedure Law

The European influence on national civil procedural law is multi-dimensional. As has been described by Bart Krans[1], a large part of the Europeanisation of national procedural law derives from what he has called the 'invisible pillar'. Krans showed us not only the existence of such a type of European influence, but also demonstrated how vast this area is and that it covers a wide variety of topics. The invisible pillar differs from two other pillars of Europeanisation described by Krans[2] because it is much less visible. It offers an intriguing interplay between European rules and decisions at one hand and national rules and court judgements at the other hand, due to the rather sneaky way in which it affects rules and procedural behaviour of judges and parties. Its impact is far-reaching and may not be underestimated as will be illustrated below.

The invisible pillar is two-headed.[3] The first part of this pillar follows from the role of national civil procedure law in enforcing EU law. The European Court of Justice stressed at several occasions the principle of procedural autonomy of Member States. which implies that the national legal system of each Member State has to regulate the procedural rules governing the actions which are to ensure respect for the rights which individuals derive from EU law. As a consequence, EU law (often) needs national civil procedure law to find its way to European citizens. National courts have the duty to apply their procedural law in accordance with the so-called Rewe/Comet rule, i.e. in compliance with the principles of equivalence and effectiveness.[4]

* Senior Full Professor Department of Interdisciplinary Study of Law, Private Law and Business Law Ghent University, Belgium.

1 Bart Krans, 'EU Law and National Civil Procedure Law: An Invisible Pillar' [2015] ERPL 567–588.

2 The first pillar concerns the ECHR and Charter of the EU Fundamental Rights; the second pillar is formed by the growing number of European regulations on various subjects concerning the crossroads of civil procedure law and private international law on the one hand, and concerning European procedure law in civil matters of a cross-border nature on the other hand.

3 Krans (n 1) 572.

4 Case C-473/00 *Cofidis v Fredout* [2002] ECLI:EU:C:2002:705, para. 28; Case C-415/11 *Mohamed Aziz* [2013] ECLI:EU:C:2013:164 paras 50 and 53: 'As regards the principle of effectiveness, it is the Court's settled case-law that every case in which the question arises as to whether a national procedural

An example of this first area of the invisible pillar highlighted by Krans[5] concerns the *ex officio* (of own motion of a judge or a court) application of EU Law in the field of consumer protection.[6] Article 6 (1) of the Directive on unfair terms in consumer contracts provides: 'Member States shall lay down that unfair terms used in a contract concluded with a consumer by a seller or supplier shall, as provided for under their national law, not be binding on the consumer and that the contract shall continue to bind the parties upon those terms if it is capable of continuing in existence without the unfair terms.' Unfair terms control is based on the idea of imbalance between the consumer and the seller or supplier. The consumer is in a weak position vis-à-vis the trader as regards both his bargaining power and his level of knowledge. Basically this leads to the consumer agreeing to so-called general business conditions drawn up in advance by the trader without being able to influence the content of those terms.[7] In order to guarantee the protection intended by the Directive, the Court has stated on a number of occasions that the imbalance may be corrected only by positive action unconnected with the actual parties to the contract.[8] In the exercise of the functions incumbent upon it under the provisions of the Directive, the national court must ascertain whether a contractual term, which is the subject of the dispute before it, falls within the scope of that Directive. If it does, that court must assess that term, if necessary, of its own motion, in the light of the requirements of consumer protection laid down by that Directive.[9]

In the *Invitel* case[10] the Hungarian national consumer protection authority brought an action for an injunction against Invitel, a fixed-line telephone network operator, concerning the use of Invitel's allegedly unfair terms in its contracts concluded with consumers. The CJEU confirmed in its preliminary ruling once more that where the unfair nature of a term in the general business conditions (GBC) has been acknowledged, national courts are required of their own motion – also with regard to the future – to ensure that consumers who have concluded a contract with the seller or supplier to which those GBC apply will not be bound by that term. The Court stressed that the declaration of invalidity of an unfair term included in the standard terms of consumers contracts in an action based on Article 7 of the Directive on unfair terms in consumer contracts,

provision makes the application of European Union law impossible or excessively difficult must be analysed by reference to the role of that provision in the procedure, its progress and its special features, viewed as a whole, before the various national bodies'.

5 Krans (n 1) 573–576.

6 See especially Council Directive (EEC) 93/13 on unfair terms in consumer contracts [1993] OJ L95/29; EP and Council Directive 2011/83 on consumer rights, amending Council Directive (EEC) 93/13 and EP and Council Directive 1999/44 repealing Council Directive (EEC) 85/577 and EP and Council Directive 97/7 [2011] OJ L304/64.

7 See references cited by Krans (n 1) footnote 25; Case C-453/10 *Pereničová-Perenič v SOS finance spol. s r. o* [2012] ECLI:EU:C:2012:144, para 27; Case C-472/10 *Nemzeti Fogyasztóvédelmi Hatóság v Invitel Távközlési Zrt.* [2012] ECLI:EU:C:2012:242.

8 Case C-241/98 *Océano Grupo Editorial and Salvat Editores* [2000] ECLI:EU:C:2000:346, para. 27; Case C-168/05 *Elisa Mostaza Claro v Centro móvil Milenium SL* [2006] ECLI:EU:C:2006:675, para. 26.

9 Case C-137/08 *Pénzügyi Lízing Zrt. V Ferenc Schneider* [2010] ECLI:EU:C:2010:659, para. 49.

10 Case C-472/10 *Invitel* 26 April 2012, ECLI:EU:C:2012:242.

affects *all* consumers who concluded with Invitel a contract to which the same GBC apply, including those consumers who were not party to the injunction proceedings.

The CJEU's decision in the *Invitel* case delivers a perfect illustration that *ex officio* application of EU law may go far beyond having a serious effect on the mutual obligations imposed on the parties. Although EU (case) law formally recognises the principle of procedural autonomy of the Member States, the European ruling in the *Invitel* case affects the Belgian rules on *res judicata*, one of the basic principles of the national justice system. Moreover, *res judicata* has been qualified by the Court of Justice as an expression of the principle of legal certainty.

According to Belgian law, *res judicata*[11] is strictly limited to the parties involved in the case that led to the judgement. Its effects work only *inter partes*. It does not affect natural or legal persons who were not involved in the legal proceedings concluded by the decision of the judge. However, in cases in which the *Invitel* ruling applies, Belgian judges will be forced to recognise an *erga omnes* effect of *res judicata* vested in those decisions. As a consequence, any consumer who has concluded a contract with e.g. the telecom provider concerned will be allowed to call upon the *res judicata* of a decision rendered against that provider upon its GBC, although this consumer was not involved in the precedent proceedings. It illustrates that EU case law may lead to inconsistency at the national level. It transforms, in a rather hidden or nontransparent way, in a particular kind of cases the significance of a fundamental principle of Belgian civil procedure law. By doing so it causes internal fragmentation.

The second area of the invisible pillar concerns procedural rules in Directives. As Krans has pointed out, a vast list of procedural topics has been touched upon by Directives.[12] Costs is one of them and recent Belgian case law offers an example of friction caused by Article 14 of the IP Rights Enforcement Directive[13], which states: 'Member States shall ensure that reasonable and proportionate legal costs and other expenses incurred by the successful party shall, as a general rule, be borne by the unsuccessful party, unless equity does not allow this.'[14] The CJEU reminded in its *Realchemie* judgment

11 A Belgian judgment deciding on (one or several aspects of) the merits of the claim is vested with *res judicata* as soon as it is pronounced by the judge, even if the judicial decision can still be reviewed (e.g. *via* appellate proceedings). *Res judicata* implies among other things that the introduction of a new claim which takes the same already adjudicated issues into account, is at that stage inadmissible (see Articles 23–25 Belgian Judicial Code (hereinafter: BJC)).

12 Krans (n 1) 572.

13 EP and Council Directive (EC) 2004/48 on the enforcement of intellectual property rights [2004] OJ L195/16.

14 Compare Article 45, section 2 TRIPS: 'The judicial authorities shall also have the authority to order the infringer to pay the right holder expenses, which may include appropriate attorney's fees. In appropriate cases, Members may authorise the judicial authorities to order recovery of profits and/or payment of pre-established damages even where the infringer did not knowingly, or with reasonable grounds to know, engage in infringing activity'. This rule does not have direct effect in Belgium. Art. 14 of the Directive served as a source of inspiration for art. 69, section 1 of the Agreement on a Unified Patent Court (2013/C 175/01): 'Reasonable and proportionate legal costs and other expenses incurred by the successful party shall, as a general rule, be borne by the unsuccessful party, unless equity requires otherwise, up to a ceiling set in accordance with the Rules of Procedure'. The United Patent court Consultation Document 'Rules on court fees and recoverable costs', acknowledges that there is no

that this provision aims to strengthen the level of protection of intellectual property, by avoiding the situation in which an injured party is deterred from bringing legal proceedings in order to protect his rights.[15] Recital 17 of the Directive explains that 'measures, procedures and remedies provided for in this Directive should be determined in each case in such a manner as to take due account of the specific characteristics of that case, including the specific features of each intellectual property right and, where appropriate, the intentional or unintentional character of the infringement'. Article 3 of the Directive provides that measures, procedures and remedies to ensure the enforcement of the intellectual property rights covered by this legal instrument shall be fair and equitable and shall not be unnecessarily complicated or costly.

Although some have pleaded that also this section of the Directive required implementation[16] because of the nature of IP-cases, especially the complexity of the legal and technical issues at stake which makes e.g. patent litigation quite expensive,[17] the Belgian legislator did not step into action and did not transpose this provision. As a result the general rules upon the recoverability of lawyers' fees are applicable. Those rules have been subject to a major statutory reform in 2007, introducing a (fixed or variable flat-rated) recoverability of lawyers' fees.[18]

Article 1022 BJC defines the expenses of a judicial procedure as a fixed compensation for the expenses and fees of the lawyer of the winning or successful party. 'Fixed' implies that not the actual fees are recoverable: they are limited to a fixed amount, in principle related to the amount of the claim. This amount is deemed to recover the lawyers' fees and costs of that party. The word 'lawyer' means that the successful party is only entitled to expenses of a judicial procedure if this party was assisted and/or represented by a lawyer during the proceedings. Hence, a party which defends its own legal interest during judicial proceedings, is not entitled to these expenses.

The (basic) amount of the judicial expenses, which are determined by Royal Decree,[19] can be increased or diminished by the judge if specifically motivated, at the request of one of the parties, as the occasion arises after interpellation by the judge (not *ex officio*), without exceeding the fixed minimum and maximum amounts. The judge has to take into account the following criteria, when increasing or decreasing the basic amount: the financial abilities of the forfeiting parties (in order to diminish the amount); the complexity of the litigation; the contractually agreed compensation for the winning party; the manifestly unreasonable nature of the situation.

common legal basis within the 25 Member States as to the question of what reasonable representation costs are and when they become excessive, <www.unified-patentcourt.org/images/documents/court_fees_and_recoverable_costs_consultation.pdf> (accessed 3 January 2016).

15 Case C-406/09 *Realchemie Nederland BV v Bayer CropSience AG* [2011] ECLI:EU:C:2011:668, para. 48.

16 Implementation of other provisions of this Directive led to the introduction of a specific type of seizure and special rules on provisional measures in IP-cases in Belgium (see Articles 1369*bis*/1–1369*ter* BJC).

17 J. Deene, 'De rechtsplegingsvergoeding in procedures inzake intellectuele rechten: een *sui generis*-regime?' [2011–12] RW 946–953.

18 Vincent Sagaert and Ilse Samoy, 'Cost and Fee Allocation in Civil Procedure' International Academy of Comparative Law (2010) <www-personal.umich.edu/~purzel/national_reports/Belgium.pdf> accessed 3 January 2016.

19 Royal Decree of 26 October 2007, Moniteur belge [Official Gazette of Belgium] 9 November 2007.

No party can be forced to pay additional compensation for the lawyer's intervention of the other party, above the amount of the expenses of judicial procedure. Since the 2007 reform the part of the lawyers' fees of the winning party exceeding the fixed expenses, cannot longer be claimed to the losing party on another basis, e.g. the rules on contractual or extra-contractual liability.

Concerning the fees and costs of technical experts assisting parties in legal proceedings, Belgian case law established that such fees and costs are only recoverable in the event the losing party has committed a (contractual[20] or extra-contractual[21]) fault and the fees and costs paid to those experts are the inevitable consequence thereof.

On several occasions, the question has been raised whether those (reformed) Belgian rules for recovery of fees and costs of lawyers and technical experts assisting a party in legal proceedings are compatible with the IP rights enforcement Directive. The Antwerp Court of Appeal ruled that these mechanisms are not in compliance with the Directive.[22] As a consequence the totality of the actual fees and costs of the lawyer assisting or representing the winning party is, in principle, to be taken into account for compensation. Several decisions of the Ghent Court of Appeal presume that the reformed rules on recoverability of lawyers' fees and costs are compliant with this Directive as they are of a more recent date than the Directive and the Agreement on Trade-Related Aspects of Intellectual Property Rights (TRIPS).[23]

Last year the Antwerp Court of Appeal[24] referred the issue to the CJEU in a patent dispute, opposing a patentee (the US-based company United Video Properties) to an alleged patent infringing party (Telenet, a major player on the Belgian telecom market). Telenet ultimately won the case but it incurred legal costs and expenses[25], which considerably exceeded those recoverable under Belgian law. It asserted that especially patent cases are extremely complex and require comprehensive written pleadings and assistance of technical experts. The Court of Appeal stated that also other, i.e. non-IP, cases might be complex and require assistance of specialists. However, the Court agreed to refer the issue to the CJEU for a preliminary ruling. It raised the two following questions to the Luxemburg based Court:

- Do the terms 'reasonable and proportionate legal and other costs' in Article 14 of the IP rights enforcement Directive oppose against Belgian legislation which allows the

20 Supreme Court AR C.13.0328.N, 24 April 2014; Supreme Court AR C.11.0656.F, 15 November 2013; Supreme Court AR C.01.0186.F, 2 September 2004; all these decisions of Belgians' Supreme Court (*Hof van Cassatie/Cour de cassation*) are accessible in Dutch and French on their date via <cassonline.be> accessed 29 December 2015.

21 Supreme Court AR C.10.0425.N, 1 March 2012; Supreme Court 16 November 2006, AR C.05.0124.F <cassonline.be> accessed 29 December 2015.

22 Court of Appeal Antwerp 15 June 2009, IRDI 2010, 286.

23 Court of Appeal Ghent 2 March 2009 Jaarboek Handelspraktijken en Mededinging 2009 761; Court of Appeal Ghent 24 June 2013 Ing. Cons. 2014 78.

24 Court of Appeal Antwerp 26 January 2015 IEF 14605.

25 Telenet paid € 185,462.55 as fees to its lawyers and € 40,400 as costs to its patent agent, of which the first judge in its contested judgment considered only an amount of € 11,000 recoverable vis-à-vis the unsuccessful party under the Belgian legal expenses and cost rules of 2007.

court to take into consideration certain specific characteristics particular to the case and provided in a system of variable fixed rates for lawyers' fees and costs?
- Do the terms 'reasonable and proportionate legal and other costs' in Article 14 of the IP rights enforcement Directive oppose against case law according to which the fees and costs of a technical expert are only recoverable in the event of fault (contractual or extra-contractual)?

The case, known as C-57/15, is still pending for the EU Court of Justice. The hearing took place on 14 January 2016. Although it is not for the first time the Court is questioned about the compatibility of detailed domestic procedural rules of a Member State governing expenses and costs of court actions with the principles of effectiveness and equivalence,[26] it remains quite difficult to predict the decision the Court will render. Most probably, taking into account the principle of procedural autonomy, the Court will confine itself to establish, on behalf of the national court, some general relevant criteria that the national court must apply in order to ensure compliance with the Directive.[27] Depending on the content of the CJEU's decision, the Belgian court will be confronted with the difficult task whether a Directive compliant result can be reached in this case, i.e. that the cost of proceedings do not appear to be objectively unreasonable.

If the Antwerp court would conclude in the wake of the anticipated CJEU decision that (some) IP-cases, given their complexity, need another and more generous regime for the recoverability of legal expenses and costs in order to reach the principle of effectiveness, its ruling risks to affect in a significant way the cost structure and recoverability of lawyers' fees in Belgian civil procedure. Complexity does not seem to be an exclusive characteristic of IP-cases. Disputes in many other fields of law governed by civil procedure rules could also lead to difficult factual and legal questions and extensive files. They sometimes require, just like IP-cases, the assistance of specialised, highly qualified lawyers and technical experts. Would it be defendable and compatible with the requirement of equal treating that holders of IP rights seeking justice, due to a higher degree of recoverability of judicial costs and expenses, get more procedural options that other litigants?

This illustration of the second area of the so-called invisible pillar shows that rules and instruments initiated by the EU may affect (legal) topics in a much more broader way than obviously was intended by the European legislator. This may not be really surprising, as it is a logical consequence of the EU Member States multi-layered legal systems. But the not always foreseeable interaction between community legislation and national legal concepts leads, at least at the national level, to new challenges and the need to pursuit new balances in order to avoid annoying inconsistencies in the legal system.

26 See e.g. Case C-172/99 *Clean Car Autoservice GmbH v Stadt Wien* [2001] ECLI:EU:C:2001:663, para. 29, in which the Court decided with regard to the principle of effectiveness: 'national rules which provide that the successful party in proceedings before a national court is entitled to recover certain of the costs incurred (...) do not appear to be of such a kind as to render virtually impossible or excessively difficult the exercise of rights conferred by Community law.'

27 Ch. Vrendenbarg, 'Toelaatbaarheid van forfaitaire proceskostenvergoeding bij handhaving van IE-rechten' [2015] IER 39 (in Dutch). The author is of the opinion that recovering only € 11,000 on an amount of paid lawyers' fees of more than € 185,000 seems quite unbalanced.

2. A New Legal Instrument Inspired by European Legislation does not seem to be in Sync with its European Counterparts

Until recently, the BJC contained only one procedure explicitly designed to provide relief for uncontested monetary claims: the summary order for payment procedure. Recently a brand new recovery track for such claims has been added by the Act of 19 October 2015.[28] This new track is largely inspired by Article 10 (1) of the Directive 2011/7/EU of the European Parliament and of the Council of 16 February 2011 on combating late payment in commercial transactions.[29] Together with the small claims procedure Regulation[30] and the order for payment procedure Regulation[31] the Directive has created a European dimension to this topic.[32]

The summary order for payment procedure was introduced in 1967, on the occasion of the enactment of the BJC.[33] It served two goals: introducing a quick and simple *ex parte* procedure for the collection of small claims and eliminating the possibility for a debtor to delay payment by way of abusive and frivolous arguments.[34] The procedure consists of two stages: an ultimate reminder for payment and the actual summary order for payment procedure. It is only applicable to claims falling under the jurisdiction of the Justice of the Peace, the Police Court or the Commercial Court. The claim must relate to an established debt of an amount not exceeding € 1,860.[35] The amount must be certain, fixed and have fallen due. Additionally, the object of claims falling under the jurisdiction of the Police Courts must be compensation for damages occurred by traffic or train accidents, even when the accident happened in a place closed to the public.[36] The claim must be substantiated by a written document drawn up by the debtor. This does not have to be an admission or acknowledgement of debt.[37] This condition is usually broadly interpreted: an ordering slip[38], a receipt of delivery signed by the debtor or an accepted

28 Loi du 19 Octobre 2015 modifiant le droit de la procédure civile et portant des dispositions diverses en matière de justice, Moniteur belge [Official Gazette of Belgium] 22 October 2015, Articles 32–40 and 51. The new track will enter into force on a date specified by the government and at latest on 1 September 2017.

29 (Recast) OJ 23 February 2011 L48/1.

30 Council Regulation (EC) on establishing a European Small Claims Procedure [2007] OJ L199/1.

31 Council Regulation (EC) on creating a European order for payment procedure [2006] OJ L399/1.

32 Compare Krans (n 1) 581.

33 The procedure was amended in 1987.

34 G. Van Mellaert, 'Order for payment under Belgian law' in W. Rechberger and G. Kodek (eds), *Orders for payment in the European Union* (2001) 91. See also <https://e-justice.europa.eu/content_order_for_payment_procedures-41-be-maximizeMS_EJN-en.do?member=1> accessed 18 January 2016.

35 A summary order for payment can only be requested at the Commercial Court from 1 July 2014 onwards. The financial limitation to claims not exceeding € 1,860 is not applicable for this Court, which aimed to make the procedure more attractive for business disputes irrespective of the value of the claim, since the financial threshold is generally regarded as being too low.

36 Article 601*bis* BJC.

37 Article 1338 BJC. Originally, the claim had to be proven by a deed from the debtor. This condition was dropped by the 1987 legislative amendments in a proved fruitless attempt to make this procedure more attractive.

38 *Contra*: Justice of the Peace of Fexhe-Slins, 26 March 1981, *JL* 1981, 175.

invoice[39] all have been accepted as a written document from the debtor. Most case law requires a document that is (explicitly) signed or accepted by the debtor and that is directly related to the product or service that has been bought. Have not been accepted as a written document from the debtor: a simple, not explicitly accepted invoice[40] or a financing/rental/insurance contract.[41] Finally, the procedure only applies when the debtor has his domicile or habitual residence in Belgium.[42]

The summary order for payment procedure has not at all proven to be a successful procedure and it is firmly criticised as well by scholars as by practitioners.[43] Statistics show that, in average, no more than 0.3% of all new (petition) cases that were brought before the Justices of the Peace between 2009 and 2013 are summary order for payment procedures.[44] The ordinary procedure, in which the summoned debtor is defaulted, is much more applied than the summary order for payment procedure. Different characteristics of the latter – in particular: claims may not exceed the amount of € 1,860 (with the exception of claims falling under the jurisdiction of the Commercial Court), the condition of a written document drawn up by the debtor, the fact that a prior formalised ultimate reminder for payment must be sent to the debtor, the impossibility to obtain a decision that is provisionally enforceable and the mandatory assistance of a lawyer – lead to the finding that the Belgian summary order for payment procedure is a burdensome, inefficient, costly and, as a consequence, not frequently used procedure for creditors to obtain relief in small and simple matters. Not surprisingly the 2002 Green Paper concluded that 'due to some structural defects the order for payment procedure has turned out to be more cumbersome than ordinary civil proceedings and has, therefore, not met broad acceptance among legal practitioners'.[45]

In the course of the last decade, many proposals were launched to amend this summary order for payment procedure. This was often done very inconsistently by totally ignoring the European context and by not paying attention to an equal treatment of the persons seeking justice. One has to keep in mind that the above mentioned European recovery procedures, which are directly applicable on cross-border cases pending in Belgium, require mirror (judicial) proceedings in national law for purely domestic cases. Only this approach avoids discrimination or unequal treatment between foreign and national creditors or cross-border and national cases. Unfortunately, the new simplified order for payment track seems to be cursed with the same deficiencies.

39 Van Mellaert (n 34) 92.

40 Justice of the Peace of Ostend, 28 November 1997, *TWVR* 1998, 44 and Justice of the Peace of Fexhe-Slins, 26 March 1981, *JL* 1981, 175.

41 Justice of the Peace of Wezet, 29 June 1987, *JL* 1987, 1011.

42 Article 1344 BJC.

43 Aude Berthe, 'L'injonction de payer en droit belge – Aspects *de lege lata* et *de lege ferenda*', Ius & Actores (2009) 67; G. Closset-Marchal, 'La procédure sommaire d'injonction de payer: un nouvel essor?', T. Vred. (1988) 35; G. De Leval, 'La procédure sommaire d'injonction de payer et l'espace européen – Principes généraux en matière d'inversion du contentieux', Act.dr. (2003) 399.

44 <http://justitie.belgium.be/nl/informatie/statistieken/hoven_en_rechtbanken/> (accessed 17 January 2016).

45 Commission, *Green Paper on a European order for payment procedure and on measures to simplify and speed up small claims litigation*, COM (2002) 746 final, at 9.

In his 2015 Justice Plan the Belgian minister of Justice announced a more efficient summary order for payment procedure[46], which eventually led to a Law of 19 October 2015.[47] The new rules deal, *inter alia*, with the recovery of uncontested monetary claims and the introduction of a new simplified recovery track (Articles 1394/20 – 1394/27 BJC). The government pointed out that these claims cause an overload of work for judges and are simply used by claimants to get an enforceable title. The legislator deliberately avoided to use the word 'procedure' in describing this new 'technique', as this new track introduced a merely administrative way for the recovery of uncontested monetary claims.[48] As it is not of a judicial nature, it is considered as not belonging to the judges core task of adjudicating disputes. The recovery of uncontested monetary claims should therefore as much as possible be kept outside the courts. In order to surround this new track with some guarantees regarding expertise and independence, a key role has been granted to the lawyers, the bailiffs and to the judge appointed as a member of the management and supervision committee of the centralised data-base where all the notices on attachments, delegations, assignments and collective settlements of debts are kept.

The new recovery track for uncontested monetary claims contains four stages. In a first step, at the request of the lawyer of the creditor,[49] the bailiff sends a final notice to pay to the debtor with a copy of the relevant items of evidence (stating the uncontested nature of the claim) and an answer form.[50] The notice has to contain, among others, a clear description of the claim and the amounts that are being claimed from the debtor (including the costs of the final notice and, where appropriate, the increments, interests and penalties), a summons to pay within one month and the modalities of the required payment. At the second stage, the debtor has one month to pay or to ask for payment facilities (e.g. payment by instalments) or to contest the claim (wholly or in part) by using the answer form. In the latter case, the debtor has to state the reasons why he or she challenges the claim. A non-motived challenge will be considered as an absence of challenge. At the third stage, the track is cut short for the debts that are paid or that are contested. In the latter case, the creditor is free to initiate an ordinary civil procedure. If, in a following procedure on the merits of the case, the challenge as formulated by the debtor is judged clearly unfounded or unreasonable, the debtor can be condemned to a fine for abuse of process. As a fourth and final step, an enforceable title is issued in case the debtor does not react in time or if no agreement was concluded on payment facilities. At the request of the creditor, the bailiff draws up a procès-verbal of non-challenge that is declared enforceable by a judge who is member of the management and supervision committee that deals with, among other things, the publication of attachment orders. Execution of the title is done by a bailiff on behalf of the creditor and starts by serving a

46 'Plain Justice' (2015) 32–33, nr 74 <www.koengeens.be/fr/justitieplan> (accessed 29 December 2015).

47 Loi du 19 Octobre 2015 modifiant le droit de la procédure civile et portant des dispositions diverses en matière de justice, Moniteur belge [Official Gazette of Belgium] 22 October 2015, Articles 32–40 and 51.

48 Although some provisions (e.g. Article 1394/27, para.1 BJC) refer explicitly to the word 'procedure'.

49 Assistance of a lawyer is mandatory. On basis of his ethics (which are regarded as a safeguard), the lawyer is presumed to act as the first judge of the case.

50 This is comparable to the prior ultimate notice for payment in the summary order for payment procedure.

copy of it on the debtor (to ensure that the latter is fully informed of the title). The enforcement will only be suspended if the debtor initiates a judicial procedure by using a petition (which is less costly than a writ of summons),[51] on condition that this petition is lodged before the totality of the debt has been paid. A full payment by the debtor is legally considered as a settlement.[52]

The new track potentially leads to a reversal of the burden to take the matter to court, which in term will lead to a reversal of the roles of the parties in the proceedings. The initiative (and the provision of the inherent costs) lies no longer in hands of the creditor as he becomes the defendant. Instead the debtor will be coerced to take legal action if he wants to challenge the enforceable title delivered at the end of this new recovery track.

The (Belgian) National Chamber of Bailiffs got the task to build up a new data bank in which all data related to this new track and relevant for supervising the course of it will be stored.[53] Every bailiff making use of this track is obliged to transfer all documents concerned (writs, notices, notifications, modalities of the payment (e.g. terms of instalment)) to the data base. Bailiffs will be able to register and consult directly those data.

This new recovery track and its scope are surrounded by a number of safeguards. First, the procedure can only be used for uncontested monetary claims. Once a claim is challenged, the ordinary procedure applies as the bailiff does not have any margin of appreciation and a judge will have to adjudicate the dispute. Second, the scope is strictly limited to commercial claims and debts, in the sense that both creditor and debtor have to be registered at the (Belgian) Central Enterprise Databank, which implies that the new track is only applicable in a Belgian business to business context. Are excluded: public debtors, private (or non-commercial) creditors and debtors, insolvency procedures and most non-contractual claims between private (or non-commercial) parties. Third, the increments, interests and penalties are legally capped at a maximum of ten percent of the claim.[54] Fourth and finally, the assistance of or representation by a lawyer is mandatory to initiate the new recovery track.

These safeguards imply that from various aspects the new Belgian recovery track for uncontested monetary claims differs substantially from its European counterparts. Especially its very limited scope *ratione personae* which excludes *inter alia* private persons, in particular consumers, making use of this most probably efficient and rather cheap track has been criticised. One can only wonder why, once again,[55] a company-debtor will be in a more favourable position if it fails to fulfil its monetary obligations towards a private person as opposed to a professional. The Explanatory memorandum of

51 Article 1394/24, section 3 BJC.

52 Article 1394/24, section 4 BJC.

53 Article 1394/27 BJC (which explains why the date of entry into force of the provisions of this new track is postponed at the latest till 1 September 2017).

54 Article 1394/20 BJC. The compensation for recovery costs is fixed at a minimum of € 40 but may not exceed an amount of € 2,500.

55 By transposing the Directive on late payment in commercial transactions the Belgian legislator offered also a more favourable position towards professional creditors.

the new Act does not supply a plausible, persuasive explanation for this difference in treatment.

The legislative section of the Council of State indicated in its advice to the parliament the exclusion of public debtors of the field of application of the new recovery track as a possible discriminatory treatment, which also needed an elaborated justification.[56] It has not been provided by the legislator.

Compared with the European instruments there is a striking difference between the swift and informal procedures created by the aforementioned Regulations and the new Belgian recovery track. The latter requires the intervention of at least two legal professionals, a lawyer and a bailiff, which makes it probably more costly than an European order for payment or a European small claims procedure. Some highly esteemed scholars have even expressed the opinion that, under circumstances, the new track may be considered contrary to the requirements of Article 6 of the European Convention on Human Rights and Article 1 of the first Protocol[57] by blocking or, at least, by making the access to the judge extremely difficult. Consequently they have pleaded for the abolishment of this new recovery track.[58]

3. To Conclude

In their introductory remarks to the workshop on the influence of EU law on national civil procedure, the editors of this book described the research subject in the subtitle as 'a smooth process or a rocky road for Member States?' As far as Belgium is concerned, I'm of the opinion that the relationship between EU (case) law and Belgian civil proceedings nowadays can be compared with a slippery road towards a – much needed but still far from obvious – cohabitation.

A thorough knowledge of and familiarity with each other are prerequisites for any well-balanced relationship. Projects as have been initiated during the last years in the Netherlands[59] to promote and reinforce the knowledge of European law and to do research about its impact on purely domestic cases, have not yet been deployed – at least not to the same extent – in Belgium. Within the framework of the European Judicial Network, the Belgian Judiciary Training Institute intends to offer with 'Eur-Alert!'[60] a monthly electronic newsletter with a hyperlinked general selection of European legislation and case-law, relevant information on this topic to judges, prosecutors and court judicial staff. Unfortunately, this newsletter is published irregularly. The European Commission's initiative to boost a true European judicial culture by training half of the EU legal professionals in EU law or in the law of another

56 Advice 57.529/2-3 11 June 2015, Parl.St. Kamer 2014–15, N° 54–1219/1, 121–122 <https://www.dekamer.be/kvvcr/showpage.cfm?section=/flwb&language=nl&cfm=/site/wwwcfm/flwb/flwbn.cfm?legislat=54&dossierID=1219> (accessed 18 January 2016).

57 Which recognises the right to peaceful enjoyment of property.

58 G. De Leval, J. Van Compernolle and F. Georges, 'La loi du 19 octobre 2015 modifiant le droit de la procédure civile et portant des dispositions diverses en matière de justice' [2015] JT (785) 804–805.

59 E.g. Eur*infra*.

60 <www.igo-ifj.be/nl/euralert> (accessed 18 January 2016).

Member State by 2020 is certainly helpful,[61] although its focus lies on training in criminal EU law areas.

There is certainly still room for a lot of improvement of knowledge and understanding of EU (case) law by judges and the legal profession via initial and continuous training. This is, among other things, proven by disputable practices in some Belgian courts. For instance, a lot of Belgian judges require that a European order for payment is signed by a lawyer. If not the request for this order is declared inadmissible. They seem to consider this request erroneously as an *ex parte* petition which has to be signed by a lawyer.[62] A recent statutory change concerning default proceedings delivers another illustration of a notable difference in the attitude of judges related to the source of the rule (EU law or a national rule). The amended Article 806 BJC stipulates that if a party does not appear in court the judge examining the merits of the claim is only allowed to verify whether the demand (or the means of defense) does (do) not violate rules of public order. The amendment gave way to a lot of critics, because making default traditionally has been considered in Belgian case-law as a manner of contesting the claim. The curious thing about this viewpoint is that Belgian judges and scholars[63] have accepted unanimously that in a European context a judgment criticism granted on default could be assimilated to an uncontested (monetary) claim.[64]

61 <http://ec.europa.eu/justice/criminal/european-judicial-training/index_en.htm> (accessed 29 December 2015).

62 Article 1026 BJC. Unfortunately the European order for payment Regulation does not provide, as the Regulation on small claims does in its Article 10, that representation by a lawyer or another legal professional shall not be mandatory.

63 G. De Leval, 'Reconnaissance et exécution de l'acte notarié dans l'espace européen' in Christine Biques, Alain Delièege, Pasvale Lecoq, Yves-Henri Leleu, Michèle Vanwijck (eds), *Liber Amicorum Paul Delnoy* (Brussels, Larcier, 2006) 671; J.-F. Van Drooghenbroeck and S. Brijs, 'Un titre exécutoire européen', Les dossiers du JT (Brussels Larcier 2006) 61; Ilse Couwenberg, 'Erkenning, exequatur en executie van vonnissen' in Benoit Allemeersch and Thalia Kruger (eds), *Handboek Europees burgerlijk procesrecht* (Cambridge-Antwerp 2015) 170; Kh. Hasselt 1 February 2006 RW [2007–08] 1259; Vred. Brussel 14 March 2007 JLMB [2007] 1199.

64 Case C-292/10, *G v Cornelius de Visser* [2012] ECLI:EU:C:2012:142, para 62: 'A judgment by default is indeed one of the enforcement titles within the meaning of Article 3 of that regulation which may be certified as a European Enforcement Order. As recital 6 in the preamble to Regulation No 805/2004 states, the absence of objections from the debtor as stipulated in Article 3(1)(b) of that regulation can take the shape of default of appearance at a court hearing or of failure to comply with an invitation by the court to give written notice of an intention to defend the case'.

Clement Salung
Petersen*

DANISH CIVIL PROCEDURE AND THE INTERNAL MARKET: IMPACT AND CHALLENGES OF SECTORAL HARMONISATION

1. Introduction

The EU has increasingly used its internal market competence in Article 114 TFEU to harmonise matters of civil procedure law. Unlike the judicial cooperation competence in Article 81 TFEU, the internal market competence is not confined to cross-border cases. Instead, harmonisation passed under Article 114 is confined to a specific subject-matter. The Intellectual Property Enforcement Directive (2004/48/EC) is the most comprehensive example of such 'sectoral harmonisation' of procedural matters. It concerns 'measures, procedures and remedies necessary to ensure the enforcement of intellectual property rights' (Article 1), and it applies both to cross-border *and* domestic disputes concerning enforcement of IP rights protected either by EU law or by national law (Article 2). Other examples are the Consumer Injunctions Directive (2009/22/EC replacing Directive 98/27/EC), which concerns injunctive relief in certain cross-border situations, and the Antitrust Damages Directive (2014/104/EU), which concerns certain actions for damages for infringement of competition law rules and, *inter alia*, lays down rather detailed rules on disclosure of evidence.

When the Commission presented its proposal[1] for the Enforcement Directive, prominent European academics voiced their concerns about the effectiveness and desirability of inserting EU law principles aimed at enforcing IP rights into parts of national procedural law that are otherwise not limited to IP disputes, emphasising that the Directive involved several complex and sensitive matters.[2] In the Nordic countries, some academics were particularly concerned that the Directive would result in a significant *fragmentation* of domestic civil procedure law, which would increase

* Associate Professor (PhD), University of Copenhagen, Faculty of Law. clement.petersen@jur.ku.dk

1 COM(2003) 46 final of 30 January 2003.

2 William R. Cornish, Josepf Drexl, Reto Hilty and Annette Kur supported by 31 law professors from 11 EU and EEA member states, 'Procedures and Remedies for Enforcing IPRs: The European Commission's proposed Directive' [2003] EIPR 25(10) 447. Several Nordic academics supported this view separately, see 'Nordic Intellectual Property Review' [2003] (NIR) 359.

complexity and legal uncertainty.[3] Academics also criticised the Enforcement Directive for focusing too much on law enforcement and thereby disregarding the fact that civil procedure rules function as a balancing instrument to achieve civil justice and that an unbalanced 'enforcement approach' to questions of civil justice might increase abuses of process.[4]

The deadline for implementing the Enforcement Directive expired almost ten years ago.[5] Since then, the Commission has made several consultations on how the Directive has improved the enforcement of IP rights, whereas the impact of the Directive on national civil procedure seems to have attracted little (if any) attention.[6] In the meantime, the newly enacted Antitrust Damages Directive takes a similar *enforcement approach* to matters of civil procedure without detailed analysis of how this will affect civil procedure law in the Member States.[7]

This chapter explores the impact of this sectoral harmonisation on Danish civil procedure law. It shows how sectoral harmonisation has significantly affected the coherent and systemic approach to civil justice by creating divergences that do not reflect the general values and principles of the Danish civil justice system, and it identifies some pertinent challenges caused by this development (*infra* 2 and 3). On this basis, it considers how internal market harmonisation of civil procedure matters can serve both the functioning of the internal market and the maintaining of a coherent and systemic approach to civil justice in the Member States (*infra* 4).

2. Sectoral Harmonisation and Danish Civil Procedure Law: Impact

Danish civil procedure law is mainly regulated in the Danish Administration of Justice Act, which reflects a largely coherent and systemic approach to civil justice. Danish civil procedure law is thus based on a coherent set of values and fundamental principles that

3 An interesting discussion of this topic amongst academics, lawyers and judges from the Nordic countries took place at the Nordic Meeting of Jurists (*Nordisk Juristmøde*) in 2006, see Thomas Riis, 'Immaterialrettens særlige procesformer' (presentation at the Nordic Meeting of Jurists 2006 with subsequent discussions, <http://jura.ku.dk/njm/english/> accessed 23 January 2016). See also Magnus Hauge Greaker, 'Direktiv 2004/48/EF av 29. april 2004 om håndhevelsen av immaterielle rettigheter og norsk rett' [2006] NIR 598, 600; Eva Storskrubb, *Civil Procedure and EU Law. A Policy Area Uncovered* (Oxford University Press 2008) 262; Bart Krans, 'EU Law and National Civil Procedure Law: An Invisible Pillar' [2015] European Review of Private Law 567, 582.

4 See Riis (n 3); Anette Kur, 'The Enforcement Directive – Rough Start, Happy Landing?' [2004] IIC 821; Gerhard Wagner, 'Harmonization of Civil Procedure – Policy Perspectives' in X. E. Kramer and C. H. van Rhee (eds), *Civil Litigation in a Globalising World* (Springer 2012) 110.

5 The Member States should comply with the Directive by 29 April 2006, cf. Article 20 of the Directive, but only five Member States complied with this deadline. Several Member States did not implement the Directive before 2009. For details, see SEC(2010) 1589 final 27.

6 The EU Commission has (for obvious reasons) focused on the enforcement of IP rights, see *e.g.* SEC(2010) 1589 and the public consultation on the evaluation and modernisation of the IPR enforcement framework launched in December 2015.

7 The Antitrust Damages Directive is based on a proposal of 11 June 2013, see COM(2013) 404 final.

guide its interpretation and gap-filling.[8] Danish civil procedure has different types of procedure, including preliminary injunctions proceedings, small claims proceedings, debt collection proceedings and 'ordinary' civil proceedings. Within any particular type of proceedings, the same procedural rules normally apply to any kind of dispute, *i.e.* regardless of the type of claim and the area of substantive law it concerns.[9] Courts with a specialised jurisdiction, such as the Maritime and Commercial Court, generally use the same procedural rules as courts with a general jurisdiction. This coherent and systemic approach contributes to legal certainty and predictability, and it is regarded as an important policy aim to maintain this coherence in the Danish civil justice system.[10]

The aim of the following analysis is to show how sectoral harmonisation can affect this coherence by requiring Member States to adopt rules for a particular type of dispute that do not reflect the general values and principles of its national civil justice system (sometimes referred to as *fragmentation*). The analysis will focus on sectoral harmonisation of disclosure of evidence, measures to preserve evidence, a right to information and legal costs (*infra* 2.1–2.4). It will then focus more generally on the implications for interpretation of Danish civil procedure law and for the division between civil and criminal procedure law (*infra* 2.5 and 2.6).

2.1. *Disclosure of Evidence*

Both the Enforcement Directive and the Antitrust Damages Directive include provisions concerning orders for disclosure of evidence.[11] However, there are significant differences between these provisions.

First, the Enforcement Directive only concerns ordering a *party* to a dispute to disclose 'specified evidence'. Under the Antitrust Damages Directive, such orders can also be directed at non-parties and they can concern 'relevant evidence' as well as 'relevant categories of evidence circumscribed as precisely and as narrowly as possible on the basis of reasonably available facts in the reasoned justification'. The latter goes beyond what is currently obtainable in Danish civil litigation.[12]

Secondly, the consequences for a person who refuses to comply with an order to disclose evidence is unregulated in the Enforcement Directive, whereas it is regulated in Article 8 of the Antitrust Damages Directive. It appears that existing Danish law on penalties does not fully live up to the requirements in the latter Directive.[13]

8 For an account of the general purposes and values of the Danish civil justice system, see the Danish Committee on Administration of Justice Report no 1401, *Reform af den civile retspleje I* (Danish Ministry of Justice 2001) 83. The general purposes, values and principles of civil justice are largely the same in the Nordic countries, see Clement Salung Petersen, 'A Comparative Perspective on Recent Nordic Reforms of Civil Justice' in Laura Ervo and Anna Nylund (eds), *The Future of Civil Litigation* (Springer 2014) 9.

9 A few exceptions follow from Chapters 42–44 in the Danish Administration of Justice Act.

10 See, *e.g.*, the report from the Danish Committee on Administration of Justice (n 8).

11 See Article 6 of the Enforcement Directive and Articles 5 and 8 of the Antitrust Damages Directive.

12 See Sections 298–301 of the Danish Administration of Justice Act.

13 This is also the position taken in the draft Bill of 2 October 2015 (*Forslag til Lov om ændring af konkurrenceloven*) 18.

Thirdly, restrictions on the duty to disclose evidence are regulated rather differently in the two Directives. In the Enforcement Directive, the only express restriction on the duty to disclose evidence is 'protection of confidential information', which is not defined in the Directive. However, it is mentioned in Recital 20 that the procedures 'should have regard to the rights of the defence and provide the necessary guarantees, including the protection of confidential information', which seems to imply that further restrictions are also acceptable. In this regard, the Antitrust Damages Directive includes a more elaborate list of restrictions concerning proportionality, protection of certain confidential information and the client-attorney privilege.[14] Furthermore, it explicitly states that the interest of undertakings to avoid actions for damages following an infringement of competition law shall *not* constitute an interest that warrants protection.[15] In Danish civil procedure law, the duty to disclose evidence is also subject to other restrictions such as protection of information sources of the media.[16]

Even though both Directives concern the same procedural matter, namely disclosure of evidence in certain types of civil litigation, it is clear that the two Directives are not based on a coherent approach to this matter. This can be seen as a reflection of the *enforcement approach* taken in both Directives; the Directives are not about civil justice, but about strengthening the enforcement of IP rights and competition law, respectively.

As mentioned, some of the requirements in the Antitrust Damages Directive go beyond current Danish law on disclosure of evidence. According to the Danish draft Bill for implementing this Directive, new special rules will therefore be implemented in a Ministerial Order to the Danish Competition Act (!) concerning disclosure of evidence in civil proceedings concerning competition law.[17] These new rules will thus introduce a significant *fragmentation* of Danish law on disclosure of evidence.

2.2. *Measures for Preserving Evidence*

In cases concerning infringement of intellectual property rights, relevant evidence may be inaccessible to right holders. This includes information about the sale of infringing copies of a product and information about the commercial use of pirated software or a patented production method. There is thus a need to provide measures for acquiring and preserving evidence, which makes these cases quite similar to many criminal cases. Since IP rights are often enforced in civil proceedings, even though criminal liability has come to play an increasing role in the gravest cases of infringement, special procedural rules have been introduced in several jurisdictions to accommodate the above-mentioned need for measures to preserve evidence. The most (in)famous European examples of such court-ordered measures are the *Anton Piller order*, which was introduced by the House of Lords in English civil procedure law in 1975 and is now known as search orders, and

14 See Article 5(3), 5(4) and 5(6) of the Antitrust Damages Directive.

15 See Article 5(5) of the Antitrust Damages Directive.

16 See Sections 169–172 of the Danish Administration of Justice Act. Compare Principle 16.2 of the ALI/UNIDROIT Principles of Transnational Civil Procedure: 'It is not a basis of objection to such disclosure that the evidence may be adverse to the party or person making the disclosure.'

17 See draft Bill of 2 October 2015 (Forslag til Lov om ændring af konkurrenceloven) 12.

the French *saisie contrefaçon*.[18] Article 7 of the Enforcement Directive is modelled on these UK and French rules and on Article 50(1)(b) of the WTO TRIPS Agreement.[19]

Article 7 imposes an obligation on Member States to ensure that the competent judicial authorities may order prompt and effective provisional measures to preserve relevant evidence in respect of the alleged infringement, subject to the protection of confidential information. Such measures may include the detailed description, with or without the taking of samples, or the physical seizure of the infringing goods, and, in appropriate cases, the materials and implements used in the production and/or distribution of these goods and the documents relating thereto. These measures shall be available even before commencement of proceedings on the merits of the case.

Before the TRIPS Agreement and the Enforcement Directive, this type of provisional measure did not exist in numerous Member States, including Denmark and Sweden. After having signed the TRIPS Agreement, Denmark and Sweden came under significant political pressure from the US to implement such measures in their national laws.[20] Eventually, it was decided to implement such measures in Danish and Swedish law, and these measures were subsequently adjusted to comply with Article 7 of the Enforcement Directive. The implementation of this new measure in Denmark and Sweden is thus a good example of a *legal transplant*.

Since this type of measure was previously unknown in Danish and Swedish civil procedure law, it was necessary to adopt new special rules. In Sweden (and Finland), these special procedural rules have been inserted in the (substantive) laws on IP protection and they apply only in disputes related to this legislation. In Denmark, it was suggested to adopt a separate *procedural* Act concerning these measures in cases concerning IP infringement, but eventually it was decided to instead insert the new special rules in a new chapter in the Danish Administration of Justice Act.[21]

In Denmark (as well as in Sweden and Finland), these new rules do not reflect the general principles of civil justice and thus constitute a significant *fragmentation* of civil procedure law.[22] By way of comparison, it is interesting to observe that the Norwegian legislator decided to introduce new *general* rules on search orders, which are not limited to cases concerning infringement of IP rights, in order to avoid such fragmentation of its civil procedure law.[23]

18 The Anton Piller order was introduced in *Anton Piller KG v Manufacturing Processes Ltd* [1976] 1 All ER 779 and renamed 'search orders' in the CPR, see *e.g.* Neil Andrews, *Three paths of justice* (Springer 2012) 161. The rules on *saisie contrefacon* are laid down in the French Intellectual Property Code (*Code de la proprieté Industrielle*).

19 See COM(2003) 46 final 21.

20 See Danish Committee Report 1385, 'Bevissikring ved krænkelse af immaterialrettigheder m.v.' (Danish Ministry of Culture 2000); Swedish report DS 1998:224, and Gunnar Karnell, 'Föregripande skydd – internationalisering av system med civilrättslig husrannsakan *inaudita altera parte*' [1997] NIR 315.

21 See Chapter 57 A of the Danish Administration of Justice Act.

22 From a Danish (and Swedish) perspective, it is thus difficult to concur with the view offered by Wagner (n 4) 104 that Article 7 of the Enforcement Directive 'would fit in well with any decent code of civil procedure, under the subchapter of preservation of evidence'.

23 See Chapter 28 of the Norwegian Dispute Act and Ot.prp. nr. 33 (2003–2004). These new rules were implemented to comply with the requirements in the TRIPS Agreement. The Enforcement Directive does not apply in Norway.

2.3. *Right to Information*

Under Article 8 of the Enforcement Directive, Member States shall ensure that the competent judicial authorities in the context of infringement proceedings may order that a certain type of information be provided by a specified group of persons that may or may not be parties to a pending dispute. This provision is modelled on German and Benelux law and similar provisions also existed in other Member States.[24] It can be used, in particular, to trace everyone involved in specific infringements and to provide a better basis for calculating damages. This provision in the Directive has been described as 'probably one of the core issues of the whole project'.[25]

Article 8 has affected several fundamental principles in Danish civil procedure law. First, it is a fundamental principle in Danish civil procedure law that if a (potential) party to a civil dispute refuses to provide information requested by another party, the only available sanction is that the court may draw adverse inferences when deciding the dispute. In particular, pecuniary sanctions are only available against non-parties who refuse to provide a witness statement or disclose relevant evidence. To adopt Article 8 in Danish law, it was therefore necessary to introduce new rules *sui generis* in the Danish Administration of Justice Act.[26] These rules apply only to IP disputes.[27]

Secondly, it is a general principle in Danish civil procedure law that the taking of evidence must be relevant for the specific dispute. The right to information can go beyond the specific dispute, because it aims (also) to enable the right holder to obtain information about any third parties involved in the IP infringements, typically in order to enable the right holder to enforce their rights against those third parties afterwards.[28] In this regard, Article 8 requires that the right to information shall be applicable 'in the context of infringement proceedings'. In Denmark, this has been interpreted to mean that the right to information might not be available before the court has rendered judgment concerning the matter of infringement. In such cases, the right to information blurs the main phases in Danish civil proceedings, *i.e.* the interim (pleadings) phase and the main hearing (trial).[29]

Thirdly, Article 8 can also affect the general restrictions on a duty to provide information in the context of civil litigation. Article 8(3) acknowledges the need for certain restrictions on the right to information, including provisions that afford an opportunity for refusing to provide information which would force a person to admit to his/her own participation (or that of his/her close relatives) in the IP infringements, and provisions that govern the protection of confidentiality of information sources or the processing of personal data. These restrictions do not fully reflect the traditional (quite far-reaching) restrictions in Danish civil procedure on the right to obtain information

24 See COM(2003) 46 final 21. Article 47 of the TRIPS Agreement includes a similar (but not mandatory) provision. On *Norwich Pharmacal orders* in UK law, see Andrews (n 18) 65.

25 See Kur (n 4).

26 See Chapter 29 A of the Danish Administration of Justice Act.

27 For details, see Section 306 of the Danish Administration of Justice Act.

28 See Article 8(1).

29 See Greaker (n 3) 601.

and documents etc. from parties and non-parties (witnesses).[30] Nevertheless, the Danish legislator decided to make the Danish transposition of Article 8 subject to all these traditional Danish restrictions. This can be seen as an endeavour to maintain coherence in Danish civil procedural law. However, this transposition of Article 8 might not comply with the Directive.[31] Article 8(3) has challenged similar restrictions in the German Civil Procedure Code, which allows a banking institution to invoke banking secrecy in order to refuse to provide information pursuant to the right to information under Article 8.[32]

2.4. Legal Costs

Under Article 14 of the Enforcement Directive, Member States shall ensure that 'reasonable and proportionate legal costs and other expenses incurred by the successful party shall, as a general rule, be borne by the unsuccessful party, unless equity does not allow this'. This principle of fee shifting (the English Rule) is well-known in most Member States.[33] However, there are differences between how to assess the 'reasonable and proportionate legal costs and other expenses', in particular when it comes to lawyers' fees. In Denmark, there is thus a significant discrepancy between, on the one hand, the actual lawyers' fees (typically) paid by a successful party and, on the other hand, the 'reasonable amount' that shall be reimbursed by the unsuccessful party.[34] Furthermore, the successful party may not be able to claim reimbursement of all costs related to expert evidence and expert assistance under Danish law.[35] These problems also exist in other Member States.[36]

The Danish legislator assumed that Danish civil procedure law already complied with Article 14. So far, this provision has therefore had no direct impact on Danish civil procedure law. By contrast, a special regime for the award of legal costs in IP cases was adopted in the Netherlands to comply with Article 14.[37]

In this regard, it is clear that the Enforcement Directive provides a basis for the CJEU to lay down more detailed principles for determining the 'reasonable amount' that shall be borne by the unsuccessful party in IP disputes.[38] So potentially, Article 14 may lead to a divergence also in Danish civil procedure law.

30 See Sections 169–172 of the Danish Administration of Justice Act.

31 See Jonas Christoffersen, 'Retten til tavshed over for håndhævelse af immaterialrettigheder' [2006] Ugeskrift for Retsvæsen (Danish Weekly Law Reports) 319.

32 See Case C-580/13 *Coty Germany GmbH v Stadtsparkasse Magdeburg* [2015] ECLI:EU:C:2015:485.

33 See SEC(2010) 1589 final 24.

34 See Clement Salung Petersen, 'Access to the Danish Civil Justice System: Recent Reforms and Current Challenges' in Laura Ervo and Anna Nylund (eds), *The Future of Civil Litigation* (Springer 2014) 281, 298.

35 In patent cases, parties often need assistance from patent attorneys. The costs related to such assistance are usually not reimbursed, see Danish Supreme Court decision of 17 December 2008 reported in the Danish Weekly Law Reports (Ugeskrift for Retsvæsen) 2009 762.

36 See SEC(2010) 1589 final 24; Krans (n 3) 576; Magdalena Tulibacka, 'Europeanization of Civil Procedures: In Search of a Coherent Approach' [2009] CMLR (46) 1527, 1548.

37 See Krans (n 3) 577; Tulibacka (n 36) 1561.

38 So far, case law from the CJEU has only concerned the field of application of Article 14, see Case C-406/09 *Realchemie Nederland BV v Bayer CropScience AG [2011] ECLI:EU:C:2011:668* (concerning an

In this connection, Article 14 is supplemented by a general obligation for Member States to ensure that all measures, procedures and remedies covered by the Directive are not 'unnecessarily complicated or costly', see Article 3(1). Court fees differ significantly between Member States, and therefore it is interesting to observe that the CJEU might use this provision to put limits on court fees in IP cases.

From a national civil justice perspective, Article 14 concerns a matter that is clearly related to the general issue of *access to justice*. The Enforcement Directive includes no general considerations about this issue, which can be seen as yet another example of the *enforcement approach*; the Directive is not about civil justice and providing access to justice but about enforcement of IP rights. Article 14 is thus based on partly different values than the general rules on legal costs in Danish civil procedure law.

2.5. *Interpretation of Civil Procedure Rules*

Sectoral harmonisation also affects the *interpretation* of national civil procedure rules. This is clear, when new national rules have been adopted to comply with specific requirements in a Directive. The fact that these rules must be interpreted in light of the relevant sectoral harmonisation emphasises the fragmentation of such special rules.

More importantly, the sectoral harmonisation can also affect the interpretation of existing (general) rules of civil procedure, which have been assumed to comply with the sectoral harmonisation. As an example, Articles 6, 9, 11 and 14 of the Enforcement Directive have not caused any legislative changes in Danish law.[39] Nevertheless, the Danish rules on disclosure of evidence (Article 6), provisional and precautionary measures (Article 9), injunctions (Article 11) and legal costs (Article 14) must be interpreted in light of the Enforcement Directive in cases falling within the subject-specific framework of this Directive (cases concerning enforcement of IP rights). In other cases, these Danish rules are not influenced by the Enforcement Directive.

In this regard, national courts must have regard to the general principles included in Article 3 of the Enforcement Directive, which lays down numerous general obligations regarding the measures, procedures and remedies covered by the Directive. Thus, these measures, procedures and remedies shall be 'effective, proportionate and dissuasive' as well as 'fair and equitable', and they shall not be 'unnecessarily complicated or costly', or entail 'unreasonable time-limits or unwarranted delays'. Moreover, they shall be applied in such a manner as 'to avoid the creation of barriers to legitimate trade' and 'to provide for safeguards against their abuse'.[40]

These obligations are clearly of a (very) general nature, and the Enforcement Directive seems to leave it to the Member States to strike a balance between these, to some extent, irreconcilable requirements. Nevertheless, compliance with these general obligations in

exequatur procedure) and Case C-681/13 *Diaego Brands BV v Simiramida-04 EOOD [2015] ECLI:EU:C:2015:471* (action for damages to compensate for the injury caused as a result of an allegedly unjustified seizure intended to prevent an IP infringement).

39 The draft Bill for adopting the Antitrust Damages Directive into Danish law also intends to largely rely on existing Danish rules on disclosure of evidence.

40 Similar obligations are laid down in Articles 41 and 42 of the WTO TRIPS Agreement.

civil litigation could come under scrutiny by the CJEU.[41] In this regard, the CJEU can either leave Member States with a wide discretion to take into account their specific procedural traditions, or they can more specifically address how the balance shall be struck in IP cases. The latter approach can lead to (additional) fragmentation of national civil procedure law.

Arguably, it would be a wise strategy for the CJEU to leave sufficient discretion for Member States to take into account the differences between their procedural traditions (see *infra* 3).[42] So far, the CJEU has not made more detailed interpretations of the general principles in Article 3.[43]

In this connection, it is interesting to observe that the Enforcement Directive is not mentioned in leading Danish textbooks on civil procedure concerning disclosure of evidence, injunctions, seizure of assets and costs.[44] The EU harmonisation of these matters is thus rather invisible to Danish lawyers and judges. When EU harmonisation is less visible to national lawyers and judges, it might lead to fewer preliminary references to the CJEU.[45] Furthermore, it might cloud the relevance of including case-law from other Member States concerning the topics covered by the harmonisation. However, from a national perspective, these aspects support the coherence of the national civil justice system.

2.6. *Civil and Criminal Procedure Law*

From a traditional Danish perspective, serious violations of the law are normally subject to criminal liability, and it is generally for the police and public prosecutors to take action against such crimes. This also includes (suspected) serious violations of IP law and competition law. To enable public authorities to do this, Danish criminal procedure law provides the police with several measures to investigate crimes and preserve relevant evidence that go far beyond the measures available under *civil* procedure law. These measures include measures to preserve evidence that are rather similar to those described in Article 7 of the Enforcement Directive. From a traditional Danish perspective, it is

41 Michel M Walter and Dominik Goebel, 'Enforcement Directive' in Michel M Walter and Silke von Lewinski (eds), *European Copyright Law - A Commentary* (Oxford University Press 2010) 1224.

42 Compare Cornish et al (n 2).

43 The CJEU referred to some of the requirements in Article 3 in Case C-324/09 *L'òreal v eBay* [2011] ECLI:EU:C:2011:474, concerning injunctions. In other case law, the CJEU has referred more generally to the Enforcement Directive (together with other directives) and emphasised the obligation to interpret the Directive in accordance with general principles of EU law such as the principle of proportionality, see Case C-275/06 *Productores de Música de España (Promusicae) v Telefónica de España* [2008] ECLI:EU:C:2008:54, and Case C-557/07 *LSG-Gesellschaft zur Wahrnehmung von Leistungsschutzrechten GmbH v Tele2 Telecommunication Gmbh*[2009] ECLI:EU:C:2009:107. See also case C-70/10 *Scarlet Extend SA v Société belge des auteurs, compositeurs et éditeurs SCRL (SABAM)* [2011] ECLI:EU:C:2011:771, and Case C-360/10 *Belgische Vereniging van Auteurs, Componisten en Uitgievers CVBA (SABAM) v Netlog NV* [2012] ECLI:EU:C:2012:85.

44 See *e.g.* Ulrik Rammeskow Bang-Pedersen and Lasse Højlund Christensen, *Den Civile Retspleje* (PEJUS, 3rd ed. 2015) and Bernhard Gomard and Michael Kistrup, *Civilprocessen* (KarnovGroup, 7th ed. 2015).

45 The number of preliminary references concerning the Enforcement Directive has been quite limited.

important that these measures are available only to public authorities and within the special procedural guarantees against abuse and excessive use provided by criminal procedure law.

From a traditional Danish perspective, the rules on measures to preserve evidence in cases concerning IP infringement (*supra* 2.2) represent an anomaly in Danish civil procedure law, because these rules provide private right holders with a measure to preserve evidence that is normally only available to the police under criminal procedure law. Sectoral harmonisation has hereby affected the traditional division between Danish civil and criminal procedure law.

2.7. *Conclusion*

The analysis shows that sectoral harmonisation has affected the coherence of the Danish civil justice system by creating divergences that do not reflect general values and principles of civil justice in Denmark. These divergences take the form of special rules or special principles for interpretation of general rules that apply only in a particular type of dispute. Sectoral harmonisation has also affected the division between Danish civil and criminal procedure law in certain cases concerning enforcement of IP rights. This development creates some pertinent challenges, which are discussed below.

3. Sectoral Harmonisation and Danish Civil Procedure Law: Challenges

When internal market harmonisation requires a Member State to introduce new procedural rules that are not based on its general values and principles of civil justice, the Member State is likely to limit the scope of such rules to what is necessary to comply with the harmonisation. There will thus be no legislative spill-over effect into other areas of civil procedure law (sometimes referred to as spontaneous harmonisation). Instead, the new rules will become special rules, often clearly separated from the remaining *general* rules of civil justice, and the harmonisation will thus create new *divergences* in the national civil justice system (*fragmentation*). As shown *supra* 2, there are several examples of this in Danish civil procedure law.

Special rules, which are clearly separated from and alien to the general civil justice system, are unlikely to affect the *general* rules of civil procedure. As an example, the special Danish rules concerning measures to preserve evidence and right to information in IP cases have not affected the general rules of civil procedure law (*supra* 2.2 and 2.3). Likewise, the proposed new special rules concerning disclosure of evidence in competition law cases are also unlikely to affect the general rules on disclosure of evidence in Danish civil procedure law (*supra* 2.1). From a national perspective, this kind of special rules is likely to be regarded as controversial and less legitimate that the general rules of civil procedure. As an example, the measures to preserve evidence in IP disputes were regarded as highly controversial when they were enacted in Denmark.[46]

46 See Clement Salung Petersen, Peter Møgelvang-Hansen and Thomas Riis, *Judicielle forbud/påbud og immaterialretsproces* (Karnov Group 2015) 276.

Special rules increase the complexity in the national civil justice system, which counteracts the general interest that judges focus on the resolution of disputes on the merits rather than using large parts of their capacities on procedural matters.[47] Several of the special rules introduced in Danish law to comply with sectoral harmonisation have raised difficult questions of interpretation and because of their special background in EU law these questions can remain unsettled for a long time until addressed by the CJEU.[48] The special rules can thus create uncertainty and make procedural law less predictable.[49]

4. Danish Civil Procedure and the Internal Market

Whereas the establishment and functioning of the internal market is an important policy area in the EU, maintaining a coherent and systemic approach to civil justice is an important policy aim in Danish civil procedure law. Therefore, the above-mentioned impact and challenges caused by internal market (sectoral) harmonisation of procedural matters are generally undesirable from the perspective of Danish civil procedure law as well as from the perspective of any other Member State that subscribes to a similar policy of maintaining a coherent and systemic approach to civil justice.

This makes it pertinent to consider whether (and how) internal market harmonisation can serve *both* the functioning of the internal market *and* the maintaining of a coherent and systemic approach to civil justice in the Member States.[50] It seems that several factors are important in this regard.

First of all, the EU legislator should acknowledge that harmonising matters of civil procedure law is not *only* a matter of ensuring *enforcement* of particular rights.[51] Civil procedure law is about *civil justice*, and this is obviously a much broader concept than enforcement of particular rights.[52] Therefore, EU harmonisation of procedural matters should be based on, and take into due consideration, generally accepted values and principles of civil justice.[53]

To do this, there is a need to clarify *what* values and principles of civil justice should guide EU action affecting the field of civil procedure law.[54] A good starting point could be the values and principles of civil justice that are common to all (or at least most) of the European Member States. The ongoing research project between the European Law

47 See Wagner (n 4) 101.
48 See *supra* 2.4 about differences of interpretation.
49 See Krans (n 3) 581.
50 The need for coherence in EU harmonisation of civil procedure law is also stressed by Zampia Vernadaki, 'Civil Procedure Harmonization in the EU: Unravelling the Policy Considerations' [2013] Journal of Contemporary European Research 9(2) 297, 299.
51 See *supra* 2 concerning the 'enforcement approach' in the Enforcement Directive and the Antitrust Damages Directive.
52 See *e.g.* Wagner (n 4) 110 and 112.
53 Vernadaki (n 49).
54 Compare Tulibacka (n 36) 1558, who recommends that new EU harmonisation of civil procedures is preceded by comprehensive research into national rules and practices, as well as any reforms which are taking place on the national level.

Institute (ELI) and the American Law Institute (ALI) entitled 'From Transnational Principles to European Rules of Civil Procedure' will probably be able to provide valuable input in this regard.[55] The similar work regarding European private law can also serve as inspiration, including when it comes to the task of finding the right level of detail in defining such common principles.[56] It should also be kept in mind that to guide internal market harmonisation of civil procedure matters, the common values and principles need not be more detailed than such harmonisation can be expected to be within the limits of the principles of subsidiarity and proportionality.[57] Thus, they do not need to address all issues of civil justice, but only those that are likely to be affected by future internal market harmonisation. When such harmonisation expands, the principles could expand with it.

Eventually, the identified values and principles of civil justice could be laid down in a soft law instrument such as Recommendation 2013/396/EU on common principles for injunctive and compensatory collective redress mechanisms in the Member States concerning violations of rights granted under Union law. Such a soft law approach is sufficient for the purposes discussed here, but it should be mentioned that the European Parliament (Committee on Legal Affairs) is currently considering the establishment of common minimum standards for civil procedure in the European Union, including in the form of a Directive.[58]

Secondly, internal market harmonisation should, as far as possible, be based on a coherent and systemic legislative approach to any procedural matter and thus create consistency across different EU instruments.[59] As an example, the requirements to disclosure of evidence should not differ between the Enforcement Directive and the Antitrust Damages Directive, unless these differences have been justified by rational reasons under generally accepted principles of civil justice.

Thirdly, national legislators should be encouraged to adjust their civil procedure law to meet the common European principles. Arguably, a set of European principles of civil procedure is more likely than stand-alone and sometimes incoherent sectoral harmonisation to inspire *national legislators* to adapt their *general* civil procedure law

55 See <www.europeanlawinstitute.eu/projects/current-projects-contd/article/from-transnational-principles-to-european-rules-of-civil-procedure/> accessed 23 January 2016. The topic has also been intensely discussed since the so-called *Storme group* published a study on the possibility of approximating the national laws of civil procedure, see Marcel Storme (ed), *Approximation of Judiciary Law in the European Union* (Springer Netherlands 1994).

56 See *e.g.* the Study Group on a European Civil Code and the Research Group on EC Private Law (Acquis Group), 'Principles, Definitions and Model Rules of European Private Law. Draft Common Frame of Reference (DCFR)' (Outline edition 2009) 9.

57 For an analysis of general civil procedure principles, see *e.g.* Neil Andrews, 'Fundamental Principles of Civil Procedure: Order Out of Chaos' in X.E. Kramer and C.H. van Rhee (eds), *Civil Litigation in a Globalising World* (Springer 2012) 19 with further references.

58 See 'Working document on establishing common minimum standards for civil procedure in the European Union – the legal basis' of 21 December 2015 (European Parliament, Committee on Legal Affairs, Rapporteur: Emil Radev, PE572.853). See also Vernadaki (n 49).

59 This need is also stressed by Burkhard Hess, 'Procedural Harmonisation in a European Context' in X.E. Kramer and C.H. van Rhee (eds), *Civil Litigation in a Globalising World* (Springer 2012) 159, 171; Tulibacka (n 36) 1559; Vernadaki (n 49).

(and thus create a *legislative spill-over effect*). This will remove (or at least minimise) the risk of divergences in national civil procedure law and, at the same time, support a general *convergence* of civil procedure law across Member States, which will in itself support the functioning of the internal market.

In conclusion, internal market harmonisation can serve *both* the functioning of the internal market *and* the maintaining of a coherent and systemic approach to civil justice in the Member States, but it requires a policy change both in the EU and in the Member States when it comes to harmonisation of procedural matters.

5. Concluding Remarks

Sectoral EU harmonisation has affected the coherent and systemic approach to civil justice in Denmark by creating divergences that do not reflect the general values and principles of the Danish civil justice system. These divergences take the form of special rules that apply only in a particular type of dispute and special principles for interpretation of general rules that apply only in a particular type of dispute. Sectoral harmonisation has also affected the division between Danish civil and criminal procedure law in certain cases concerning enforcement of IP rights. Such consequences of sectoral harmonisation constitute a fragmentation of the Danish civil justice system, which increases its complexity and might also affect its legitimacy. Such divergences are therefore generally undesirable from the perspective of Danish civil procedure law – and from the perspective of any other Member State that subscribes to a coherent and systemic approach to civil justice.

On this basis, it is argued that internal market harmonisation of civil procedure matters should, as far as possible, take into due consideration the policy aim of maintaining a coherent and systemic approach to civil justice. The analysis suggests that several factors are important in this regard. In particular, the EU legislator should acknowledge that harmonising matters of civil procedure law is not only about enforcement of particular rights, but about civil justice, and find a coherent and consistent approach to such harmonisation based on the values and principles of civil justice that are common to most (if not all) Member States. At the same time, national legislators should be encouraged to adjust their civil procedure law to meet such common European principles. Consequently, the analysis concludes that it *is* possible for internal market harmonisation of civil procedure matters to serve *both* the functioning of the internal market *and* the maintaining of a coherent and systemic approach to civil justice in the Member States, but that it requires a policy change both in the EU and in the Member States when it comes to such harmonisation of procedural matters.

Neil Andrews*

EUROPEAN INFLUENCES UPON ENGLISH CIVIL JUSTICE: TEMPESTS OR GENTLE BREEZES?

1. Introduction

At any rate in legal matters, adverse weather is not confined to that approaching from the West, that is, from the Atlantic Ocean, Bristol Channel and the Irish Sea. European civil justice initiatives continue to sweep across the North Sea to London (the seat of the UK Parliament). These initiatives take the form of EU Regulations, or Directives, or Recommendations issued by the European Union authorities, or European Court of Justice case law, or the jurisprudence of the Strasbourg court on the European Convention on Human Rights.

But how bad is it? Is this easterly weather system nothing more than intermittent gentle breezes or have there been severe storms? The answer is that weather from the East has mostly involved gentle breezes (so gentle as almost to escape notice). But (on some occasions) easterly blasts have exceeded gale force 10: see discussion in section III of the European Court of Justice's ban on anti-suit injunctions and examination in section VII of the Constitutional Reform Act 2005 where the British Parliament created a new United Kingdom Supreme Court, to secure complete separation of functions between the legislature and judicial system, and to ensure that the Lord Chancellor (that is, the Minister of Justice) can no longer sit as a judge. These tempests have changed the landscape of British law and of its institutions and remedies.

2. European Statutory Changes to English Civil Procedure

Six statutory projects within European Union law have been mandatorily absorbed within the United Kingdom, and other Member States, under the authority of the EU legal framework.[1] Those changes can be listed as follows.

* Professor of Civil Justice and Private Law, University of Cambridge.

1 B Hess, *Europäisches Zivilprozessrecht* (CF Müller Publications, Heidelberg, 2010); A Layton and H Mercer (eds), *European Civil Practice* (2nd edn, Sweet & Maxwell, London, 2004); E Storskrubb, *Civil Procedure and EU Law: A Policy Area Uncovered* (Oxford University Press, 2008); see also C Crifò,

(1) Undoubtedly the most significant of these measures is the system for allocation of jurisdiction and the mutual recognition and enforcement of judgments under the Brussels Convention (1968), which was later adopted by the UK Parliament (the Civil Jurisdiction and Judgments Act 1982), and later embodied as the Brussels I bis (Brussels recast) Regulation (2012).[2] However, the Common Law system was disturbed by the European Court of Justice's ban on anti-suit injunctions vis-à-vis litigious conduct which constitutes a breach of a jurisdiction or arbitration clause (see the trilogy of cases discussed in section III).

In addition, there are:

(2) the Evidence Regulation (2001);[3]
(3) the Enforcement Order Regulation (2004);[4]
(4) the European Payment Order Regulation(2006);[5] and
(5) the European Small Claims Procedure (2007);[6]
(6) the Service Regulation (2007).[7]

'Civil Procedure in the European Order: an Overview of the Latest Developments' in Déirdre Dwyer (ed), *The Civil Procedure Rules Ten Years On* (Oxford University Press, 2009), ch 19; Elena Alina Ontanu and Ekaterina Pannebakker, 'Tackling Language Obstacles in Cross-Border Litigation: The European Order for Payment and the European Small Claims Procedure Approach' (2012) 5 Erasmus LR 169.

2 Council Regulation (EU) 1215/2012: (Brussels I bis) 'on jurisdiction and the recognition and enforcement of judgments in civil and commercial matters', of 12 December, 2012 (effective 10 January, 2015); superseding Council Regulation (EC) No 44/2001 of 22 December 2001.

3 Council Regulation (EC) 1206/2001 on cooperation between the courts of the Member States in the taking evidence in civil or commercial matters [2001]; Eva Storskrubb, *Civil Procedure and EU Law: A Policy Area Uncovered* (Oxford University Press, 2008) ch 7; Case C-283/09 *Werynski v Mediatel 4B spólka zoo* [2012]. See also Laddie J in *Dendron GmbH v University of California* [2004] EWHC 589 (Pat); [2005] 1 WLR 200.

4 Council Regulation (EC) 805/2004 on creating a European Enforcement Order for uncontested claims [2004] OJ L143/15; E Storskrubb, op cit, ch 9.

5 Council Regulation (EC) 1896/2006 on creating a European order for payment procedure [2006] OJ L399/1; implemented at CPR Part 78, section I (since 12 December 2008); Eva Storskrubb, *Civil Procedure and EU Law: A Policy Area Uncovered* (Oxford University Press, 2008) ch 12; Carla Crifò, 'Civil Procedure in the European Order: an Overview of the Latest Developments' in Déirdre Dwyer (ed), *The Civil Procedure Rules Ten Years On* (Oxford University Press, 2009), ch 19, at 370–74.

6 Council Regulation (EC) 861/2007 on establishing a European Small Claims Procedure [2007] OJ L199/1; implemented at CPR Part 78, section II (since 1 January 2009); Eva Storskrubb, *Civil Procedure and EU Law: A Policy Area Uncovered* (Oxford University Press, 2008) ch 13; Carla Crifò, 'Civil Procedure in the European Order: an Overview of the Latest Developments' in Déirdre Dwyer (ed), *The Civil Procedure Rules Ten Years On* (Oxford University Press, 2009) 374–8; and Carla Crifò (2011) 30 CJQ 283.

7 Council Regulation (EC) 1393/2007 on the service in the Member States of judicial and extrajudicial documents in civil or commercial matters [2007] OJ L324/79, repealing Council Regulation (EC) 1348/2000 on the service in the Member States of judicial and extrajudicial documents in civil or commercial matters [2000] OJ L325/79; Eva Storskrubb, *Civil Procedure and EU Law: A Policy Area Uncovered* (Oxford University Press, 2008), ch 6.

3. The EU Ban on Anti-suit Injunctions Concerning Litigation Conducted before Member States

This judicial prohibition (for the European Court of Justice's decisions in the three seminal cases, see below) has hit hard within England and Wales. The ban is much regretted by Common Law lawyers.

Jurisdiction clauses within the EU or for Lugano Convention countries. The European Court of Justice's decision in *Turner v Grovit* (2005)[8] prevents the English courts from issuing anti-suit injunctions to enforce exclusive English jurisdiction clauses where the offending court proceedings have been commenced within the European jurisdictional zone.

Arbitration clauses within the EU or for Lugano Convention countries. The European Court of Justice's decision in *Allianz SpA v West Tankers* (2009)[9] prevents the Common Law anti-suit injunction from being issued to counter breach of arbitration clauses by the commencement of inconsistent *court* litigation within the *same* European jurisdictional zone. But Recital 12 of the Jurisdiction Regulation (2012) (effective from 10 January 2015) makes clear that a judgment by a Member State court on the substance of a civil or commercial case is binding even though that decision involved an incidental decision that the dispute was not subject to a valid arbitration clause.

In the *Gazprom* case (2015),[10] the European Court of Justice, confirming the *West Tankers* case (2009) noted that it is incompatible with the Jurisdiction Regulation for the court of a Member State to issue a decision prohibiting the respondent from continuing, or initiating, civil or commercial proceedings covered by the Jurisdiction Regulation[11] in another Member State. This is because the latter court must be permitted to determine for itself whether it has jurisdiction[12] and this includes determining whether there is a valid arbitration clause in respect of the relevant civil or commercial matter.[13]

However, the European Court of Justice in the *Gazprom* case (2015) distinguished[14] the grant by an arbitral tribunal of an anti-suit order from the issue by a Member State

8 Case C-159/02 *Turner v Grovit* [2005] ECLI:EU:C:2004:228, 1 AC 101, ECJ; for comment, see Neil Andrews, 'Abuse of Process and Obstructive Tactics under the Brussels Jurisdictional System …' (2005) European Community Private Law Review 8–15 (this journal is also entitled *Zeitschrift für Gemeinschaftsprivatrecht* and *Revue de droit privé international*).

9 Case C-185/07 [2009] ECLI:EU:C:2009:69, 1 AC 1138, [2009] 1 Lloyd's Rep 413 (noted by E Peel (2009) 125 LQR 365).

10 Case C-536/13 *Gazprom OAO* case [2015] ECLI:EU:C:2015:316.

11 The *Gazprom* case (2015), ibid, was decided under the pre-2012 Jurisdiction Regulation, Council Regulation (EC) 44/2001 on jurisdiction and the recognition and enforcement of judgments in civil and commercial matters [2000] OJ L012/0001, but it is clear from the Opinion of Advocate General Wathelet (delivered 4 December 2014) that Recital 12 in the preamble to the Brussels 1 Regulation (recast) (Regulation (EU) 1215/2012 on jurisdiction and the recognition and enforcement of judgments in civil and commercial matters [2012] OJ L361/1) is a 'retroactive interpretative law', which 'explains how [the arbitration] exclusion must be and always should have been interpreted' (*per* A-G Wathelet, Opinion, 4 December 2014, at [91] ff).

12 Case C-536/13 *Gazprom OAO* case (n 10) at [32] and [33].

13 Ibid at [34].

14 Ibid at [35].

court of an anti-suit injunction (as in the *West Tankers* case). A Member State court does not act inconsistently with the Jurisdiction Regulation if it decides to recognise or enforce such an arbitral award. The result of such recognition might be that the relevant Member State court decides not to receive or continue to hear a civil or commercial matter (wholly or partially). Such a decision is compatible with the Jurisdiction Regulation because:

(1) issues of arbitration fall outside the scope of the Jurisdiction Regulation,[15] so that any decision on such a matter made by one Member State court cannot be binding under the same Regulation on the courts of other Member States; and
(2) an 'anti-suit' arbitral award (that is, one which prohibits a party from pursuing or continuing court proceedings) is unobjectionable under the Jurisdiction Regulation because the arbitral tribunal is not a Member State court; and so the arbitral award involves no attempt by a Member State court to preclude or constrain (whether directly or indirectly) another Member State court's determination concerning its jurisdiction; there is no conflict between courts in the matter of jurisdiction;[16] and
(3) the arbitral tribunal, unlike the Member State court in the *West Tankers* context, has no direct power to issue penalties against the party who fails to comply with the anti-suit prohibition;[17] this means that the party who is subject to an arbitral tribunal's prohibition has an opportunity to contest[18] whether the prohibitive arbitral award (the 'anti-suit' arbitral award) should be recognised and enforced (in the case of a foreign arbitral award by applying the New York Convention's criteria).[19]

The European Court of Justice in the *Gazprom* case (2015)[20] did not endorse Advocate General Wathelet's Opinion[21] that *West Tankers* has been impliedly reversed by Recital 12 of the Brussels I Regulation (recast).[22] And so the *Gazprom* case (2015) confirms that courts in Member States still lack capacity to issue anti-suit injunctions to give effect to arbitration clauses.

15 Ibid at [36] (and at [28]).
16 Ibid at [37].
17 Ibid at [40].
18 Ibid at [38].
19 Ibid at [38], [41], [42], [43].
20 Ibid.
21 Opinion of Advocate General Wathelet (delivered 4 December 2014), at [130] to [152].
22 Council Regulation (EU) 1215/2012 on jurisdiction and the recognition and enforcement of judgments in civil and commercial matters (Brussels I bis) [2012] OJ L012/0001 (effective 10 January, 2015), superseding Council Regulation (EC) 44/2001 on jurisdiction and the recognition and enforcement of judgements in civil and commercial matters [2001] OJ L012/1.

4. European Account Preservation Order

The UK Government opted out of the European Account Preservation Order Regulation.[23] At the same time the UK Government expressed interest in future proposals.[24] The proposed European order for the preservation of bank accounts in favour of claimants follows the non-English model of operating *in rem* rather than *in personam*, but the element of surprise would be retained by its grant 'without notice' or *ex parte*.

5. Cross-Border Mediation within the EU

English law has implemented the European Directive on Mediation (2008)[25] by an addition to the CPR;[26] by Regulations;[27] by amending the Limitation Act 1980,[28] and by implementing (in the form of Regulations)[29] the confidentiality regime contained within the Directive.

Substantively, the European Directive on Mediation (2008)[30] is of modest significance, for two reasons: its concrete contents are slight;[31] and its 'cross-border' scope renders it of marginal significance. Regrettably, this European intervention has consumed countless hours of official time, both at the European hub and among the Member States. On any sensible cost-benefit analysis this exercise in law-making has hardly been worthwhile.

However, the Directive does at least draw attention to the widespread phenomenon of mediation. And it incidentally underlines the 'voluntary' nature of mediation. This important restatement of fundamental principle occurs in the Preamble to the Directive:

23 Council Regulation (EC) 655/2014 [2014] OJ L189/59 (effective 18 January, 2017); see also: European Commission, Proposal for a Regulation of the European Parliament and of the Council Creating a European Account Preservation Order to facilitate cross-border debt recovery in civil and commercial matters, COM (2011) 445 final <(http://ec.europa.eu/justice/civil/files/comm-2011-445_en.pdf> (accessed 10 March 2016); Emily Lew, Speedy Cross-Border Debt Recovery? The New Europe-Wide Freezing Order' (2011) 11 JIBFL 699.

24 UK Government's Statement, 31 October 2011, www.publications.parliament.uk/pa/cm201011/cmhansrd/ cm111031/wmstext/111031m0001.htm#1110311000006.

25 Council Directive 2008/52/EC on certain aspects of mediation in civil and commercial matters [2008] OJ L136/0003; N Trocker and A De Luca (eds), *La Mediazione Civile alla Luce della Direttiva 2008/52/CE* (Firenze University Press, 2011); Frédérique Ferrand 'Discussion of Directive's reception in Germany and in France' (2011) 16 ZZP Int 29; Carlos Esplugues-Mota 'A New General Legal Regime for Mediation in Spain' (2011) 16 ZZP Int 95.

26 CPR Part 78, section III.

27 Directive Cross-Border Mediation (EU Directive) Regulations 2011/1133, regulation 26.

28 Limitation Act 1980, s 33A (where mediation proceedings are commenced before the limitation period has expired, and that period would otherwise elapse during those proceedings, the period is postponed so as to elapse eight weeks after those proceedings have ended).

29 Cross-Border Mediation (EU Directive) Regulations 2011/1133, regulations 9 and 10.

30 See (n 10) above.

31 For implementation of the Directive Cross-Border Mediation (EU Directive) Regulations 2011/1133: Part 2 introduces provisions concerning mediation privilege in the context of cross-border mediation; and Part 3 introduces provisions to ensure interruption of the limitation period, amending the Limitation Act 1980, by inserting a new s 33A; and amending the Foreign Limitation Periods Act 1984 by inserting a new s 1A.

(para 13) The mediation provided for in this Directive should be a voluntary process in the sense that the parties are themselves in charge of the process and may organise it as they wish and terminate it at any time. However, it should be possible under national law for the courts to set time-limits for a mediation process. Moreover, the courts should be able to draw the parties' attention to the possibility of mediation whenever this is appropriate.

(para 14) Nothing in this Directive should prejudice national legislation making the use of mediation compulsory or subject to incentives or sanctions provided that such legislation does not prevent parties from exercising their right of access to the judicial system...

Thus the authors of the Directive have acknowledged that mediation cannot be thrust upon parties. But the same authors also acknowledge at paragraph (14) that state-controlled incentives and sanctions, ultimately administered by civil courts, can be used to encourage resort to mediation.

Incentives are unproblematic. Sanctions are more controversial. They should be cautiously administered. A sanction should apply only to support a limited duty: this restricted duty is confined to considering mediation, when this possibility is suggested by the other side or by the court.

Other than to exhort Europeans to consider mediation, one wonders why the Directive was introduced at all. Perhaps it is merely a centralist tendency to meddle with something new. Certainly, its scope is very small. Article 2 of the Directive is confined to 'cross-border' mediations of 'civil and commercial' disputes, that is, where the parties are domiciled or habitually resident in different Member States, or the host Member State is different from the parties' Member State. This is a small, arguably even a tiny, category.

A more benevolent view is that the Directive provides a valuable stimulus within the Member States to the expansion of mediation in civil and commercial matters and that certain cross-border issues were perceived by the European authorities as a helpful occasion for 'flagging' the general importance of developing a vibrant culture of mediation.

6. Opt-in and Opt-out Collective Proceedings within Competition Law

In 2013 the EU issued recommendations concerning an opt-out 'collective redress mechanisms'.[32] The Directive on anti-trust damages actions (2014)[33] did not require

32 Commission, 'common principles for injunctive and compensatory collective redress mechanisms in the Member States concerning violation of rights granted under Union law' COM (2013), OJ 2013 L201/60; Commission. 'Collective Redress' (Communication) COM(2013) 401 final; Burkhard Hess, 'European Perspectives on Collective Litigation', in V. Harsagi and C.H. van Rhee (eds), *Multi-Party Redress Mechanisms in Europe: Squeaking Mice?* (Intersentia, Cambridge, 2014) 3–14; Christopher Hodges, 'Collective Redress: A Breakthrough or a Damp Squib?' (2014) 37 Journal of Consumer Policy 67; John Sorabji, 'Reflections on the Commission Communication on Collective Redress' [2014] 17 Irish Journal of Euro Law 62–76; Astrid Stadler, 'The Commission's Recommendations on Common Principles of Collective Redress and Private International Law Issues' [2013] 4 Netherlands Journal of Private International Law 483.

33 Preamble (13) to the Directive of the European Parliament and of the Council on certain rules governing actions for damages under national law for infringements of the competition law provisions

Member States to adopt such mechanisms in order to facilitate claims for competition law damages. But schedule 8 of the Consumer Rights Act 2015 has introduced both an opt-in and an opt-out judicial mechanism (and associated settlement mechanisms) for dealing with claims for damages arising in the competition law context (for details, see below).

Schedule 8 to the Consumer Rights Act 2015 has introduced (by amendment to the Competition Act 1998) both an opt-out and opt-in mechanism for claims before the Competition Appeal Tribunal ('the Tribunal') in respect of competition infringements. The claims can be either for injunctions[34] or money.[35] Exemplary or punitive damages are unavailable.[36]

Such collective proceedings can be commenced by a representative,[37] but that person must obtain from the Tribunal a 'collective proceedings order'.[38] The three effects of such an order are (i) to authorise the representative party to proceed,[39] (ii) to delineate the relevant class of person whose claims are eligible for inclusion in the proceedings,[40] and (iii) to specify whether the proceedings will be opt-in or opt-out.[41] The representative might or might not be a person who is a co-victim within the relevant class.[42] Damages-based agreements are unenforceable in opt-out proceedings.[43]

These collective proceedings do not affect the right to 'bring any other proceedings in respect of the claim'.[44] Limitation periods are suspended during the currency of such collective proceedings, subject to specified termination points.[45]

of the member States and of the European Union ((2013/0185 (COD)), 24 October 2014 http://ec.europa.eu/competition/antitrust/actionsdamages/damages_directive_final_en.pdf (accessed 10 March 2016).

34 Competition Act 1998, s 47D, substituted by Schedule 8 to the Consumer Rights Act 2015.

35 Competition Act 1998, s 47A, substituted by Schedule 8 to the Consumer Rights Act 2015; on these changes, see the Explanatory Notes to section 81 of the 2015 Act, at paras 418 to 450 <www.legislation.gov.uk/ukpga/2015/15/notes/contents>.

36 Competition Act 1998, s 47C (1).

37 Ibid s 47B(2).

38 Ibid s 47B(4) to (9.

39 Ibid s 47B(7)(a).

40 Ibid s 47B(7)(b).

41 Ibid s 47B(7)c).

42 Ibid s 47B(8).

43 S 47C(8), ibid, adopting, ibid at s 47C(9)(c), the definition of DBAs in Courts and Legal Services Act 1990, s 58AA(3).

44 Competition Act 1998, s 47B(13), substituted by Schedule 8 to the Consumer Rights Act 2015.

45 Competition Act 1998, s 47D(4).

Opt-in and opt-out proceedings in this context are defined as follows:[46]

A. opt-in collective proceedings are '*collective proceedings which are brought on behalf of each class member who opts in by notifying the representative, in a manner and by a time specified, that the claim should be included in the collective proceedings*';
B. opt-out collective proceedings are '*collective proceedings which are brought on behalf of each class member except – (a) any class member who opts out by notifying the representative, in a manner and by a time specified, that the claim should not be included in the collective proceedings, and (b) any class member who – (i) is not domiciled in the United Kingdom at a time specified, and (ii) does not, in a manner and by a time specified, opt in by notifying the representative that the claim should be included in the collective proceedings.*'

Judicial decisions (whether judgments or orders) made under these collective regimes are binding on all represented persons.[47]

In both opt-out and opt-in proceedings before the Tribunal compensatory damages (or other pecuniary awards)[48] can be awarded in such proceedings by the Tribunal 'without undertaking an assessment of the amount of damages recoverable in respect of the claim of each represented person'.[49] In opt-out proceedings, the damages will normally be paid to the representative party for distribution amongst the class.[50] In opt-out proceedings damages might remain unallocated to class members after a specified date. These will either be paid to the nominated charity,[51] or the Tribunal might order that such unallocated damages will be paid to the representative in respect of the costs incurred in connection with the proceedings.[52] Injunctions can be awarded in opt-out or opt-in competition law collective proceedings.[53]

Appeals (which can be brought only by the representative)[54] are possible on points of law or concerning money awards or the grant of an injunction.[55]

In the case of opt-out proceedings, the Tribunal can approve a collective settlement,[56] but 'only if satisfied that its terms are just and reasonable'.[57] Such a settlement will then

46 Ibid s 47B(11).
47 Ibid s 47B(12).
48 Ibid s 47C(9)(d).
49 Ibid s 47C(2).
50 Ibid s 47C(3).
51 Ibid s 47C(5). The charity currently nominated is the Access to Justice Foundation, as mentioned at Explanatory Notes to section 81 of the 2015 Act, at para 438 <www.legislation.gov.uk/ukpga/2015/15/notes/contents>.
52 Competition Act 1998, s 47C(6).
53 Ibid s 47D.
54 Ibid s 49(2A).
55 Ibid s 49(1A) to (1D).
56 Ibid s 49A.
57 Ibid s 49A(5).

be binding on all represented persons domiciled in the United Kingdom or those who positively opted in to the collective proceedings.[58]

There is also a (detailed) mechanism for gaining the Tribunal's approval of a collective settlement even where no substantive collective proceedings have already begun. But this requires the Tribunal to make a collective settlement order.[59]

Another aspect peculiar to competition law concerns the doctrine of legal advice privilege and the position of in-house counsel, The European Court of Justice in *Akzo Nobel European Commission* (2010)[60] confirmed that an in-house lawyer's advice does not attract legal advice privilege for the purpose of EU competition law. By contrast, the position in English law is that in-house counsel can give privileged legal advice. This was confirmed in *Alfred Crompton Amusement Machines Ltd v Customs & Excise Commissioners (No 2)* (CA, 1972),[61] where the Court of Appeal noted a long-standing practice,[62] which can be traced to at least the early part of the nineteenth century (in the case of the Treasury Solicitor, the main body of lawyers responsible for conducting much of the litigation affecting the government). According to the English line of authority, salaried in-house counsel can be relied upon to maintain independence and professional probity when advising their client-employer in legal matters. The same respect has been extended to private sector in-house lawyers.

7. Separation of Powers and the European Convention on Human Rights

The Human Rights Act 1998, which took effect in October 2000, rendered the European Convention on Human Rights directly applicable in English courts. Article 6(1) of the Convention states:[63]

> *Right to a Fair Trial: In the determination of his civil rights and obligations or of any criminal charge against him, everyone is entitled to a fair and public hearing within a reasonable time by an independent and impartial tribunal established by law.*

58 Ibid s 49A(8), (9).

59 Ibid s 49B.

60 Case C-550/07 *Akzo Nobel Chemicals Ltd v European Commission* [2011] ECLI:EU:C:1010:512; noted Dr. Andrew Higgins, (2011) 30 CJQ 113; and Lucas Bastin, 'Should 'Independence' of In-House Counsel be a Condition Precedent to a Claim of Legal Professional Privilege...?' (2011) 30 CJQ 33.

61 [1972] 2 QB 102, 129, CA; not challenged on appeal, [1974] AC 405, 430–1, HL.

62 [1972] 2 QB 102, 120, CA, *arguendo*, citing the Revenue Solicitors Act 1828, the Attorneys and Solicitors Act 1874, and the Solicitors Act 1932.

63 (Cmd 8969); Human Rights Act 1998, s 1(3), and Sch 1, incorporates the European Convention on Human Rights into UK law; Jack Beatson et al, *Human Rights: Judicial Protection in the United Kingdom* (Sweet & Maxwell, London, 2008); Mark W. Janies, Richard S. Kay and Anthony W. Bradley, *European Human Rights Law: Text and Materials* (3rd edn, Oxford University Press, 2008); Rickhard Clayton and Hugh Tomlinson QC, *The Law of Human Rights* (2nd edn, Oxford University Press, 2008).

That important codification of fundamental principle comprises the following elements:

(1) The right to 'a fair hearing': this is a wide concept embracing:[64]
   (a) the right to be present at an adversarial hearing;
   (b) the right to equality of arms;
   (c) the right to fair presentation of the evidence;
   (d) the right to cross examine opponents' witnesses;
   (e) the right to a reasoned judgment;[65]
(2) 'a public hearing': including the right to a public pronouncement of judgment;
(3) 'a hearing within a reasonable time'; and
(4) 'a hearing before an independent[66] and impartial[67] tribunal established by law'.

Undoubtedly the most significant impact of the European Convention on Human Rights is the decision to abolish the traditional judicial role of the Lord Chancellor and to reconstitute the Appellate Committee of the House of Lords as the United Kingdom Supreme Court (which first sat on 1 October 2009).

These events unfolded as follows. The European Court of Human Rights in *McGonnell v UK* (2000), in a case concerning legal arrangements on the island of Guernsey, a 'mini-legal system' within the British Isles, had signalled the need for there to be complete separation of judicial, executive, and legislative functions. In the *McGonnell* case the European Court of Human Rights held that the United Kingdom had infringed this requirement because the Bailiff of Guernsey (a judge and a member of the Guernsey legislature) had sat in a civil case concerning planning legislation which had been enacted when he was presiding over the legislative chamber on the island.[68]

The Strasbourg Court in *McGonnell v UK* (2000) held that such a confusion of legislative and judicial roles is '*incompatible with the requisite appearance of independence and impartiality*' demanded by Article 6(1) of the European Convention on Human Rights. The Strasbourg Court declared:

> '*Any direct involvement in the passage of legislation or of executive rules is likely to be sufficient to cast doubt on the judicial impartiality of a person subsequently called to determine a dispute*

64 Richard Clayton and Hugh Tomlinson, op cit.

65 In *Bond v Dunster Properties Ltd* [2011] EWCA Civ 455 Arden LJ explained that the Article 6(1) right to 'a fair hearing within a reasonable time' included the delivery of judgment, hence judgment must be delivered within a reasonable time; but '*what is a reasonable time may well vary according to the complexity of the legal issues, the volume and nature of the evidence and other matters*' (ibid, [4]).

66 *Starrs v Ruxton* 2000 JC 208, 243; 17 November 1999, *The Times* (High Court of Justiciary) *per* Lord Reed; *Millar v Dickson* [2002] 1 WLR 1615, PC.

67 *Porter v Magill* [2001] UKHL 67, [2002] 2 AC 357, HL.

68 *McGonnell v United Kingdom* (2000) 30 EHRR 289; on which, A Le Sueur, 'Access to Justice Rights in the United Kingdom' [2000] 5 EHRLR 457, 467; and R Cornes, '*McGonnell v UK*, the Lord Chancellor and the Law Lords' [2000] PL 166; and D Woodhouse, 'The Office of Lord Chancellor' (1998) PL 617; and 'The Office of Lord Chancellor: Time to Abandon the Judicial Role...' (2002) 22 LS 128, 141–3; and, generally, D Woodhouse, *The Office of the Lord Chancellor* (Hart, Oxford, 2001).

over whether reasons exist to permit a variation from the wording of the legislation or rules at issue.'[69]

The same court said that once a person has presided over a legislative chamber he should be precluded from adjudicating in any civil or criminal case which requires interpretation of the relevant enactment.[70]

The *McGonnell* decision (2000) raised doubts concerning the Lord Chancellor's capacity to adjudicate in judicial cases (in practice the Lord Chancellor would sit in modern times only in appeals heard by the House of Lords or the Privy Council). This is because the Lord Chancellor combined executive, legislative, and judicial functions.[71]

Indeed, the main reason for abolition of the Appellate Committee of the House of Lords was the perceived need to dismantle the three-fold responsibilities of the Lord Chancellor, the so-called 'universal joint' of the British Constitution.[72] For the pre-Constitutional Reform Act 2005 Lord Chancellor combined Cabinet status (with Ministerial responsibility for an Executive branch of government, for a Department of State, for a long time known as the Lord Chancellor's Office, more recently re-named as the Department for Constitutional Affairs, and now called the Ministry of Justice); the Lord Chancellor was also Speaker of the House of Lords, and so he had a legislative capacity; and, thirdly, he was a judge, able to preside in appeals heard by the House of Lords or the Privy Council.[73]

Building on the *McGonnell* case (2000), constitutional purists[74] contended that it would be desirable, even – as they further argued – necessary, to detach the judicial House of Lords from the legislative House of Lords so that (i) the Law Lords would be physically separate from the legislature and (ii) they would no longer be allowed to participate in legislative debates.[75]

As Lord Neuberger (now the President of the UK Supreme Court; formerly a member of the House of Lords in its judicial capacity) diplomatically put it, with a note of agnosticism: 'whether one agrees with it or not', after the Human Rights Act 1998, the

69 *McGonnell* case, (2000) 30 EHRR 289, ECHR, at [55].

70 Ibid [57].

71 For a list of the Law Lords' various roles, R Cornes, '*McGonnell v UK*, the Lord Chancellor and the Law Lords' (2000) PL 166, 174; D Woodhouse, 'The office of Lord Chancellor: time to abandon the judicial role – the rest will follow' (2002) 22 LS 128, 141 ff.

72 Andrew Le Sueur, 'From Appellate Committee to Supreme Court: A Narrative' in Louis Blom-Cooper, Brice Dickson and Gavin Drewry (eds), *The Judicial House of Lords: 1876–2009* (Oxford University Press, 2009) 66–70.

73 On the Law Lords' roles, R Cornes, '*McGonnel v UK*, the Lord Chancellor and the Law Lords' (2000) PL 166, 174; D Woodhouse, 'The office of Lord Chancellor: time to abandon the judicial role–the rest will follow' (2002) 22 LS 128, 141 ff.

74 For example, anticipating the Constitutional Reform Act 2005, Lord Steyn (now retired as a Lord of Appeal in Ordinary), in his 2002 'All Souls College, Neill Lecture', had criticised the multi-faceted role of the Lord Chancellor: Steyn, 'The Case for a Supreme Court' (2002) 118 LQR 382.

75 Non-retired Law Lords had already eschewed participation in Parliamentary debates concerning party-political matters; some had even vowed individually not to speak at all in the legislative chamber: for details, L Blom-Cooper, B Dickson, G Drewry (eds), op cit, at 269, and ibid, David Hope, ch 11, especially at 175 ff.

fact that the House of Lords' appellate committee remained in form 'part of the legislature' was bound to be 'regarded as a constitutional impropriety, at least by the more purist or literalist public lawyers.'[76]

On 12 June 2003, the Labour Government (led by Prime Minister 'Tony' Blair) announced its plan to abolish the ancient judicial function of the Lord Chancellor, to scrap the judicial House of Lords, and to transfer its function to a new Supreme Court. As was well-known, this would end the complex set of offices held by Mr Blair's former pupil-master, then Lord Chancellor, Lord Irvine of Lairg. This Press Release came as a shock, notably to the former pupil-master, who was in 2003 the Lord Chancellor.[77]

In 2005 the Constitutional Reform[78] Act was enacted, leading to the House's abolition in 2009. On 28 July 2009, the Lords of Appeal in Ordinary last gave judgment in the Chamber of the House of Lords (the very last case concerned the question of assisted suicide).[79]

The Constitutional Reform Act 2005 has now stripped out the judicial role from the ancient office of the Lord Chancellor. He has ceased to be a judge. Instead he is merely a representative of the Executive, a Minister of the Crown, and a Cabinet member. Furthermore, since the 2005 Act, the Lord Chancellor need not be legally qualified.

Once the Lord Chancellor had been down-graded to a non-judicial Minister, the ground was cleared for creating a Supreme Court. On 1 October, 2009, the United Kingdom Supreme Court sat for the first time.

The constitutional purists have prevailed. Whether or not there was any constitutional necessity to disturb the settled traditions of the House of Lords, the new court is now manifestly insulated from any 'legislative or executive contamination': none of its judges is involved in the legislative process, or in the practice of Government. But it is still a matter for political debate whether it was necessary to create the Supreme Court and to annihilate the judicial House of Lords.

8. Other Tentacles of European Human Rights Law

'Access to Court' Principle. The European Court of Human Rights in *Golder v U.K.* (1975)[80] divined an implicit fundamental right of 'access to court'. Lord Bingham in *Brown v Stott* (2001) explained:[81]

76 D Neuberger, 'The Supreme Court: Is the House of Lords 'Losing Part of Itself'' (2 December 2009), at [17].

77 Lord Irvine, LC, had not seen the need (2 April 2003): Andrew Le Sueur, 'From Appellate Committee to Supreme Court: A Narrative' in Lois Blom-Cooper QC, Brice Dickson and Gavin Drewry (eds), *The Judicial House of Lords: 1876–2009* (Oxford University Press, 2009) 65 nn 6, 7; although Lord Bingham had advocated such a change: Bingham, 'The Evolving Constitution' [2002] EHRLR 1; and Lord Steyn had also favoured this change, 'The Case for a Supreme Court' (2002) 118 LQR 382.

78 'Reform! Reform! Don't talk to me about reform. Aren't things bad enough already?', *per* Astbury J, as noted by Lord Neuberger, 'The Supreme Court: Is the House of Lords 'Losing Part of Itself'' (2 December 2009), at [13].

79 D Neuberger (n 76), at [2].

80 (1975) 1 EHRR 524, 536, at [35].

81 [2003] 1 AC 681, 694, PC.

'Article 6(1) contains no express right of access to justice, but in Golder v U.K. (1975)[82] *the European Court of Human Rights said that it was 'inconceivable' that this provision should give detailed procedural guarantees without protecting access to justice. The court in the Golder case conceded that this implied right was not absolute and so admitted limitations.'*[83]

Duty to Give Reasoned Judgments. The Court of Appeal in *English v Emery Reimbold & Strick Ltd* (2002) noted that Article 6(1) requires a court to provide a reasoned judgment.[84]

Compatibility of the English 'Striking Out' Procedure and Article 6 of the European Convention on Human Rights. The power to strike out a pleading (now known as a 'statement of case', whether it is a claim, defence, reply, or counterclaim, or any part of one) is exercisable in any of these situations: *the statement of case discloses no reasonable grounds for bringing or defending the claim; or the statement of case is an abuse of the court's process*[85] *or is otherwise likely to obstruct the just disposal of the proceedings; or failure to comply with a rule, practice direction or court order.*[86]

One of the grounds for striking out (because '*the statement of case discloses no reasonable grounds for bringing or defending the claim*') can overlap with the court's jurisdiction to award summary judgment under CPR Part 24 (on which see above). Both pre-trial procedures serve the function of enabling the court to weed out bad or tenuous claims or defences. Both are subject to the evidential constraint that the court can only receive oral evidence at trial. As we shall see, the summary judgment sieve has a slightly finer mesh than the striking out jurisdiction.

The European Court of Human Rights in *Osman v UK* (1998)[87] castigated the English courts for employing striking out to dismiss *legally* unfounded claims. It held that there had been a violation of Article 6 on the facts of that litigation. But the European Court in *Z v UK* (2001) acknowledged that such a pre-trial filter is compatible with the human right to a 'fair hearing', provided the English court only decides to strike out a claim (or possibly a defence) after considering possible pertinent differences between factual situations.[88]

82 (1975) 1 EHRR 524, 536, at [35].

83 Ibid [38].

84 [2002] EWCA Civ 605, [2002] 1 WLR 2409, CA, at [12] (adumbrated by *Flannery v Halifax Estate Agencies Ltd* [2000] EWCA Civ 811 [2000] 1 WLR 377, CA; noted JA Jolowicz [2000] CLJ 263 (judge must give intelligible reasons for rejecting one side's expert testimony and preferring the other side's; a common law decision which ante-dated commencement of the Human Rights Act on 2 October 2000).

85 Generally on abuse of process, Neil Andrews, *English Civil Procedure* (Oxford University Press, 2003), ch 16.

86 CPR 3.4(2)(a) to (c).

87 *Osman v UK* (1998) BHRC 293; (1999) 29 EHRR 245.

88 *Z v United Kingdom - 29392/95* [2001] ECHR 333 (10 May 2001); (2001) 10 BHRC 384, (2002) 34 EHRR 333, [2001] 2 FCR 246, [2001] 2 FLR 612; ECtHR, not following *Osman v UK* (1998) BHRC 293; (1999) 29 EHRR 245; ACL Davies (2001) 117 LQR 52.

The Court in *Z v UK* (2001) said:[89]

> '*There is no reason to consider the striking-out procedure which rules on the existence of sustainable causes of action as per se offending the principle of access to a court. In such a procedure, the plaintiff is generally able to submit to the court the arguments supporting his or her claims on the law and the court will rule on those issues at the conclusion of an adversarial procedure...*'[90] It added: '*the inability of the applicants to sue the local authority flowed not from an immunity but from the applicable principles governing the substantive right of action in domestic law. There was no restriction on access to a court...*'[91]

An example of the English courts acting on this requirement, and considering whether an immunity has been over-stretched, is the Supreme Court of the United Kingdom's abolition in *Jones v Kaney* (2011)[92] of party-appointed expert's immunity.

The Privilege Against Self-Incrimination. In English law the privilege is defined broadly by section 14 of the Civil Evidence Act 1968 as follows:

> '*The right of a person in any legal proceedings other than criminal proceedings to refuse to answer any question or produce any document or thing if to do so would tend to expose that person [or his or her spouse] to proceedings for an offence or for the recovery of a penalty [under UK law]*'

But there is a loose-end concerning pre-existing documents. A majority of the (English) Court of Appeal in *C plc v P* (2007)[93] held that there is no privilege in things or documents existing prior to the order compelling their production, applying the European Court of Human Rights' decision in *Saunders v UK* (1996),[94] where the European Court of Human Rights said:

89 *Z v United Kingdom*, ibid.

90 Ibid at [97].

91 Ibid.

92 [2011] UKSC 13, [2011] 2 AC 398.

93 [2007] EWCA Civ 493, [2008] 1 Ch 1, at [26] to [38], per Longmore LJ, and Sir Martin Nourse at [74]; noted R Moules [2007] CLJ 528.

94 (1996) 23 EHRR 313, at [69]; the ECHR in JB v Switzerland added that the same applies to evidence obtained by means of a tachograph compulsorily fitted to a lorry (1996) 23 EHRR 313, ECHR; Saunders case is noted Neil Andrews [1997] CLJ 243; G Stessens, 'The Obligation to Produce Documents vs the Privilege Against Self-Incrimination' (1997) 22 ELRev Supp HRS 45, 54–5 supports a distinction between (i) (non privileged) bare production of pre-existing material known to exist and (ii) (privileged) admission by 'testimonial' self-incrimination that documents exist, are authentic, have been lost, or destroyed, or information concerning their current location, discernible in US jurisprudence (Fisher v US 425 US 391, 423–3 (1976), US v Doe 465 US 605, 1984); for other comment on the Saunders case, John Andrews, 'Hiding Behind the Veil: Financial Delinquency and the Law' (1997) 22 ELRev 369; and Eriksen and Thorkildsen, 'Self-Incrimination, the Ban on Self-Incrimination after the Saunders Judgment' (1997) 5 Journal of Financial Crime 182.

'The right not to incriminate oneself is primarily concerned... with respecting the will of an accused person to remain silent... [It] does not extend to the use in criminal proceedings of material which may be obtained from the accused through the use of compulsory powers but which has an existence independent of the will of the suspect such as... documents acquired pursuant to a warrant, breath, blood or urine samples and bodily tissue for the purpose of DNA testing.'

9. Concluding Remarks

The English legal system is mature and developed, although not of course beyond improvement.

Most cross-border measures have been absorbed without any disturbance and operate satisfactorily (see section II): the Service Regulation (2007), the Evidence Regulation (2001), the Enforcement Order Regulation (2004), the European Payment Order Regulation (2006), and the European Small Claims Procedure (2007).

The most important European legislative change is the UK's adoption of the Brussels Convention (1968) in the Civil Jurisdiction and Judgments Act 1982 (now Brussels I bis (Brussels recast) Regulation (2012).[95] For the most part this system operates satisfactorily. However, one disturbing result of this jurisdictional system is the European Court of Justice's ban on anti-suit injunctions vis-à-vis litigious conduct which constitutes a breach of a jurisdiction or arbitration clause (see the trilogy of cases discussed in section III).

In so far as it retains the power to choose, England (and the United Kingdom) is not keen to be drawn into European measures which would appear to conflict with traditional techniques and even constitute a retrograde step. This explains, as mentioned in section IV, British unwillingness to adopt the European Account Preservation Order.

In section V we noted the European Directive on Mediation (2008). This instrument's `cross-border' scope renders it of marginal significance. Caution is required. This European intervention has consumed countless hours of official time, both at the European hub and among the Member States. It is doubtful whether this exercise in law-making is worthwhile. It has not made any significant impact within the UK. Its content is narrow. This seems an example of legislation designed to draw attention to an attractive and developing practice.

As noted in section VI, the UK has introduced both an opt-out and opt-in collective proceedings mechanism in respect of competition law infringements. These measures go beyond the requirements of the relevant Directive,

The greatest impact of European law concerns Human Rights law. As noted at section VII, in the Constitutional Reform Act 2005 the British Parliament decided (ostensibly compelled by European human rights jurisprudence) to create a new United Kingdom Supreme Court, to secure complete separation of functions between the legislature and judicial system, and to ensure that the Lord Chancellor (that is, the Minister of Justice) can no longer sit as a judge. This dismantling of long-standing arrangements was a

95 Council Regulation (EC) 1215/2012 OJ L351/1.

dramatic, surprising, and controversial 'spin-off' from the separation of powers notion, more exactly, the concept of 'judicial independence', contained within the European Convention on Human Rights. But it would be incorrect to attribute the entire impetus for this change to the external influence of Strasbourg jurisprudence. Instead some British jurists seized on this external prod in order to bolster their case that constitutional changes were necessary.

Other legal undercurrents are noted at section VIII, notably the Strasbourg case law on the privilege against self-incrimination.

Isabelle Després*

EUROPEAN UNION AND NATIONAL CIVIL PROCEDURE: THE FRENCH PARADOX

1. Introduction

The phrase 'French paradox' usually designates a French singularity which is the relatively low incidence of cardiovascular disease in spite of the rather large proportion of saturated fats in the diet. Can this phrase also be applied to other aspects of French culture?[1] This is the question that comes to mind when one tackles the issue of the links between European Union Law[2] and national civil procedure.

Indeed, a priori, because of the principle[3] of procedural autonomy of States that are members of the European Union (however tempered by the necessities of equivalence and effectiveness), the influence of the European Union on national civil procedures, and specifically on French national civil procedure, would seem extremely limited, and that should be the end of the matter. Nevertheless, some authors[4] observe that 'the actions

* Full Professor at the University of Nantes, Faculty of Law and Political Sciences. Special thanks to my dearest brother Charles, whose help translating this paper into English was so precious to me.

1 For more information about the links between culture and procedural law, see *Droit et culture: Travaux de l'association Henri Capitant, tome LVIII, Journées louisianaises, 19–23 mai 2008* (Bruylant 2010), 407 ff and especially Loïc Cadiet, 'Culture et droit processuel: questionnaire relatif au thème n° 3,' No 3 ff. <www.henricapitant.org/sites/default/files/Culture_et_droit_processuel.pdf> accessed 5 March 2016. In No 4.4 (p 6), the author quotes Wouter De Vos: 'The close link between civil procedural law and the cultural milieu in which it developed is a well-known phenomenon among proceduralists.' However, in No 4.5 (p 9), the author also quotes Alfredo Buzaid, according to whom 'contrary to other fields of juridical science, which reflect the character of peoples throughout their long traditions, civil procedure must be given exclusively rational means in order to enforce the law.'

2 There will be no discussion here of the better-known links between European human rights law and national civil procedure, ie the impact of article 6(1) of the European Convention on Human Rights (Right to a fair trial). Nor will article 47 of the Charter of Fundamental Rights of the European Union (Right to an effective remedy and to a fair trial), which is very similar to article 6(1) above, be discussed.

3 For a brief reminder of European Court of justice case law, see *Le juge administratif et le droit de l'Union européenne: Les dossiers thématiques du Conseil d'Etat* (23 September 2015) 9 <www.conseil-etat.fr/content/download/47718/416523/version/5/file/juge-adm-et-droit-ue.pdf> accessed 5 March 2016, esp Cases 33/76 *Rewe v Landwirtschaftskammer Saarland* and 45/76 *Comet v Produktschap voor Siergewassen* [1976], as well as Case 265/78 Ferwerda v Produktshap voor Vee en Vlees [1980] ECLI:EU:C:1980:66.

4 Serge Guinchard, Frédérique Ferrand and Cécile Chainais, *Procédure civile* (4th edn, Dalloz 2015) para 1553.

taken by the European Union in the creation of the so-called 'area of freedom, security and justice' is considerable' and conclude that 'these regulations have a direct impact on French civil procedure' (although they do not go into further detail).

These two contrasting views confirm the theory put forth by our Dutch Colleague, Mr Krans, of an 'invisible pillar'[5] that is leading us, according to him, to the Europeanisation of procedural law. Naturally, this extremely interesting hypothesis[6] emanating from a Dutchman leads one to consider the question as regards France. How can the situation be invisible to the naked eye of some, while it seems blindingly obvious to others? Probably because the phenomenon manifests itself mostly in indirect ways.

Because of the segmentation of the disciplines that are taught and the fields of research that are investigated, specialists tend to ignore problems that are part of other academic fields. Thus, for example, in France,[7] conflicts of jurisdiction are traditionally studied by internationalists[8] and consumer law procedure by consumer law specialists.[9] This is the reason why, notably in these fields where the work done by the European Union is considerable, its greater consequences on the general theory of private judicial law are not really studied. Although they are alluded to here and there, they are never studied in depth.

5 Bart Krans, 'EU Law and National Civil Procedure Law: An Invisible Pillar' [2015] European Review of Private Law 567.

6 Krans (n 5) 581 'the invisible pillar is a large pillar and in fact of course not really invisible. This [...] pillar is not created for the purpose of a pillar of European influence on national civil procedure law but has, as such, risen more or less accidentally. EU law has gained a significant degree of influence on national civil procedure law of the Member States. This pillar does not concern cross-border cases but procedural topics relevant for purely national issues. Of course, this pillar will not have the same size in every Member State.'

7 In other countries, the situation is sometimes different: in Germany, 'civil procedure law (...) includes (...) international conflicts of jurisdiction. Private international law thus only concerns itself with conflicts of laws' and the legislators chose 'not to write a separate consumer code', and put all the laws relative to consumer protection in the *Bürgerliches Gesetzbuch* (German civil code) instead when they reformed German law on November 26, 2001 (Act on the Modernisation of the Law of Obligations). See Claude Witz, *Le droit allemand*, (2nd edn, Dalloz 2013) 87 and 92.

8 It is almost certain that the first one to break with that tradition was Mr Cadiet, *Droit judiciaire privé* (Litec 1992). He justified it thus, 'One should have a comprehensive view of private judicial law (...) The double dimension of private judicial law (domestic and international) must be seen. (...) Traditionally, in France, the international dimension of private judicial law is studied as part of private international law. (...) Nevertheless, conflicts of jurisdiction have as much to do with judicial law as with international law. (...) The creation of European rules to enforce individual rights across borders further embeds international judicial law in civil judicial law, thus widening its span.' Loïc Cadiet, *Droit judiciaire privé* (2nd edn, Litec 1998) para 25. He has always maintained this view of things. See also Loïc Cadiet and Emmanuel Jeuland, *Droit judiciaire privé* (8th edn, LexisNexis 2013). Other authors have adopted the same point of view. That is why, in 2006, they changed the name of their book, 'Civil Procedure', to 'Civil Procedure: Domestic Law and Law of the European Union'. Serge Guinchard, Cécile Chainais and Frédérique Ferrand, *Procédure civile: droit interne et droit de l'Union européenne* (32nd edn, Dalloz 2014).

9 Consumer law books devote numerous pages to consumer law procedure. Jean Calais-Auloy and Henri Temple, *Droit de la consommation* (9th edn, Dalloz 2015) para 586–698, Jérôme Julien, *Droit de la consommation* (LGDJ 2015) para 415–473 (about 100 pages or 15% of each book).

In order to check the validity of this initial intuition of creeping Europeanisation, the reflection in this paper will follow three consecutive lines of thought, ie an approach through private international law, an approach through consumer law and finally, an approach through civil procedure itself.

2. The Private International Law Approach

To think that private international law, and more specifically European private international law, could be a vector of change in national procedural law may seem strange, but it is not a simple figment of the imagination, which is quickly proved by a glance at the three fields concerned with conflicts of jurisdiction (direct jurisdiction, procedure and indirect jurisdiction).

First, one must remind the reader that, in the presence of an international element, the main rules that define the *direct jurisdiction* of French courts 'are simply the transposition, on the international plane, of the criteria of national territorial jurisdiction.'[10] It may be true that these are general rules of law, which only apply in the absence of special rules, and that these general rules of law are often superseded by special jurisdiction rules elaborated within the framework of the European Union, particularly by those emanating from the new Brussels I regulation.[11] Nevertheless, there is evidence that, like a two-stage rocket, interactions between European law and general law can have an impact on domestic law in the long run.

The following is an illustration of how European international private law can lead to modifications in national law (and thus, by ricochet, in general international private law, if it still has to come into play). In an unpublished judgment of November 5, 2008, the *Cour de cassation* (French supreme court for private disputes)[12] applied article 16(1) of the Brussels I regulation[13] to enable a consumer to refer to a local judge.[14] A few months after this judgement, article L 141-5 was added[15] to the French consumer code (as opposed to the civil procedure code),[16] specifying that 'the consumer is free to choose to refer to, in addition to one of the territorially competent courts under the civil

10 Cadiet and Jeuland, (n 8) para 13.

11 Regulation (EU) 1215/2012 of the European Parliament and of the Council of 12 December 2012 on jurisdiction and the recognition and enforcement of judgements in civil and commercial matters, also called Brussels Ia.

12 Cass civ (1) 5 November 2008, Case 07-18064.

13 Council Regulation (EC) 44/2001 of 22 December 2000 on jurisdiction and the recognition and enforcement of judgements in civil and commercial matters.

14 Hélène Gaudemet-Tallon, *Compétence et exécution des jugements en Europe, Matières civile et commerciale: Règlements 44/2001 et 1215/2012, Conventions de Bruxelles (1968) et de Lugano (1988 et 2007)* (5th edn, LGDJ 2015) para 289. The author explains that the consumer is free to refer to a local court and that European law has evolved subtly on this point over the years (article 14 Brussels Convention, article 16(1) Brussels I Regulation, article 18 Brussels Ia Regulation).

15 *Loi* n° 2009-526 du 12 mai 2009 de simplification et de clarification du droit et d'allègement des procédures (article 24).

16 Thus bridging the gap between the private international law and consumer law approaches dealt with in this paper.

procedure code, the court of his place of residence at the time when the contract was entered into or when the harmful event occurred.' The adoption of the forum actoris in French domestic law is indeed posterior to its consecration in European law.

Secondly, even if 'questions of *procedure* have traditionally been resolved under the law of the forum since the origins of the science of conflicts of laws,'[17] Mrs Niboyet[18] still chose to speak 'against the systematic use of the lex fori when it comes to procedure.' It is in all probability in the field of evidence that the most spectacular changes are likely to take place, making use of European Council regulation 1206/2001 of May 28, 2001.[19] Article 10(3) of this regulation, which allows[20] a court to request from another court the execution of an investigatory measure under a special form[21] existing in its national law (and not in that of the requested court), seems likely to 'disturb habits' but there is reason to think 'that, after a possibly difficult transitional period, the implementation of this regulation will result in a smooth harmonisation of judicial practices as regards investigatory measures, by mutual impregnation' and even that, after some time, it will be 'difficult to discriminate between purely national procedures and cross-border procedures, as it seems obvious that judges will deal with both of them in the same way, without distinction' and as a result, in the end, 'the regulation will no longer apply only to cross-border matters but will progressively [infiltrate] national litigation.'[22] Before we reach that point,[23] the ability to apply foreign procedures already gives States the benefit of 'a means to curb the instrumentalisation of their judicial institutions by litigants'[24] looking for more efficient methods to defend their interests.

17 Marie-Laure Niboyet and Géraud de Geouffre de la Pradelle, *Droit international privé* (4th edn, LGDJ 2013) para 653.

18 Marie-Laure Niboyet, 'Contre le dogme de la *lex fori* en matière de procédure' in *Vers de nouveaux équilibres entre ordres juridiques: Mélanges en l'honneur de Hélène Gaudemet-Tallon* (Dalloz 2008) 365.

19 Regulation on cooperation between the courts of the Member States in the taking of evidence in civil or commercial matters.

20 Such special procedures are not new, since article 9 of the Hague Convention of 18 March 1970 on the Taking of Evidence Abroad in Civil and Commercial Matters had opened the door to such practices. The novelty in regulation 1206/2001 lies in the possibility for judges to communicate directly, without any intermediary.

21 For example, an English judge can ask a French judge to submit a witness to cross-examination, even though the procedure does not exist in French law. Marie-Laure Niboyet, 'Les nouvelles figures de la coopération judiciaire civile européenne' (2004) 131 Droit et patrimoine 53.

22 Daniel Lebeau and Marie-Laure Niboyet, 'Regards croisés du processualiste et de l'internationaliste sur le règlement CE du 28 mai 2001 relatif à l'obtention des preuves civiles à l'étranger' (19–20 February 2003) Gazette du Palais 6.

23 In 2009, Niboyet described an 'excessive discrepancy between the potential applications of the laws and actual practice', because of 'force of habit and perhaps overworked judges, more than a lack of knowledge or the complexity' of said laws. Marie-Laure Niboyet, 'Propos conclusifs' in Fabienne Jault-Seseke, Juliette Lelieur and Christian Pigache (eds), *L'espace judiciaire européen civil et pénal: regards croisés* (Dalloz 2009) 181, 185–186.

24 Niboyet and de Geouffre de la Pradelle, (n 17) para 657.

As far as the adoption of European order for payment[25] and small claims[26] procedures is concerned, a 'fierce controversy'[27] erupted between the Commission and member states about whether or not their application should be restricted to cross-border litigation. An interpretation that 'did not abusively wring meaning'[28] from the text[29] won[30] and, as a consequence, the optional instrument method[31] was chosen for each procedure. One notable result is that French[32] and European[33] order for payment procedures coexist and come into play according to the type of litigation at hand. Currently, they are just separate entities. However, one cannot exclude that, in time, they might influence each other.

Thirdly, as regards *indirect jurisdiction*, it is 'by a sort of imitation [of European liberalism that French] general law about foreign rulings'[34] ended up more streamlined.[35]

In addition, article 54(1) of the Brussels Ia regulation probably offers new prospects in the standardisation of national laws. The text makes it possible to adapt foreign rulings issuing a measure or an order that is not provided for in the law of the petitioned state. One author[36] wrote about this topic that the field 'of provisional and interim measures could prove to be the main field of application of the new provision. Indeed, it is largely known that the specific laws of member states vary widely in this domain. The example of English interim measures issued as in personam orders is one of the best illustrations of this fact. An English freezing order (old Mareva injunction) will thus have to be acknowledged and enforced in France, with the exception of in rem seizures. Identifying

25 Regulation (EC) 1896/2006 of the European Parliament and of the Council of 12 December 2006 creating a European order for payment procedure.

26 Regulation (EC) 861/2007 of the European Parliament and of the Council of 11 July 2007 establishing a European small claims procedure.

27 Marie-Laure Niboyet, '2005: la coopération judiciaire européenne prend sa vitesse de croisière' (2006) 145 Droit et patrimoine 110, 112.

28 Cyril Nourissat, 'Droit civil de l'Union européenne: panorama 2005' [2006] Recueil Dalloz 1259, 1265.

29 Formerly article 65 TEC, now article 81 TFEU.

30 Rafal Manko, *Europeanisation of civil procedure: towards common minimum standards?* (European Parliamentary Research Service, 2015) 11, 'the requirement of a cross-border element has been maintained under Lisbon, which means that EU involvement in civil justice is possible only if there are connecting factors in a case (eg residence, place of performance etc) pointing to at least two different Member States.'

31 'So-called optional instruments (...) supplement national laws without replacing them. Even if it is spreading slowly, the use of optional instruments deserves to become more common. It allows, better than other methods, to abide by the European motto, 'United in diversity'. Nevertheless, resolute implementation of optional instruments in Europe will require considerable information efforts.' Bénédicte Fauvarque-Cosson, 'Le droit des contrats au cœur de l'innovation juridique' in *Liber amicorum Camille Jauffret-Spinosi* (Dalloz 2013) 323, 335 and 336–337.

32 Articles 1405 ff of the *Code de procédure civile* (French civil procedure code).

33 Articles 1424–1 ff of the *Code de procédure civile* (French civil procedure code).

34 Niboyet and de Geouffre de la Pradelle, (n 17) para 6.

35 Cornelissen Case, Cass civ (1) 20 February 2007, Bertrand Ancel and Horatia Muir Watt [2007] Revue critique de droit international privé 420 (note), François-Xavier Train [2007] Journal du droit international 1195 (note), Louis d'Avout and Sylvain Bollée [2007] Recueil Dalloz 1115, Marie-Laure Niboyet, 'L'abandon du contrôle de la compétence législative indirecte (le 'grand arrêt' Cornelissen du 20 févr. 2007)' (29 April – 3 May 2007) Gazette du Palais 2.

36 Gilles Cuniberti, 'La réforme du règlement Bruxelles I' (February 2013) Droit et procédures 26, 31.

such equivalent mechanisms will not be easy.' Nonetheless, this will be something to strive for. Anyway, it seems that the adaptation method concretised[37] by the Brussels regulations bears the seeds of future change in domestic law.

Thus, it can be said that the private international law approach reveals the strong prospective dimension of the question of the influence of European law on national civil procedure, which is by all means much stronger than that which appears in the consumer law approach to be delineated below.

3. The Consumer Law Approach

For a long time,[38] the protection of consumers has been a major concern[39] of the European Union. The standards set in relation to this 'reflect three lines of thought: the protection of their health and their safety, the protection of their economic interests, notably in contractual relationships with professionals, and finally, action taken in defense of their individual or collective rights in litigation, and especially cross-border litigation, with said professionals.'[40] Indeed, one must understand that, 'in order to really protect consumers, it is not enough to set substantive rules. It must be ensured that those rules are enforced, thanks to efficient procedures.'[41] And this is where European Union law meets national civil procedure, and in our case, French civil procedure. The two (unfruitful?) encounters described below have to do with, on the one hand, the extent of the judge's role regarding laws, and on the other hand, the introduction of class action as a judicial tool destined to federate the interests of consumers.

It is well-known that, to the Court of justice,[42] the protection that the directive on unfair terms[43] offers to consumers 'implies that a national judge is able to appreciate *ex officio* the unfairness of a clause of a contract that is submitted to him when he assesses the admissibility of a claim brought to a national court'. The Court of justice confirmed the above-mentioned landmark ruling when other directives were concerned (directive relative to consumer credit,[44] directive regarding contracts signed away from business

37 'This adaptation method is possible under regulation 44/2001'. Case C-235/09 *DHL Express v Chronopost* [2011] ECLI:EU:C:2011:238. Hélène Gaudemet-Tallon (n 14) para 374.

38 'In the beginning, the EEC did not pay special attention to consumers' interests. Although the Treaty of Rome of 25 March 1957 did mention the 'consumer' in various places, it did not propose a consumer protection policy.' Over time, the situation has evolved significantly. Gilles Paisant, *Défense et illustration du droit de la consommation* (LexisNexis 2015) para 24.

39 'Consumer safety and consumer rights are described as 'priorities of European Union policies.'' Paisant (n 38).

40 Paisant (n 38).

41 Calais-Auloy and Temple, (n 9) para 586.

42 Cases C-240/98 *Oceano Grupo Editorial SA v Rocio Murciano Quintero* [2000] and C-241/98 *Salvat Editores SA v José M Sanchez Alcon Prades* [2000] ECLI:EU:C:2000:346. See also Case C-473/00 *Cofidis v Fredout* [2002] ECLI:EU:C:2002:705.

43 Council Directive 93/13/EEC of 5 April 1993 on unfair terms in consumer contracts.

44 Council Directive 87/102/EEC of 22 December 1986 for the approximation of the laws, regulations and administrative provisions of the Member States concerning consumer credit, as amended by Directive 98/7/EC of the European Parliament and of the Council of 16 February 1998. See Case C-429/05 *Rampion v Franfinance* [2007] ECLI:EU:C:2007:575.

premises,[45] directive on certain aspects of the sale of consumer goods and associated guarantees)[46] and even increased its reach when deciding that 'the national court is required to examine, of its own motion, the unfairness of a contractual term where it has the legal and factual elements to do so.'[47]

In contrast, in France, the *Cour de cassation*,[48] most certainly 'out of fear of a dramatic (…) surge in appeals',[49] had spoken against the possibility for a judge to apply consumer laws ex officio, the reason being that such laws, being part of a public order of protection (as opposed to a public order of direction, the rules of which are set with general interest in mind), could therefore only be invoked by the person that they protect (that is to say, the consumer, who unfortunately is often unaware of the rights granted to him). Despite widespread outcry, as many deemed it contrary to the provisions of the civil procedure code,[50] this stance was maintained, until new legislation resulted in a sudden about-face.[51] The Chatel Act[52] (after the name of the Secretary of State in charge of consumer affairs and tourism) gave birth to article L 141–4 of the consumer code, which specifies that 'the judge can take into account any provision of the present code, ex officio, in litigation arising from its application.' The Hamon Act[53] (after the name of the Minister of social and solidarity-based economy and consumer affairs) went further and added a paragraph to the article, reading thus: 'After listening to the parties involved, he rejects, ex officio, the application of any clause the unfairness of which emerges from the discussion.' Since the indicative

45 Council Directive 85/577/EEC of 20 December 1985 to protect the consumer in respect of contracts negociated away from business premises. See Case C-227/08 *Eva Martin v EDP Editores SL* [2009] ECLI:EU:C:2009:792.

46 Directive 1999/44/EC of the European Parliament and of the Council of 25 May 1999 on certain aspects of the sale of consumer goods and associated guarantees. See Case C-32/12 *Soledad Duarte Hueros v Autociba SA* [2013] ECLI:EU:C:2013:637.

47 Case C-243/08 *Pannon v Erzsébet Sustikné Gyorfi* [2009] ECLI:EU:C:2009:350.

48 Cass civ (1) 15 February 2000, Case 98–12713 [2000] Bulletin civil I 49, 'The only person that can bring before a court violations of articles L 311–2, L 311–8 and L 311–10 of the consumer code, even if these are public policy provisions, is the person these provisions are destined to protect; therefore, these violations cannot be taken into account ex officio by the judge before whom the beneficiary has not appeared.'

49 Ghislain Poissonnier, 'Office du juge en droit de la consommation: une clarification bienvenue' [2008] Recueil Dalloz 1285, 1288.

50 Article 12 of the *Code de procédure civile* (French civil procedure code), 'The judge shall resolve the dispute according to the applicable laws. He shall name the facts and contracts, disregarding any denominations the parties may have used. (…)'. However, the *Cour de cassation* decided that 'Even though, as a general principle, article 12 of the *Code de procédure civile* requires the judge to name the facts and contracts, disregarding any denominations the parties may have used, it does not require him, in the absence of special rules, to change the choice of legal rule being invoked. Cass Ass plén 21 December 2007, Case 06–11343 [2007] Bulletin civil AP 10, Régis de Gouttes (11 January 2008) Gazette du Palais 13 (note), Olivier Deshayes, 'L'office du juge à la recherche de sens (à propos de l'arrêt d'assemblée plénière du 21 déc. 2007)' [2008] Recueil Dalloz 1102.

51 Cass civ (1) 22 January 2009, Case 05–20176 [2009] Bulletin civil I 9, 'Violations of the public order provisions of the consumer code can be taken into account ex officio by a judge'.

52 *Loi* n° 2008–3 du 3 janvier 2008 pour le développement de la concurrence au service des consommateurs (article 34).

53 *Loi* n° 2014–344 du 17 mars 2014 relative à la consommation (article 81).

usually stands for the imperative in legal texts, the compliance of French law with European requirements now seems to be a done deal. In spite of the progress made thanks to the amendments to the consumer code, 'criticism can be aimed against article L. 141-4 (...). Technically, this [article has to do with] procedure [and, if necessary, should have been codified in the civil procedure code]. As far as its content is concerned, [it should have appeared that] this reform was useless, since a judge had, and still has, the power to take into account a legal text [ex officio],'[54] while still abiding by both the principle of the right to a fair hearing[55] and the principle of party disposition.[56]

As regards *class action*, the European impulse results from a number of initiatives. The Commission first raised the question in a Green Paper[57] about class action for consumers and then opened the debate[58] with a public consultation[59] in order to try to unify the European approach to these matters. In addition, the Parliament passed a resolution[60] on this issue. And finally, on June 11, 2013, the Commission issued a recommendation[61] inviting, 'without being a binding obligation,[62] Member States to implement collective redress mechanisms in order to ensure their citizens' effective access to justice in the event of a violation of the rights that the European Union grants to them.'[63] In addition, collective redress should manifest itself not only as injunctive redress, but also as compensatory redress.

Injunctive collective redress and unfair terms removal action, as defined in article L. 421-6 of the consumer code, was created in 1988 and has been modified several times since. The above-mentioned Hamon Act,[64] 'spurred by a landmark European Union Court of Justice decision[65], tried to widen the reach of rulings,'[66] by allowing associations to ask the judge to declare that the terms recognised as unfair be deemed unwritten 'in

54 Poissonnier (n 49) 1291.

55 Article 16 of the *Code de procédure civile*, a judge 'cannot make a decision based on the legal texts he has taken into account ex officio without having first consulted the parties concerned.'

56 Article 5 of the *Code de procédure civile*, 'A judge must render a judgement about everything that is in question and only about what is in question.'

57 Green Paper of 27 November 2008 on Consumer Collective Redress, COM(2008) 794 final.

58 Communication from the Commission to the European Parliament, the Council, the European Economic and Social Committee and the Committee of the Regions of 31 March 2010, COM(2010) 135 final 8.

59 Commission staff working document of 4 February 2011, Public Consultation: Towards a Coherent European Approach to Collective Redress, SEC(2011) 173 final.

60 European Parliament resolution of 2 February 2012 on 'Towards a Coherent European Approach to Collective Redress', 2011/2089(INI).

61 Commission recommendation of 11 June 2013 on common principles for injunctive and compensatory collective redress mechanisms in the Member States concerning violations of rights granted under Union Law, 2013/396/EU.

62 Nevertheless, it is mentioned (para 38) that 'The Member States should implement the principles set out in this Recommendation in national collective redress systems by 26 July 2015 at the latest.'

63 Daniel Mainguy, *L'action de groupe en droit français après la loi Hamon du 17 mars 2014* (Gazette du Palais 2014) para 54.

64 See *supra* text and footnote 53.

65 Case C-472/10 *Nemzetti Fogyasztovédelmi Hatosag v Invitel Tavközlési Zrt* [2012] ECLI:EU:C:2012:242.

66 Paisant (n 38) para 73.

all identical contracts established by the same professional with consumers,'[67] whether those contracts be 'running or not.'[68]

In the case of compensatory collective redress, French-style class action[69] was born[70] in 2014 with the passing of the Hamon Act.[71] Under articles L. 423-1 and those following of the consumer code (which have already been modified),[72] nationally representative and approved consumer rights organisations, and those exclusively, are granted standing 'to seek compensation for individual losses sustained by consumers who are in similar or identical situations, such losses having for common cause breach of their legal or contractual obligations by one or more professionals.' In addition, it is specified right away (as it has a bearing on the procedure that naturally follows) that the infringement resulting in the damage may either take place following the sale of goods or during the providing of services, or stem from anticompetitive practices. Finally, it must be pointed out that 'Class action can only concern redress of property loss resulting from material damage sustained by consumers.' Viewed in this light, class action seems rather tightly regulated. Nevertheless, step by step, it is slowly encroaching upon other fields,[73] which makes all the more regrettable the choice of an approach through consumer law rather through civil procedure itself.[74]

4. The Approach through Civil Procedure Itself

The approach through civil procedure itself is rarely chosen. Nevertheless, mediation and the duty to give reasons constitute two examples worth mentioning.

67 Article L 421-6 of the *Code de la consommation* (French consumer code).

68 Article L 421-6 of the *Code de la consommation*, in the part modified by article 40 of the Macron Act (after the name of the Minister of economy, industry and digital affairs). *Loi* n° 2015-990 du 6 août 2015 pour la croissance, l'activité et l'égalité des chances économiques.

69 Serge Guinchard, 'Une *class action* à la française?' [2005] Recueil Dalloz 2180.

70 Before that, there was jointly represented action, adopted in 1992 and described thus in articles L 422-1 ff of the *Code de la consommation*, 'when several consumers who are identified natural persons have sustained individual losses because of violations committed by the same professional (...), any nationally representative and approved consumer rights organization (...) can, if it has been mandated by at least two of the concerned consumers, bring the matter before any court in the name of those consumers.' 'Because of its specific constraints – such as requiring a mandate and the inability for organizations to solicit consumers – it was abandoned (...). Curiously, the law introducing class action did not do away with jointly represented action'. Maria José Azar-Baud, 'Réflexions autour de l'efficacité de l'action de groupe' in Linda Arcelin-Lécuyer (ed), *Le droit de la consommation après la loi du 17 mars 2014* (Presses universitaires de Rennes 2015) 105, 109.

71 See *supra* text and footnotes 53 and 64 (article 1).

72 By article 42 of the Macron Act (n 68) and article 3 of *Loi* n° 2015-1268 du 14 octobre 2015 d'actualisation du droit des outre-mer.

73 *Loi* n° 2016-41 du 26 janvier 2016 de modernisation de notre système de santé created a specific class action procedure for healthcare products, as described in articles L 1143-1 ff of the *Code de la santé publique* (French public health code). K Haeri and B Javaux, 'L'action de groupe en matière de produits de santé: une procédure complexe à l'efficience incertaine' [2016] Recueil Dalloz 330. As regards class action against discrimination, a law is pending.

74 Louis Boré, 'Pour l'introduction d'une action de groupe dans le nouveau Code de procédure civile' in Jean Foyer and Catherine Puigelier (eds), *Le nouveau Code de procédure civile (1975-2005)* (Economica 2006) 131.

The preference for amicable dispute resolutions 'broadly corresponds with the contemporary contractualisation of social relations.'[75] Therefore, it is not surprising that, when it comes to cross-border litigation, the European Union adopted the directive of May 21, 2008 on certain aspects of *mediation* in civil and commercial matters.[76] According to article 3(a) of the directive, 'Mediation means a structured process, however named or referred to, whereby two or more parties to a dispute attempt themselves, on a voluntary basis, to reach an agreement on the settlement of their dispute with the assistance of a mediator. This process may be initiated by the parties or suggested or ordered by a court or prescribed by the law of a Member State (§1). It includes mediation conducted by a judge who is not responsible for any judicial proceedings concerning the dispute in question. It excludes attempts made by the court or the judge seized to settle a dispute in the course of judicial proceedings concerning the dispute in question (§2).' In the end,[77] this definition, as well as the whole directive ended up inspiring the French legislator in charge of its transposition. It was a sizeable task despite the fact that it had initially been claimed[78] that the European framework could be accommodated 'with total peace of mind,' since it 'hardly affected' the state of the law.

In truth, leaning on the European Union allows the national government to use a 'powerful lever'[79] to promote alternative dispute resolution in domestic law. Thus it becomes easier to understand that, to go along with the transposition of the

[75] Yvon Desdevises, 'La médiation en France et la directive 2008/52/CE du Parlement européen et du Conseil du 21 mai 2008' in Nicolo Trocker and Alessandra De Luca, *La mediazione civile alla luce della direttiva 2008/52/CE* (Firenze University press 2011) 35, 43.

[76] Directive 2008/52/EC of the European Parliament and of the Council of 21 May 2008 on certain aspects of mediation in civil and commercial matters. Earlier, on 19 April 2002, the Commission had presented a Green Paper on alternative dispute resolution in civil and commercial law, COM(2002) 196 final. After the Directive, additional legislation was adopted: on the one hand, Directive 2013/11/EU of the European Parliament and of the Council of 21 May 2013 on alternative dispute resolution for consumer disputes and amending Regulation (EC) 2006/2004 and Directive 2009/22/EC (Directive on consumer ADR) and on the other hand, Regulation (EU) 524/2013 of the European Parliament and of the Council of 21 May 2013 on online dispute resolution for consumer disputes and amending Regulation (EC) 2006/2004 and Directive 2009/22/EC (Regulation on consumer ODR).

[77] The directive had to be implemented in national law by member states before 21 May 2011. France was late, as well as 9 other member states, and implemented it in *Ordonnance* n° 2011-1540 du 16 novembre 2011 portant transposition de la directive 2008/52/CE du Parlement européen et du Conseil du 21 mai 2008 sur certains aspects de la médiation en matière civile et commerciale, and in *Décret* n° 2012-66 du 20 janvier 2012 relatif à la résolution amiable des différends. As regards the Directive on consumer ADR (see n 76), it was implemented in the *Code de la consommation* by *Ordonnance* n° 2015-1033 du 20 août 2015 relative au règlement extrajudiciaire des litiges de consommation, and by *Décret* n° 2015-1382 du 30 octobre 2015 relatif à la médiation des litiges de la consommation (which also modified the *Code monétaire et financier* (French monetary and financial code), the *Code des assurances* (French insurance code) and the *Code de la sécurité sociale* (French social security code), in order to allow the implementation of consumer mediation in those fields).

[78] Desdevises (n 75) 35.

[79] Pierre Chevalier and Marielle Thuau, 'Les MARL: perspectives et enjeux européens' in Pierre Chevalier, Yvon Desdevises and Philip Milburn (eds), *Les modes alternatifs de règlement des litiges: les voies nouvelles d'une autre justice* (La documentation française 2003) 37, 44.

aforementioned directive, a new book (book V) was appended to the civil procedure code.[80] Article 1530 gives a definition that is very close to that of the directive, although it does not mention the lineage:[81] 'Conventional mediation and conciliation (...) refer (...) to any structured process, whereby two or more parties strive to reach an agreement, excluding any judicial proceedings, with a view to amicably resolving their dispute, with the help of a third party of their choice, who fulfils his role with impartiality, competence and diligence.'

The effect of European law on *the duty to give reasons* is both less conspicuous and more controversial. There is no doubt whatsoever that the Court of Justice of the European Union – as well as the European Human Rights Court (ECtHR) – abundantly[82] justify their rulings.

The justification of rulings is a guarantee of good justice, as stated in article 455 of the civil procedure code[83] and naturally, it also applies to all domestic courts. Nevertheless, 'the differences in style between supreme rulings have generated a lot of debate. The problem is a classic: the syllogistic form and the structure of the rulings of the French *Cour de cassation* have been commented on numerous times.'[84] Recently, Mr Louvel[85] 'suggested that the influence of the Court of Strasbourg was leading to a questioning of the 'French legalist *cassation* model' and its replacement by an application of the law 'suitable for the present circumstances, necessary because of the circumstances and proportionate to those circumstances.''[86] The debate thus opened[87] is not restricted to

80 The *Code de procédure civile* consists of 6 books: general rules for all courts, special rules for each specific court, special rules for specific types of litigation, arbitration, ADR, rules regarding overseas territories.

81 On the contrary, there is a reference to *Loi* n° 95-125 du 8 février 1995 relative à l'organisation des juridictions et à la procédure civile, pénale et administrative. After this law, *Décret* n° 96-652 du 22 juillet 1996 relatif à la conciliation et à la médiation judiciaires had added articles 131-1 to 131-15, which are specifically devoted to judicial mediation, to the *Code de procédure civile*. Articles 128 to 131, concerning judicial conciliation had been part of the *Code* since it had been created and explain in detail how to apply article 21, 'a judge shall seek reconciliation between the parties in a trial.'

82 Gautier talks of 'copious' justifications. Pierre-Yves Gautier, 'Eloge du syllogisme' [2015] La semaine juridique 902.

83 It says, among other things, 'a ruling must be justified.'

84 Frédérique Ferrand, 'La juridiction judiciaire suprême en droit comparé: missions, filtrage, intensité du contrôle' in Guillaume Drago, Bénédicte Fauvarque-Cosson and Marie Goré (eds), *L'accès au juge de cassation* (Société de législation comparée 2015) 147, 210.

85 The current president of the *Cour de cassation*.

86 Philippe Théry, 'Cours suprêmes: essai – manqué – de typologie et de définition' in Guillaume Drago, Bénédicte Fauvarque-Cosson and Marie Goré (eds), *L'accès au juge de cassation* (Société de législation comparée 2015) 15, 18 (footnote omitted).

87 In the speech he gave upon his appointment on 16 July 2014, Mr Louvel declared, 'The increasing influence of European courts, which pronounce judgements based both on facts and law, is leading our court to consider, in some cases, slight changes to its strict tradition of simply verifying the correct application and interpretation of the law while disregarding the facts themselves. The multiple facets of their rulings should encourage us to better assess the social, economical, national and international impact of our decisions, beyond the strictly theoretical legal analysis which makes up the culture of the *Cour de cassation*.' Bertrand Louvel, 'Conseil de justice et autorité judiciaire: quel avenir en France?', (17 July 2014) Les annonces de la Seine 6 para 31.

the ECtHR,[88] it also concerns the Court of Luxembourg.[89] It is currently very heated between those who defend the idea that 'concision is the genius proper to syllogism; lengthiness impedes thinking and obscures the educational value of the decision (...); the judges' analytical method results in legal uncertainty typical of case law, which is much less graspable, in spite of appearances,'[90] and those who are in favour of a 'methodological revolution', invoke Gény 'urging his peers to resolve legal questions, which all boil down to conflicts of interest, by accurately appreciating and judiciously comparing the interests at stake and trying to balance them in accordance with the desired social ends' and conclude that 'in today's era of globalisation, proportionality is establishing itself as the unchaining of facts kept under the sway of law for too long.'[91] Everyone agrees, though, that 'It is in the highest interest of the French *Cour de cassation* to ensure that its image does not become blurred and that its authority is bolstered by the quality and clarity of its rulings',[92] which goes hand in hand with the idea that it would be 'extremely beneficial [for it to] adopt more explicit motivation.'[93]

5. Conclusion

In view of all of the above, it seems all the more difficult to unequivocally answer the question as to whether the links created between the European Union and French civil procedure are of harmonious or discordant nature that they can often only be perceived through the prism of other disciplines. Is this reserved conclusion, which echoes the contradiction observed in limine, not simply the 'procedural avatar of the ambition and difficulties encountered in the construction'[94] of the European Union?

88 As argued in the following papers: Philippe Jestaz, Jean-Pierre Marguénaud and Christophe Jamin, 'Révolution tranquille à la Cour de cassation' [2014] Recueil Dalloz 2061 and Serge Guinchard, Frédérique Ferrand and Tony Moussa, 'Une chance pour la France et le droit continental: la technique de cassation, vecteur particulièrement approprié au contrôle de conventionnalité' [2015] Recueil Dalloz 278.

89 As argued in Pierre-Yves Gautier, 'Contre la 'balance des intérêts': hiérarchie des droits fondamentaux', [2015] Recueil Dalloz 2189.

90 Gautier, 'Eloge du syllogisme' (n 82).

91 Jestaz, Marguénaud and Jamin (n 88) 2069 and 2070.

92 Ferrand (n 84) 214.

93 Gautier, 'Eloge du syllogisme' (n 82).

94 Etienne Pataut, 'L'espace judiciaire européen: un espace cohérent?' in Anne-Marie Leroyer and Emmanuel Jeuland (eds), *Quelle cohérence pour l'espace judiciaire européen?* (Dalloz 2004) 31, 49.

Wolfgang Hau*

THE EUROPEAN UNION AND CIVIL PROCEDURE FROM A GERMAN PERSPECTIVE

1. Background

Three German peculiarities should be mentioned at the outset: Firstly, German law (and thus this paper) adheres to a very narrow concept of 'civil procedure', which means that employment law proceedings, administrative proceedings, tax proceedings, and social welfare proceedings are not only dealt with by separate courts applying their own special codes of procedure but are not even regarded as matters of civil procedure. Secondly, in Germany civil litigation is traditionally not only considered as a matter of practice, but also cultivated at universities as a full-fledged academic discipline. Thirdly, the Federal Republic of Germany was among the six founding states of the European Economic Community of 1957, and Article 220 of the Treaty of Rome[1] made it clear that a common market could not work without the reciprocal recognition and enforcement of judgments.

Against this backdrop, it is not surprising that German legal scholars very early pointed out that the European Single Market must have certain consequences with regard to procedural law and law enforcement in civil and commercial matters.[2] But at least in the early years of European integration such occasional observations were not really deepened. Rather, particular attention was paid to the implementation of the Brussels Convention of 1968 on jurisdiction and the enforcement of judgments in civil and commercial matters.[3] Very soon after its entry into force in 1973, this convention gained practical importance in German courts, and since 1976 it was frequently called to mind by important decisions of the European Court of Justice (ECJ; meanwhile: Court of Justice of the European Union – CJEU).[4] Naturally, this concerned only cross-border

* Professor, Chair for Private Law, Civil Procedure, and Private International Law at the University of Passau.

1 Treaty establishing the European Economic Community [1997] OJ C340/173.

2 Cf Murad Ferid, 'Methoden, Möglichkeiten und Grenzen der Privatrechtsvereinheitlichung' [1962] ZRVgl 193, 200 et seq.; Walter Hallstein, 'Angleichung des Privat- und Prozessrechts in der Europäischen Wirtschaftsgemeinschaft' [1964] RabelsZ 211, 222 et seq.

3 [1972] OJ L 299/32.

4 Case C-12/76 *Tessili v Dunlop* [1976] ECR 1473, ECLI:EU:C:1976:133; Case C-14/76 *De Bloos v Bouyer* [1976] ECR 1497, ECLI:EU:C:1976:134; Case C-29/76 *LTU v Eurocontrol* [1976] ECR 1541, ECLI:EU:C:1976:137; Case C-21/76 *Bier v Mines de Potasse d'Alsace* [1976] ECR 1735, ECLI:EU:C:1976:166.

cases, and the early development of legislation in this field at EEC/EC level ran parallel to the establishment of the law of international civil procedure, which in Germany was increasingly considered as an independent discipline, emancipated from its former ambiguous position between the traditional law of domestic civil procedure on the one hand and private international law on the other.

This development is remarkable, not only as an example for the increasing academic differentiation of legal disciplines, but rather because the relation between European law and civil procedure was normally analyzed within a very narrow perspective: only with regard to cross-border cases and only with regard to particular legal instruments, namely the Brussels Convention. However, the more fundamental questions, how far European law can also affect mere domestic cases and which role European primary law should play in this context, were, at least in Germany, discussed to a much lesser extent. In fact, in the first decades after the Second World War, German scholars were especially concerned (not to say: navel-gazing) with the further development of the theoretical system of civil procedure and with intensive discussions about its constitutionalisation, i.e. the relevance of the fundamental rights and constitutional principles as provided for in the Basic Law of 1949.[5] And at the same time, German practitioners were fully taken up by numerous reform projects – some bigger, some smaller – with which the German legislator was trying to rationalise and expedite civil proceedings.[6] In other words: the early years of the EEC saw the German Code of Civil Procedure of 1877 (Zivilprozessordnung – ZPO) almost constantly under construction, and maybe this is why scarcely anybody spared a thought about its Europeanisation.

Only in the nineties of the last century, more careful consideration was given to the relation between European law and civil procedure. One case of 1993, not decided by the ECJ, but the European Court of Human Rights, gained particular attention in Germany, even though not concerning German but Dutch law: In its decision of the case *Dombo Beheer v Netherlands*,[7] the ECHR derived important guidelines for the domestic law of evidence in civil and commercial matters from the principle of equality of arms as guaranteed in Article 6 of the European Convention on Human Rights. Following that, an intensive debate started in Germany about the impact of the Convention on the interpretation of the Code of Civil Procedure.

Almost simultaneously, as a consequence of much-noticed decisions of the ECJ, the question emerged whether European primary law affects issues of international civil procedure, especially through the general principle of non-discrimination and the fundamental freedoms. In 1993, in the case *Hubbard v Hamburger*,[8] the ECJ objected

5 For a retrospective analysis of these discussions see Rolf Stürner, 'Die Rolle des dogmatischen Denkens im Zivilprozessrecht' [2014] 127 ZZP 271, 283 et seq.

6 Cf. Wolfgang Hau, 'Recent German reforms of civil procedure' in Volker Lipp and Halvard H. Fredriksen (eds), *Reforms of Civil Procedure in Germany and Norway* (Mohr Siebeck 2011) 61 et seq.; Paul Oberhammer and Tanja Domej, 'Germany, Switzerland, Austria' in C.H. van Rhee (ed), *European Traditions in Civil Procedure* (Intersentia 2005) 103, 113 et seq.

7 App no 14448/88 (ECHR, 27 October 1993), ECLI:CE:ECHR:1993:1027JUD001444888. Thereto Peter F. Schlosser, 'EMRK und Waffengleichheit im Zivilprozeß' [1995] NJW 1404.

8 Case C-20/92 [1993] ECR I-3777, ECLI:EU:C:1993:280.

to §110 of the German Code of Civil Procedure: The former version of this provision stated that a foreign claimant, unlike a German citizen, must provide security for the costs of the defendant, and the ECJ declared that this was not in line with the standards of the EC-Treaty. And in 1994, only a few months later, the ECJ opposed another provision of the German Code of Civil Procedure: In the case *Mund & Fester v Hatrex*[9] the ECJ criticised the former version of §917, which discriminated against debtors residing outside Germany in proceedings for provisional measures.

In addition and parallel to the evolution of European case law, remarkable steps were taken and important groundwork was done by legal scholars.[10] Surely the most prominent and ambitious landmark project was the Final Report for the Approximation of the Civil Procedural Law in Europe, drawn up by the working group headed by *Marcel Storme* and published in 1994.[11] This report gained some attention in Germany: academic circles politely took note and it was discussed in much detail by the German Association of Procedural Law Scholars at their conference in 1996 – though the reactions were mainly critical.[12]

But in the end neither the courts nor academics but rather the legislator tipped the balance towards the Europeanisation of procedural law: In 1999 the Treaty of Amsterdam came into force which made it possible for the EU to enact instruments in the field of judicial cooperation. Since then, the catchphrase 'European civil procedure' ('Europäisches Zivilprozessrecht' respectively 'Europäisches Zivilverfahrensrecht') gained currency and more and more attention in Germany. This term, however, is used inconsistently: Sometimes it labels the law of international civil procedure insofar as regulated by European secondary instruments. In this respect, it is the antonym to the German rules on international civil procedure and the relevant Hague conventions. It seems, however, more reasonable to understand the term 'European civil procedure' in a broader sense: on the one hand, including secondary as well as primary law relevant for cross-border civil cases, and, on the other hand, also dealing with the question to what extent even mere domestic proceedings are affected by EU law (and the ECHR, too). This distinction between cross-border cases and mere national cases is also the starting point for the following discussion.

9 Case C-398/92 [1994] ECR I-467, ECLI:EU:C:1994:52.

10 For important early contributions to this point from a German perspective cf Peter Gottwald, Reinhard Greger and Hanns Prütting, *Dogmatische Grundfragen des Zivilprozesses im geeinten Europa* (Gieseking 2000); Wolfgang Grunsky, Rolf Stürner, Gerhard Walter and Manfred Wolf, *Wege zu einem europäischen Zivilprozeßrecht* (Mohr Siebeck 1992); Burkhard *Hess*, 'Der Binnenmarktprozeß – neuer Verfahrenstyp zwischen nationalem und internationalem Zivilprozeßrecht' [1998] JZ 1021; Walther Habscheid, 'Die Europäisierung des Zivilprozessrechts' in Peter-Christian Müller-Graff (ed), *Gemeinsames Privatrecht in der Europäischen Gemeinschaft* (Nomos 1993) 449; Hanns Prütting, 'Auf dem Weg zu einer Europäischen Zivilprozeßordnung' in Hanns Prütting (ed), *Festschrift für Gottfried Baumgärtel zum 70. Geburtstag* (Heymann 1990) 457.

11 Marcel Storme, *Final Report on the Approximation of Judiciary Law in the European Union* (Kluwer 1994).

12 See Herbert Roth, 'Die Vorschläge der Kommission für ein europäisches Zivilprozeßgesetzbuch – das Erkenntnisverfahren' [1996] 109 ZZP 271; Eberhard Schilken, 'Die Vorschläge der Kommission für ein europäisches Zivilprozeßgesetzbuch – einstweiliger und summarischer Rechtsschutz und Vollstreckung' [1996] 109 ZZP 315.

2. EU Law and Civil Procedure: Cross-border Cases

2.1. *EU Primary Law*

The architecture of the European law of international civil procedure is most strikingly reflected in the relevant regulations. Nevertheless, the primary EU law should be taken into account, too.[13] Domestic procedural provisions must be in line with fundamental freedoms, the principle of non-discrimination (Article 18 TFEU), and the European *effet utile*. The ECJ has had many opportunities to deal with such issues. A recent example concerns Italian law: In the case *Grauel Rüffer v Pokorná*,[14] the ECJ clarified that Italy must allow the use of the German language in the region of Bolzano not only to German-speaking Italians but also to foreign litigants. Further examples referring to German law, as already mentioned, are the case *Hubbard v Hamburger*[15] dealing with the requirement of security for procedural costs imposed on foreign claimants and the case *Mund & Fester v Hatrex*[16] dealing with the preconditions of provisional measures against foreign respondents. In both cases, the German law was found irreconcilable with EC law and each time the German legislator reacted soon, tamed the relevant provisions of the Code of Civil Procedure ensuring that parties from other EU Member States are not discriminated against anymore.

2.2. *EU Secondary Law*

2.2.1. Overview

As already mentioned, since the entry into force of the treaty of Amsterdam in 1999, the EC (meanwhile: the EU) is in the position to make secondary law 'in civil matters having cross-border implications, when necessary for the proper functioning of the internal market' (Article 65 EC-Treaty[17], now Article 81 TFEU[18]). This expressly includes the elimination of 'obstacles to the good functioning of civil proceedings, if necessary by promoting the compatibility of the rules on civil procedure applicable in the Member States', and this new competence was exercised without any delay: The EC almost immediately took the opportunity to enact regulations dealing with almost all major issues of international litigation within Europe. The first relevant instruments, already enacted in May 2000, were the Regulation on insolvency proceedings,[19] the Regulation on jurisdiction and the recognition and enforcement of judgments in matrimonial

13 For more detailed discussions cf Burkhard Hess, *Europäisches Zivilprozessrecht* (C.F. Müller 2010) §4; Christian Heinze, 'Europäisches Primärrecht und Zivilprozess' [2008] EuR 654; Christian Heinze, 'Zivilprozessrecht unter europäischem Einfluss' [2011] JZ 709, 712.

14 Case C-322/13 [2014] EuZW 393, ECLI:EU:C:2014:189.

15 *Hubbard (n8).*

16 *Mund & Fester (n9).*

17 Consolidated Version of the Treaty establishing the European Community [2002] OJ C 325/33.

18 Consolidated Version of the Treaty on the Functioning of the European Union [2012] OJ C 326/47.

19 Council Regulation (EC) 1346/2000 [2000] OJ L160/1.

matters and in matters of parental responsibility ('Brussels II'),[20] and the Regulation on the service in the Member States of judicial and extrajudicial documents.[21] Only a couple of months later, in December 2000, an eminently important instrument followed: the Brussels I Regulation on jurisdiction and the recognition and enforcement of judgments,[22] i.e. the successor of the long-standing Brussels Convention. This first legislative phase was concluded in May 2001 with the Regulation on cooperation between the courts of the Member States in the taking of evidence.[23]

The following years saw the replacement of such early instruments by more detailed ones, such as the 2003 Regulation concerning jurisdiction and the recognition and enforcement of judgments in matrimonial matters and the matters of parental responsibility ('Brussels IIa')[24] and the 2007 Regulation on the service in the Member States of judicial and extrajudicial documents.[25] Furthermore, in 2008 a separate regulation was enacted dealing with international aspects of maintenance (Regulation on jurisdiction, applicable law, recognition and enforcement of decisions and cooperation in matters relating to maintenance obligations[26]). Another set of regulations allowed for the enforcement of titles in all Member States without the need for a special exequatur procedure, as it was still required under the Brussels Convention and the Brussels I Regulation. This was the object of the Regulation creating a European Enforcement Order for uncontested claims of 2004[27] and the already mentioned Maintenance Regulation. The next step was the invention of standardised European procedures for obtaining enforceable instruments. This heading includes the 2006 Regulation creating a European Order for Payment Procedure[28] and the 2007 Regulation establishing a European Small Claims Procedure.[29]

The second decade of the new judicial cooperation is characterised by further modernisation of the existing instruments, especially through the updated 2012 Brussels I Regulation[30] and the 2015 version of the Insolvency Regulation.[31] Another feature is the progressive extension of the scope of EU provisions through new instruments, such as the Regulation of 2012 on jurisdiction, applicable law, recognition and enforcement of decisions and acceptance and enforcement of authentic instruments

20 Council Regulation (EC) 1347/2000 [2000] OJ L160/19.

21 Council Regulation (EC) 1348/2000 [2000] OJ L160/37.

22 Council Regulation (EC) 44/2001 [2001] OJ L12/1.

23 Council Regulation (EC) 1206/2001 [2001] OJ L174/1; German implementation: §§1072–1075 ZPO.

24 Council Regulation (EC) 2201/2003 [2003] OJ L338/1; German implementation: Internationales Familienrechtsverfahrensgesetz (International Family Law Procedure Act) [2005] BGBl. I 162.

25 Council Regulation (EC) 1393/2007 [2007] OJ L324/79; German implementation: §§1067–1069 ZPO.

26 Council Regulation (EC) 4/2009 [2009] OJ L7/1; German implementation: Auslandsunterhaltsgesetz (Foreign Maintenance Act) [2011] BGBl. I 898.

27 Council Regulation (EC) 805/2004 [2004] OJ L143/15; German implementation: §§1079–1086 ZPO.

28 Council Regulation (EC) 1896/2006 [2006] OJ L399/1; German implementation: §§1087–1096 ZPO.

29 Council Regulation (EC) 861/2007 [2007] OJ L199/1; German implementation: §§1097–1109 ZPO.

30 Council Regulation (EU) 1215/2012 on jurisdiction and the recognition and enforcement of judgments in civil and commercial matters (recast) (Brussels Ia Regulation) [2012] OJ L351/1; German implementation: §§1110–1117 ZPO.

31 Council Regulation (EU) 2015/848 on insolvency proceedings (recast) [2015] OJ L141/19.

in matters of succession[32] and the Regulation of 2014 establishing a European Account Preservation Order Procedure to facilitate cross-border debt recovery.[33] The latter regulation is particularly remarkable because it is obviously only the pilot project for further European instruments on enforcement law issues – an area which was, so far, almost exclusively left to the national legal regimes.[34]

In addition to such regulations, the EC/EU enacted various directives which complete the contemporary picture of cross-border judicial cooperation. This heading includes early examples such as the 1998 Directive on injunctions for the protection of consumers' interests[35] and the 2003 Directive to improve access to justice in cross-border disputes by establishing minimum common rules relating to legal aid for such disputes.[36] More recent instruments deal with alternative dispute resolution: Whereas the Directive of 2008 on certain aspects of mediation in civil and commercial matters[37] only covers cross-border cases, the Directive of 2013 on alternative dispute resolution for consumer disputes expressively relates to extrajudicial settlements of both national and international disputes.[38]

2.2.2. German Reactions

In Germany there are consistently voices cautioning against the intensive legislative practice of the EU in the area of international procedural law. They worry that the domestic German rules, but also those of the Hague Conference on Private International Law, will lose their significance.[39] But the prevailing opinion seems to be more open-minded:[40] the unification respectively harmonisation of rules achieved at European level so far and the discharge of national special approaches are welcomed and considered rather helpful. This position might, inter alia, be due to the fact that the EU solutions in many respects comply with the German legal tradition. Since procedural law in Germany is mainly determined by the legislator, not by case law, for German lawyers the handling of a regulation is not too much different from dealing with the Code of Civil Procedure. This familiarity is further enhanced by the fact that the German legislator meanwhile prefers to incorporate the provisions implementing European instruments in the Code

32 Council Regulation (EU) 650/2012 [2012] OJ L201/107; German implementation: Internationales Erbrechtsverfahrensgesetz (International Succession Law Procedure Act) [2015] BGBl. I 1042.

33 Council Regulation (EU) 655/2014 [2014] OJ L189/59.

34 For an early discussion cf Burkhard Hess, 'Europäisches Zwangsvollstreckungsrecht – Herausforderungen und rechtspolitische Perspektiven' [2010] DGVZ 45.

35 Directive 98/27/EC [1998] OJ L166/51.

36 Directive 2003/8/EC [2003] OJ L26/41; German implementation: §§1076–1078 ZPO.

37 Directive 2008/52/EC [2008] OJ L136/3; German implementation: Mediationsgesetz (Mediation Act) [2012] BGBl. I 1577.

38 Directive 2013/11/EU [2013] OJ L165/63.

39 Strong warnings came, for example, from Haimo Schack, 'Die EG-Kommission auf dem Holzweg von Amsterdam' [1999] ZEuP 805; Herbert Roth, 'Zum Bedeutungsverlust des autonomen internationalen Zivilprozessrechts' in Herbert Roth (ed), *Europäisierung des Rechts* (Mohr Siebeck 2010) 163.

40 See, for example, Burkhard Hess, 'Deutsches Zivilprozessrecht zwischen nationaler Eigenständigkeit und europäischem Anpassungszwang' [2010] 27 Ritsumeikan Law Review 191.

of Civil Procedure instead of enacting special statutes. For this purpose, a new eleventh book on 'judicial cooperation within the European Union' was added to the Code (§§1067–1117 ZPO).

Even with regard to content, EU legislation in the field of international procedural law suits traditional German thinking in many respects. This is clearly shown by the fact that both systems leave very little room for judicial discretion in matters of jurisdiction[41] or in the coordination of multi-fora disputes.[42] On the other hand, German law has retained some peculiarities in areas where the national rules are still applicable. Thus, German law still asserts that the location of defendant's assets in Germany is sufficient to establish international jurisdiction of our courts (§23 Code of Civil Procedure), despite the fact that this ground of jurisdiction has been abolished with regard to intra-European cases. On the other hand, German law abstains from incorporating European concepts when considered irreconcilable with our procedural tradition or system. A good example is jurisdiction based on joinder of defendants: Article 8 No 1 Brussels Ia Regulation provides for such a head of jurisdiction, but the German legislator refuses to invent a corresponding rule applicable to defendants domiciled in third states.

Below the line, it seems as if in practice German parties and courts meanwhile adapt quite well to the European rules. This might be due to the fact that the regulations are – as mentioned – closely interlocked with the Code of Civil Procedure and are explained in much detail in all standard commentaries and handbooks for practitioners. Moreover, German courts are not unduly reserved to submit questions to the ECJ for a preliminary ruling if interpretation of a provision seems doubtful, and the answers from Luxembourg normally find attention in major periodicals dealing with issues of civil procedure. Even the European Order for Payment Procedure has gained significant importance in German practice, although there is a well-established competing German court collecting procedure, whereas the European Small Claims Procedure still leads a rather shadowy existence in Germany as well as in other Member States.

3. EU Law and Civil Procedure: Domestic Cases

3.1. *European Procedural Standards*

The European Commission makes no secret of its ambition to invent European procedural rules for mere domestic civil cases, i.e. cases having no relation whatsoever to further Member States and/or third countries.[43] Accordingly, more than once the Commission explicitly refrained from limiting the scope of application of its proposals to cases with significant international elements: Its consecutive drafts for instruments on legal aid, the order for payment procedure, the small claims procedure and mediation

41 For the Brussels I regime, cf ECJ Case C-159/02 *Turner v Grovit* [2004] ECR I-3565, ECLI:EU:C:2004:228.

42 For the Brussels I regime, cf ECJ Case C-116/02 *Gasser v MISAT* [2003] ECR I-14693, ECLI:EU:C:2003:657.

43 As regards the following see Wolfgang Hau, 'Zivilsachen mit grenzüberschreitendem Bezug' in Stefan Arnold and Stephan Lorenz (eds), *Gedächtnisschrift für Hannes Unberath* (Beck 2015) 139.

again and again suggested that the proposed regulations respectively directives should apply to mere domestic cases as well as to international cases. In doing so, the Commission used to warn of a growing disparity between European and national rules on civil procedure. Nevertheless, the Commission did not prevail in any of the cases mentioned: During every single legislative process, the European Council limited the scope of the instrument in question to specified cross-border situations.

In any case, the crucial question is not so much whether European law-making in the area of civil procedural law seems appropriate, but rather whether the EU has the required legislative competence. This is more than doubtful, since Article 81 TFEU (former Article 65 EC-Treaty) unmistakably refers to 'judicial cooperation in civil matters having cross-border implications' only. Therefore, there is simply no basis for directives or regulations mainly dealing with domestic civil procedural law,[44] let alone a basis for a European Code of Civil Procedure. And it is not to be expected that this will change over the next few years. Therefore, at least in the foreseeable future, the Commission will have to make do with much smaller steps. This became apparent in the field of collective redress where the only result after years and years of discussion was a mere recommendation within the meaning of Article 292 TFEU.[45]

However, it must be taken into consideration that binding standards for the national law of civil procedure may as well be an indirect result of secondary legislation which primarily deals with matters of substantive law. Since the aims of European substantive law can only be achieved if the beneficiaries are enabled to enforce their rights effectively, the European legislator occasionally provides for procedural requirements in its secondary legislation. The 2004 Directive on the enforcement of intellectual property rights[46] may serve as a classic example: Although this directive almost exclusively regulates substantive law issues, its Article 6 invents a detailed provision as regards court orders on the presentation of evidence. This genuine procedural concept is expected to provide for particular protection of intellectual property rights and is supposed to outperform traditional national solutions which – like German law – rather try to protect the applicant by means of information rights granted under substantive law. Another, more recent example in this respect is the 2014 Directive on certain rules governing actions for damages under national law for infringements of the competition law provisions of the Member States and of the European Union.[47]

Various directives on consumer protection for example in doorstep selling situations, distance selling or selling of consumer goods do neither require the parties to be

44 Most recently, there is an intense discussion in Germany whether it was rightful to enact the Directive 2013/11/EU of 21 May 2013 on alternative dispute resolution for consumer disputes, [2013] OJ L165/63, referring to Article 114 of the TFEU: Some authors argue that Article 81 is applicable instead and that, in consequence, the directive's scope should have been limited to cross-border cases. See Martin Engel, 'Außergerichtliche Streitbeilegung in Verbraucherangelegenheiten – Mehr Zugang zu weniger Recht' [2015] NJW 1633, 1634.

45 Commission Recommendation of 11 June 2013 on common principles for injunctive and compensatory collective redress mechanisms in the Member States concerning violations of rights granted under Union Law [2013] OJ L201/60; Commission's communication thereto: COM (2013) 401.

46 Directive 2004/48/EC [2004] OJ L195/16.

47 Directive 2014/104/EU [2014] OJ L349/1.

domiciled in different states nor any other cross-border element of the case. Although such directives dealing with consumer protection only address issues of substantive law, it is recognised that the Member States are obliged to effectively implement those directives as well in procedural regard. The unharmonised national laws on civil procedure are used as a vehicle to ensure the standards of protection granted by European substantive law. In this context, the ECJ has identified two guiding principles: 'By laying down the procedural rules for proceedings designed to ensure protection of the rights which individuals acquire through the direct effect of Community law, Member States must ensure that such rules are not less favorable than those governing similar domestic actions (principle of equivalence) and are not framed in such a way as to render impossible in practice the exercise of rights conferred by Community law (principle of effectiveness).'[48] The ECJ has applied the same principles as regards national rules for execution procedures.[49]

In 2013, for example, dealing with a sale of consumer goods, the ECJ came up with procedural guidelines in order to avoid disadvantages to the consumer resulting from excessively strict requirements with regard to the complaint when bringing an action against the seller: 'Directive 1999/44/EC of the European Parliament and of the Council of 25 May 1999 on certain aspects of the sale of consumer goods and associated guarantees must be interpreted as precluding legislation of a Member State (…) which does not allow the national court hearing the dispute to grant of its own motion an appropriate reduction in the price of goods which are the subject of a contract of sale in the case where a consumer who is entitled to such a reduction brings proceedings which are limited to seeking only rescission of that contract and such rescission cannot be granted because the lack of conformity in those goods is minor, even though that consumer is not entitled to refine his initial application or to bring a fresh action to that end.'[50]

And in another interesting decision of 2012, the ECJ addressed the question to what extent a Member State's court collecting proceedings may result in an unfair disadvantage to a consumer borrower: 'Council Directive 93/13/EEC of 5 April 1993 on unfair terms in consumer contracts must be interpreted as precluding legislation of a Member State (…) which does not allow the court before which an application for an order for payment has been brought to assess of its own motion, in limine litis or at any other stage during the proceedings, even though it already has the legal and factual elements necessary for that task available to it, whether a term relating to interest on late payments contained in a contract concluded between a seller or supplier and a consumer is unfair, in the case where that consumer has not lodged an objection.'[51]

In Germany, such decisions are usually followed immediately by a discussion addressing the question to what extent the German law is compliant with the requirements formulated by the ECJ. More often than not, such discussions come to the conclusion

48 Case C-234/04 *Kapferer v Schlank & Schick* [2006] NJW 1577, ECLI:EU:C:2006:178.

49 See Case C-415/11 *Mohamed Aziz* [2013] EuZW 464, ECLI:EU:C:2013:164.

50 Case C-32/12 *Duarte Hueros v Autociba* [2013] EuZW 918, ECLI:EU:C:2013:637; thereto: Ulrich Korth, 'Zur Auslegung des Tatbestandes der 'geringfügigen Vertragswidrigkeit' in der Verbrauchsgüterkaufrichtlinie' [2014] GPR 87.

51 Case C-618/10 *Banco Español de Crédito v Camino* [2012] NJW 2257, ECLI:EU:C:2012:349.

that German law already meets the requirements and that therefore the legislator is not obliged to modify the relevant German provisions.[52]

In this context, however, it seems remarkable that the European law, as understood by the ECJ, anyhow takes into account national procedural rules. For example, primary law, namely the principle of sincere cooperation (Article 4 (3) TEU), does not require a national court to refrain from the application of national rules on res judicata only because the decision which has become final is potentially inconsistent with European law. In this regard, the ECJ stated: '[A]ttention should be drawn to the importance, both for the Community legal order and national legal systems, of the principle of res judicata. In order to ensure both stability of the law and legal relations and the sound administration of justice, it is important that judicial decisions which have become definitive after all rights of appeal have been exhausted or after expiry of the time-limits provided for in that connection can no longer be called into question (…). Therefore, Community law does not require a national court to disapply domestic rules of procedure conferring finality on a decision, even if to do so would enable it to remedy an infringement of Community law by the decision at issue (…).'[53]

3.2. *EU Law as Model for National Rules*

In order to take effect in the area of procedural law, European law is not necessarily dependent on imposing binding requirements on the Member States. On the contrary, indirect methods are not necessarily less rewarding when it comes to implementing

52 See, for a recent example, the in-depth discussion on the compatibility of the German court collecting procedure (§§688 et seq. ZPO) and European rules: Anatol Dutta, 'Nationales Mahnverfahren und die Effektivität des europäischen Verbraucherschutzes' [2013] 126 ZZP 153; Wolfgang Hau, 'Zur Frage der Klauselkontrolle bei Mahnanträgen' [2012] JZ 964; Michael Stürner, 'Amtsprüfung im Mahnverfahren und Unzulässigkeit der Vertragsanpassung bei missbräuchlicher Verzugszinsklausel' [2013] ZEuP 666.

53 Cf Case C-234/04 *Kapferer v Schlank & Schick* [2006] NJW 1577, ECLI:EU:C:2006:178; thereto: Stefanie Schmahl and Michael Köber, 'Durchbrechung der Rechtskraft nationaler Gerichtsentscheidungen zu Gunsten der Effektivität des Unionsrechts?' [2010] EuZW 927; Dieter Leipold, 'Volle Wirksamkeit des Europäischen Rechts versus Bindung nach einzelstaatlichem Verfahrensrecht' in Alexander Bruns (ed), *Festschrift für Rolf Stürner zum 70. Geburtstag* (Mohr Siebeck, 2013) 1291. To the same effect cf Case C-69/14 *Târşia* [2015] EuZW 917, ECLI:EU:C:2015:662: 'European Union law, in particular the principles of equivalence and effectiveness, must be interpreted as not precluding, in circumstances such as those in the dispute in the main proceedings, a situation where there is no possibility for a national court to revise a final decision of a court or tribunal made in the course of civil proceedings when that decision is found to be incompatible with an interpretation of EU law upheld by the Court of Justice of the European Union after the date on which that decision became final, even though such a possibility does exist as regards final decisions of a court or tribunal incompatible with EU law made in the course of administrative proceedings.' Difficult to reconcile with this, however, seems to be Case C-505/14 *Klausner Holz Niedersachsen* [2015] ECLI:EU:C:2015:742: 'EU law precludes, in circumstances such as those at issue in the main proceedings, the application of a rule of national law enshrining the principle of res judicata from preventing a national court which has held that contracts forming the subject-matter of the dispute before it constitute State aid, within the meaning of Article 107(1) TFEU, implemented in breach of the third sentence of Article 108(3) TFEU, from drawing all the consequences of that breach because of a national judicial decision which has become definitive, which court, without examining whether those contracts constitute State aid, has held that the contracts remain in force.'

particular procedural concepts. In other words: beyond the genuine scope of application, European rules can have a role model function for corresponding national rules.

The Commission, as already mentioned, consistently warns against the growing disparity of procedural law applicable to international and to mere national cases and therefore encourages the Member States to voluntarily adopt the European rules to mere domestic disputes. In other words: the scope of application of European regulations and directives might be restricted to cross-border disputes, but nevertheless they can serve as a blue-print for the national legislators. A recent example is the Commission's proposal of November 2013 for reform of the Small Claims Regulation.[54] The proposed Recital No 7 reads as follows: 'This Regulation should apply only in cross-border disputes, but nothing should prevent Member States from applying identical provisions also to purely internal proceedings concerning claims of a low value.' It is very unlikely that Germany will seize this suggestion, since there is some fundamental skepticism towards the architecture of the European small claims procedure. However, this does not mean that such suggestions from Brussels always fall on deaf ears in Germany. Take, for example, the 2008 Directive on mediation[55] which per se only applies to cross-border cases. The German legislator, however, following the recommendation made in Recital No 8 of the Directive, deliberately opted for a further reaching implementation and enacted the same rules for international and mere national cases.[56]

In this context, a phenomenon seems remarkable that can be described as regulation-induced national law of civil procedure.[57] The best example is the 2004 Regulation creating a European Enforcement Order for uncontested claims.[58] Its Recital No 19 reads: 'This Regulation does not imply an obligation for the Member States to adapt their national legislation to the minimum procedural standards set out herein. It provides an incentive to that end by making available a more efficient and rapid enforceability of judgments in other Member States only if those minimum standards are met.' According to Article 6 (1) lit. c, a judgment delivered in a Member State shall only be certified as European Enforcement Order if service of process and the summons met the minimum requirements set out in Chapter III of the Regulation.[59] It is striking that this can stimulate national legislation even as regards cases without any cross-border element: When one considers that in many cases enforcement in another Member State might be unlikely at the outset, but can nevertheless turn out to be necessary, it shows that the Regulation creates a

54 COM (2013) 794.

55 Directive 2008/52/EC [2008] OJ 2008 L136/3.

56 Cf Bundestags-Drucksache 17/5335, 11.

57 For details cf Carl Friedrich Nordmeier, 'Verordnungsveranlasstes Zivilprozessrecht: Zum Einfluss der EuVTVO auf die Auslegung von §338 S. 2 ZPO' [2011] GPR 158; Christoph Althammer, 'Mindeststandards im Zivilprozess' [2013] 126 ZZP 3, 22 et seq.

58 Regulation (EC) 805/2004 [2004] OJ 2004 L143/15.

59 Cf Recital No 19 and thereto Case C-300/14 *Intech Marine Belgium v Radio Hellenic* [2016] EuZW 235, ECLI:EU:C:2015:825.

considerable incentive for the Member States to enhance their national laws even with regard to mere domestic cases. And indeed, the German legislator showed prompt reaction by including new provisions even for domestic proceedings in the Code of Civil Procedure, complying with the requirements set out in the Regulation (cf §215, §276 ZPO). It seems to be worth discussing whether in future such an attempt to harmonise the national laws of civil procedure by 'gentle pressure from Brussels' – respectively by some sort of 'nudging' in the sense of libertarian paternalism[60] – could be adopted more often.

Eventually, legal scholars play a key role in the Europeanisation of procedural laws. In Germany, for example, it is under consideration whether the broad concept of lis alibi pendens as developed by the ECJ as regards Article 21 Brussels Convention (now: Article 29 Brussels Ia Regulation) seems suitable to replace the much narrower German concept.[61] A similar debate in Germany concerns the questions to what extent the European Evidence Regulation will lead to harmonisation of the national laws of evidence and to what extent this seems desirable. It can be expected that the provisions on the European order for payment procedure will have a similar impact on national court collecting proceedings. And last but not least: the Commission has realised that funding plays an important role when it comes to encouraging the participation of legal scholars, namely by tender procedures in connection with the review of existing instruments and the preparation of new ones.

4. Outlook

It seems obvious that the evolvement of European procedural law, at least for cross-border cases, will not come to rest in the near future: Further reforms of the existing instruments are pending and we will probably see the Europeanisation of new areas, e.g. by means of rules for international disputes over matrimonial property.[62] At least scholars will follow new projects with great interest, such as the long announced green book on minimum standards in civil proceedings.[63] However, it is rather unlikely that such documents will, in short term, have any significant impact on the German legislator respectively on the German procedural rules applicable to mere domestic cases. In fact,

60 For a general introduction to this concept of law-making see Cass R. Sunstein, *Why Nudge? The Politics of Libertarian Paternalism* (Yale University Press 2014).

61 For detailed discussions cf Helmut Rüßmann, 'Die Streitgegenstandslehre und die Rechtsprechung des EuGH – nationales Recht unter gemeineuropäischem Einfluß?' [1998] 111 ZZP 399; Peter Gottwald, 'Streitgegenstandslehre und Sinnzusammenhänge' in: Peter Gottwald, Reinhard Greger and Hanns Prütting (eds), *Dogmatische Grundfragen des Zivilprozesses im geeinten Europa* (Gieseking 2000) 85, 94; Dieter Leipold, *Wege zur Konzentration von Zivilprozessen* (Gruyter 1999) 20 ff; Christoph Althammer, *Streitgegenstand und Interesse* (Mohr Siebeck 2012).

62 Cf the Commission's new proposals: COM (2016) 106, 107 & 108.

63 Cf European Parliamentary Research Service, *Europanisation of civil procedure – Towards common minimum standards?* (European Parliament 2015); Christoph Althammer, 'Mindeststandards im Zivilprozess' [2013] 126 ZZP 3; Matthias Weller and Christoph Althammer, *Mindeststandards im europäischen Zivilprozessrecht – Grundvoraussetzung für gegenseitiges Vertrauen* (Mohr Siebeck 2015) 221.

most German observers and stakeholders seem to be more interested in whether it will be possible to systematise the very heterogeneous strings of European procedural law and to elaborate common principles.[64] The crucial precept, thus, is coordination and consolidation, but not yet codification.

It remains to be seen whether the 'European Rules of Civil Procedure', which the European Law Institute plans to draft by means of various international working groups,[65] will serve as a toolbox to avoid a fragmentary and haphazard growth of European procedural law in the not too far future. But even in the not unlikely event that such European Rules will never get officially adopted by the European Union, the academic community will benefit, since this project will compile a lot of significant information, suitable to promote further comparative studies and valuable as teaching material.

64 For different recent German perspectives in this regard see for example: Jens Adolphsen, 'Konsolidierung des Europäischen Zivilverfahrensrechts' in Reinhold Geimer (ed), *Festschrift für Athanassios Kaissis zum 65. Geburtstag* (Sellier 2012) 1; Reinhold Geimer, 'Law Making in Europa – Bemerkungen zur Justiziellen Zusammenarbeit' in J Gudowski and K Weitz (eds), *Festschrift für Tadeusz Ereciński: Aurea Praxis, Aurea Theoria* (LexisNexis Polska 2011) 1003; Burkhard Hess, 'Unionsrechtliche Synthese: Mindeststandards und Verfahrensgrundsätze im acquis communautaire' in Matthias Weller and Christoph Althammer (eds), *Mindeststandards im europäischen Zivilprozessrecht – Grundvoraussetzung für gegenseitiges Vertrauen* (Mohr Siebeck 2015) 221; Stefan Huber, 'Koordinierung europäischer Zivilprozessrechtsinstrumente' in Reinhold Geimer (ed), *Festschrift für Athanassios Kaissis zum 65. Geburtstag* (Sellier 2012) 413; Stefan Leible, 'Die Zukunft des Europäischen Zivilprozessrechts' in Jens Adolphsen (ed), *Festschrift für Peter Gottwald zum 70. Geburtstag* (Beck 2014) 381; Mary-Rose McGuire, 'Kodifikation des Europäischen Zivilprozessrechts?' [2011] ecolex 218; Felix Netzer, *Status quo und Konsolidierung des Europäischen Zivilverfahrensrechts – Vorschlag zum Erlass einer EuZPO* (Mohr Siebeck 2011); Hanns Prütting, Grundlagen und aktuelle Entwicklungstendenzen im Europäischen Zivilprozessrecht, in J Gudowski und K Weitz (eds), *Festschrift für Tadeusz Ereciński: Aurea Praxis, Aurea Theoria* (LexisNexis Polska 2011) 1255; Rolf A. Schütze, 'Der Europäische Justizraum – Utopie oder Wirklichkeit' in Jens Adolphsen (ed), *Festschrift für Peter Gottwald zum 70. Geburtstag* (Beck 2014) 585; Rolf Wagner, 'Justizielle Zusammenarbeit in Zivilsachen – quo vadis?' [2015] ZEuP 1.

65 Cf www.europeanlawinstitute.eu and various articles in [2014] Unif. Law Rev. 173 et seq.

Viktória Harsági*

INTERACTION BETWEEN EUROPEAN LAW AND HUNGARIAN CIVIL PROCEDURE LAW

1. Introduction

The influence exerted by European Union civil procedure on the national laws of the Member States has been greatly influenced by the path the individual States had to follow in order to acquire full rights of membership. This does not only mean how much time the given States had to spend as a candidate country, but also whether before their entry they had become parties to such international agreements or organisations that had made it necessary for them or even required them to harmonise their national legal systems with those agreements. As an example one might mention admission into the Council of Europe and ratification of the European Convention on Human Rights, as a consequence of which some fundamental human rights also having an effect on the administration of justice (e.g. the principles of fair process or adversarial hearing) have become built into the national legal systems.[1] Countries having joined the Hague Convention of 1965 on the Service of Court Documents or the Hague Convention of 1970 on the Taking of Evidence had become well-versed in applying rules that were later, even if with a changed content, to form part of regulations issued in the frames of European judicial cooperation.[2] The greatest experience in the application of rules of European civil procedure law – while not being a member of the European Union – was afforded by participation in the Lugano Convention[3]: The Convention concluded in 1988 was ratified by Austria in 1996 and Poland in 2000. However, in the case of Austria the application of the Lugano Convention only meant a mere two-year 'advantage', since

* Professor, Head of Department, Pázmány Péter Catholic University (Budapest), Faculty of Law, Department of Civil Procedure Law, lecturer at the Andrássy Gyula German Speaking University (Budapest), e-mail: harsagi.viktoria@jak.ppke.hu.

1 Hungary acquired membership of the Council of Europe in 1990 and she ratified the European Convention on Human Rights in 1993.

2 The Hague Convention on the Service of Court Documents was joined by Latvia in 1995, Estonia and Poland in 1996, Bulgaria in 2001, Romania in 2003 and Hungary in 2005. The Hague Convention on the Taking of Evidence was ratified by the legal predecessor Czechoslovakia among the first, and it was joined by Estonia, Poland and Latvia in 1996, Bulgaria in 2001 and Hungary in 2004.

3 Convention on jurisdiction and the enforcement of judgments in civil and commercial matters, done at Lugano on 16 September 1988.

following her accession to the European Union in 1995, beginning from 1998 she was able to apply the *Brussels Convention*.[4] Poland had gained four years' experience in the application of the common rules relating to the recognition and enforcement of court judgements prior to her accession to the European Union in 2004. The loser in this process was undoubtedly Hungary, which announced its intention to join the Lugano Convention in 1997, but having made the required statements and declarations, she failed to obtain support for her entry from the participating states.[5]

During the preparations preceding the accession of 2004, new codes of civil procedure were *born in several former Eastern-European socialist countries*, which did not only mean getting rid of the burdensome heritage of the past, but also alleviated the reception of Community norms. Codes of civil procedure falling into this line include the one adopted by Slovenia in 1997, and those passed by Latvia in 1999, Lithuania in 2002, Estonia in 2005 and Bulgaria in 2008. Where the earlier socialist code of civil procedure – for various reasons – had not yet been replaced by a new Act (like in the case of the codes of civil procedure of Hungary (1952), of the Czech Republic (1963) or of Poland (1964), the necessary changes were executed through amending Acts.[6] In the latter countries the codification of new codes of civil procedure has been launched only in recent years.

As the antecedents to the present paper and also as a starting point for it mention should be made of the research started nearly ten years ago, which was coordinated by the author of the present paper in cooperation with Professor Miklós Kengyel and the results of which have been summed up in the volume published by the German Nomos Publishers.[7] It was in the frames of this research that the following conclusions were made.

Despite the different paths leading to European Union membership, none of the Member States having joined the EU in 2004 or 2007 applied for *provisional measures* in the field of civil procedure law. All Member States considered that they had taken all measures that may ensure 'the coordinated and effective application of Community law'.

Despite the direct applicability of regulations on judicial cooperation, the approximation of national legal systems to the rules of civil procedure of the European Union *took place in a different way in each Member State*. Against the adoption of separate

4 Brussels Convention of 27 September 1968 on Jurisdiction and the Enforcement of Judgments in Civil and Commercial Matters.

5 Viktória Harsági and Miklós Kengyel, 'Generalbericht – Der Einfluss des Europäischen Zivilverfahrensrechts auf die nationalen Rechtsordnungen' in Miklós Kengyel and Viktória Harsági (eds), *Der Einfluss des Europäischen Zivilverfahrensrechts auf die nationalen Rechtsordnungen* (Nomos 2009) 195–196; Miklós Kengyel, 'Ungarn vor dem Tor des Lugano-Übereinkommens' in Geimer Reinhold and Schütze Rolf A. (eds), *Wege zur Globalisierung des Rechts: Festschrift für Rolf A. Schütze zum 65. Geburtstag* (Beck 1999) 345–358; Miklós Kengyel, 'Lugano innerhalb des Tors des Lugano Übereinkommens' in Reinhold Geimer and Rolf A Schütze (eds), *Recht ohne Grenzen: Festschrift für Athanassios Kaissis zum 65. Geburtstag* (Sellier 2012) 469–479.

6 For more detail, see: Thomas Sutter-Somm and Viktória Harsági Viktória (eds), *Die Entwicklung des Zivilprozessrechts in Mitteleuropa um die Jahrtausendswende. Reform und Kodifikation – Tradition und Erneuerung* (Schulthess 2012).

7 Miklós Kengyel and Viktória Harsági (eds), *Der Einfluss des Europäischen Zivilverfahrensrechts auf die nationalen Rechtsordnungen* (Nomos 2009).

Acts *several counter-arguments* may be raised. Because of their direct applicability it is unnecessary to repeat the contents of Community regulations; however, without this, references to domestic regulation can be interpreted only with difficulty.[8] Because of the fast development of the given field of law, the need for frequent amendments may come into conflict with the interest related to the stability of laws. Therefore in the Member States under analysis legislators favoured framework acts or amending acts as the way for carrying out the modifications. It was raised as a further question *in which act of Parliament* it would be expedient to lay down provisions relating to the application of European civil procedure law.

Hungary – hoping to join the Lugano Convention – modified her Code of Private International Law (Law-Decree No. 13 of 1979) as early as 2000 and thereby she started preparations for the application of the rules of European civil procedural law. For this very reason, before the accession only a short *framework act* was needed to be issued (Act XXX of 2003). Following the accession the rules of the Hungarian Code of Civil Procedure were amended and several changes were made to the Enforcement Act as well, but unlike in other countries no *separate chapter* on the application of European civil procedural rules was inserted into either of these acts.[9]

Hungary's accession to the Union and the preparation for it took place at a time when the regulation of civil proceedings involving a cross-border element was undergoing a change in paradigm in the European integration itself. At the turn of the millennium Community law-making in this field of law started at a great pace, as a result of which during her preparations for accession to the Union and also since then as a Union Member State with full rights of membership, Hungary has had to adapt to a pliable Community acquis being in a state of formation.[10]

2. Directions of the Research

The effect exerted by European Union civil procedure on the national legal systems should be examined, on the one hand, in its thematic diversity and, on the other hand, differentiating both in space and time.[11]

The norms of Community law do not exist and function in themselves; instead, there is functional interaction between European norms and the national legal systems. It is not rare that a Community rule cannot even be interpreted without a national legal rule. In order to reveal the content of the individual norms, during the application of traditional means of legal interpretation, European and national rules must be treated uniformly.[12] In numerous cases it is the Community norm that contains a referencing

8 Reinhold Geimer and Rolf A. Schütze, *Europäiches Zivilverfahrensrecht* (Beck 2004) 4.

9 Harsági and Kengyel (n 7).197–203.

10 Tibor Szőcs, 'A magyar nemzetközi polgári eljárásjog reformja – szabályozást igénylő kérdések' in János Németh and István Varga (eds), *Egy új polgári perrendtartás alapjai*, (HVG-Orac, 2014) 673.

11 Ibid.

12 Mátyás Kapa, 'Tétova feltevések az integrálódó európai polgári eljárásjog köréből' in Anikó Ernszt (ed), *De iuris peritorum meritis. Studia in honorem János Bruhács.* (Károli Gáspár Református Egyetem Állam- és Jogtudományi Kara, 2009) 39–40.

rule based on which concerning some questions the rules of national law must be applied (e.g. in the order for payment or small claim regulations), while in other cases during the application of the Community norm, even without a referencing rule, the rules of national law must be invoked.[13] We will start our examination by exploring this phenomenon.

The second major pillar of the field under discussion is constituted by judicial practice. Here two types of effect can be mentioned. In the first case the case-law of the Court of Justice of the European Union (CJEU) stimulates the legislator to modify legal regulation, while the other is rather an indirect effect. By this latter that situation is meant where based on the legal interpretation expounded by the CJEU in its case-law, the trial court starts interpreting and applying a procedural legal instrument differently without any change in the text of the relevant procedural legal norm.[14]

3. Court Structure

Participation in judicial cooperation has not had a significant impact on the organisation of courts. However, regardless of this (due to other causes) several fundamental changes have taken place. As a result of the justice reform of 2011, the names of courts have changed in Hungary (Act CLXI of 2011 on the Organisation and Administration of Courts). Apart from this, the reform has also brought about some structural changes in the court structure. Thus, beginning from 1 January 2012 the Hungarian court system continues to have four levels and the system of civil remedy ensures one level of appeal. The lowest level courts are the local courts (helyi bíróság), the name of which changed to district courts (járásbíróság) with effect from 1 January 2013. The second level is constituted by the 19 courts of justice (törvényszék) and the Municipal Court of Justice. The latter were substituted for the county courts and the Municipal Court of Budapest after 1 January 2012. The five courts of appeal were inserted in the court system (in two stages, in 2003 and 2005) as the third level. And finally, at the top of the hierarchy is the Curia, which replaced the Supreme Court following 1 January 2012. Cases are tried at first instance by the local courts (district courts after 2013) and the courts of justice. In civil cases local courts have general first-instance jurisdiction. Cases falling within the first-instance jurisdiction of the courts of justice can be appealed to the courts of appeal. Review petitions are heard by the Curia [§10 Hungarian Code of Civil Procedure]. However, the Curia may also serve as a forum of appeal within a narrow circle of cases; it ensures the uniformity of judicial practice. The labour courts have functioned as first instance courts since 1973. Despite the fact that their area of jurisdiction (venue) extends to a whole county, they exclusively try cases at first instance. The adjudication of appeals against the decision of labour courts forms part of the tasks of the courts of justice. Labour courts try cases arising from employment relations and employment contracts, and review social security decisions and specific administrative decisions relating to employment, and they also proceed in other cases falling within their subject-matter

13 Ibid 39–40, 44.

14 Róbert Muzsalyi, 'Az EU-jog hatása a magyar eljárásjogra' (2015) Magyar Jog 354.

jurisdiction by provision of law. After 1 January 2013, administrative courts function as specialised courts, proceeding – within one structural unit with labour courts – beginning from 1 January 2013. The jurisdiction of administrative courts extend to cases of judicial review of administrative decisions. Appeals submitted against the decisions of administrative courts is tried by the courts of justice.[15]

4. The Impact of the Norms of European Civil Procedure Law on Hungarian Legislation

4.1. General Remarks

The fundamental principles of the HCCP were modified in 2000 already with respect to Article 6 of the European Convention on Human Rights. In accordance with §2 (1) HCCP, the court shall seek to enforce the parties' right to reach a settlement in disputes and respect their right to a fair trial, and to reach a conclusion within a reasonable time period. In the event of the court's non-compliance with its obligations relating to the fair conduct of lawsuits and their resolution within a reasonable time, the party affected may seek reasonable compensation provided that the injury to his right cannot be remedied by way of redress procedures. This rule ensures the implementation of *the right of access to courts* both within and outside the scope of application of EU law.[16]

With a view to the future accession, the purpose of facilitating the application of European Community law was served by Act CX of 2000, which approximated Hungarian rules of jurisdiction to the Brussels and Lugano Conventions. It applies to this Act as well as to later legislation that they have been included mainly in Law-Decree № 13 of 1979 on Private International Law or some separate Act regulating non-litigious procedures. Only a small fraction of amendments had to be carried out through the Code of Civil Procedure. Thus, for example, Act XLI of 2005 adjusted certain rules of the Act on Enforcement to the regulations existing in this field in order to facilitate the enforcement of court judgments.[17] Out of the legislative acts amending the text of the Code of Civil Procedure – with regard to Community law – it is worth mentioning Act XXX of 2003, which is aimed at facilitating the applicability of the preliminary ruling procedure. Act XXXVI of 2005 amended the rules relating to the legal consequences of the omissions of parties in connection with the Regulation on the service of documents, which was repeatedly altered in 2008 with regard to the new Regulation on service. Act LXXX of 2003 on Legal Aid was designed to introduce essential changes in available cost reductions, especially with regard to our obligations of legal harmonisation. It was under

15 Miklós Kengyel and Viktória Harsági, 'Hungary – Civil Law' in Mariolina Eliantionio et al. (eds), *Standing up for Your Right(s) in Europe. A Comparative Study on Legal Standing (Locus Standi) before the EU and Member State Courts* (Intersentia 2013) 324–325.

16 Ibid pp. 344.

17 See: Miklós Kengyel and Viktória Harsági (eds), *Der Einfluss des Europäischen Zivilverfahrensrechts auf die nationalen Rechtsordnungen* (Nomos 2009) 111–131; Viktória Harsági and Miklós Kengyel, 'Anwendungsprobleme des Europäischen Zivilverfahrensrechts in Mittel- und Osteuropa' (2009) IPRax 533–539.

the influence of Community law that rules relating to the service of process agent were inserted as new rules in the Hungarian Code of Civil Procedure. Having regard to the Regulation on the European order for payment procedure, in 2010 new rules were incorporated into the Hungarian Code of Civil Procedure,[18] and the Act on the order for payment procedure.

4.2. *Regulation Brussels I (Old and New) and Brussels IIa*

Having regard to the fact that the harmonisation of laws and conscious preparation for entry started as early as the 90s, at the time of the accession only a short framework act had to be adopted, to be followed later by several amendments of the Code of Civil Procedure and the Enforcement Act. However, in contradistinction to other countries no separate chapter on the application of the civil procedure rules of the European Union was inserted into either Act.[19] The Brussels I Regulation and the implementing rules relating to Regulation (EC) No 805/2004 are contained partly in Chapter XII on foreign court judgments of the Enforcement Act (§§205–210/B), and partly in other chapters of the Act *in a sporadic form*.

It also applies to *Regulation (EC) No 2201/2003* replacing the short-lived Regulation (EC) No 1347/2000 that, due to the direct applicability of the Community legal rule, at the level of Member States room is only left for the adoption of norms of a supplementary, implementing character. The former regulation is silent on the implications of dual citizenship. This gap in the law has led to the submission of the first request for a preliminary ruling containing a Hungarian element, which was filed by the Cour de cassation (France) on 21 April 2008 in the case of László Hadadi v. Csilla Márta Mesko, Mrs. Hadadi.[20] The court requested the European Court to interpret point *b)* of Article 3 (1) as applied to a situation 'where both spouses have dual citizenship and both have their habitual residence in France. The court held that where the court of the Member State addressed must verify, pursuant to Article 64(4) of Council Regulation (EC) No 2201/2003 whether the court of the Member State of origin of a judgment would have had jurisdiction under Article 3(1)(b) of that regulation, the latter provision precludes the court of the Member State addressed from regarding spouses who each hold the nationality both of that State and of the Member State of origin as nationals only of the Member State addressed. That court must, on the contrary, take into account the fact that the spouses also hold the nationality of the Member State of origin and that, therefore, the courts of the latter could have had jurisdiction to hear the case. Where spouses each hold the nationality of the same two Member States, Article 3(1)(b) of Regulation No 2201/2003 precludes the jurisdiction of the courts of one of those Member States from being rejected on the ground that the applicant does not put forward other links with that State. On the

18 Viktória Harsági, "Downstream or Up the Stream' – Influence of Different Legal Cultures on Hungarian Civil Procedure Law' in Dmitry Maleshin (ed.), *Civil Procedure in Cross-cultural Dialogue: Eurasia Context* (Statut Publishing House 2012) 287–288.

19 Harsági and Kengyel, (IPRax 2009) (n 17) 533–539.

20 Case C-168/08 *László Hadadi v. Csilla Márta Mesko, Hadadiné* [2008], ECR I-6871, 13–14.

contrary, the courts of those Member States of which the spouses hold the nationality have jurisdiction under that provision and the spouses may seise the court of the Member State of their choice.'

4.3. *European Enforcement Order*

For the effective application of Regulation (EC) No 805/2004 it was indispensable to modify the domestic regulations of the Member States with regard to some questions of detail, which task was solved by the Member States using rather *different regulatory techniques*. In Hungary the amendments concerned Acts on judicial enforcement.

As a matter of fact, the *'possible' effect* of the Regulation *on the national laws of the Member States* differs to some extent from that of earlier regulations: although it does not directly regulate the procedure in which the enforceable judgement is delivered – and which is conducted based on the national law –, but through the minimum standards protecting the debtor it may still have an effect on the procedure. Albeit the Member States are not bound to adjust the rules of procedures regulated in their national laws to the system of minimum standards contained in the Regulation (see: Articles 12–17), however, if they wish that the enforcement orders arising from the procedures conducted based on their national laws could be declared – where the situation should so require – European enforcement orders, then this may nevertheless encourage them to review their procedural rules and harmonise them with the so-called minimum standards. Thus, Regulation (EC) 805/2004 may *give rise* – even if indirectly – *to the amendment of* those *domestic legal procedural rules* that are also applied by the Member States concerning purely domestic legal disputes. This phenomenon may also be perceived as a kind of expansion of European Community law. The practical importance of the issue is manifested by the fact that pursuant to the report on the application of Regulation (EC) 44/2001[21] – which in some places also deals with the problems arising from the application of Regulation (EC) 805/2004 – the experiences of the thirty German courts asked show that only approximately 50% of applications for a declaration of the original order to be a European Enforcement Order are successful and the cause of failure usually lies in the fact that the requirements prescribed by the minimum standards contained in Articles 12–17 of Regulation (EC) 805/2004 have not been met. A source of problem among others may be the *application of forms of service that do not conform to the Regulation (e.g. fictitious service).*[22]

The most important novelty of Regulation (EC) 805/2004, also referred to as a change in paradigm, was the *abolition of the exequatur procedure.*[23] It is this that gives rise to a part of the problems relating to application at the points of intersection, or 'in the field of tension' between the Regulation and national laws. The *Hungarian solution* differs somewhat from the solutions applied in other countries: here the European Enforcement

21 Burkhard Hess et al. *Report on the Application of Regulation Brussels I in the Member States*, Final version, September 2007, Study JLS/C4/2005/3, p. 22.

22 Harsági and Kengyel, (IPRax 2009) (n 17) 537.

23 Miklós Kengyel and Viktória Harsági, *Európai polgári eljárásjog* (Osiris 2006) 147–152, 501–523.

Order does not replace the issuance of a writ of execution (i.e. the ordering of enforcement). This solution proceeds from the proposition that the Regulation is aimed at the abolition of the procedure for the declaration of enforceability and at rendering the foreign judgment declared to be a European Enforcement Order equivalent to a domestic enforceable title. Therefore raising the European Enforcement Order to the same rank as a domestic enforceable title means in practice that similarly to domestic judgments and documents, the European Enforcement Order should also undergo that stage of the procedure in which the certificate of enforceability or writ of execution are issued. The above train of thoughts considered from a Hungarian point of view necessarily means that such a judgment qualified as an enforceable title – similarly to domestic judgments – 'must undergo' the first phase of the enforcement procedure, the stage of *ordering enforcement* as well, before the effectuation of enforcement could begin. This means that based on the foreign judgment the court issues a certificate of enforcement or affixes a writ of execution to a public document under conditions laid down in the national law (and identical to those applicable to domestic judgments).

4.4. *Matters Relating to Maintenance or Succession*

Some years ago, due to a fundamental change in the European acquis, a comprehensive re-regulation was carried out relating to tasks performed by the central authority proceeding in matters of maintenance. The Act provides a coherent and clear regulation of the obligations and tasks of central authorities and of the domestic legal procedure for the assertion of claims. As a shortcoming of the Act academic literature has pointed out that its scope does not extend to the implementation in Hungary of the New York Convention on Recovery Abroad of Maintenance.[24]

With respect to matters relating to succession, the latest piece of legislation is Act LXXI of 2015 on the adaptation procedure under Article 31 of Regulation (EU) No 650/2012 of the European Parliament and of the Council. It provides that where there is need for adaptation, the application concerning this may be filed with the court in Hungary. The Act concentrated the procedure in the Central District Court of Buda, which is to decide exclusively on the basis of documents, and against its decisions an appeal lies to the court of justice. The cost of the procedure is to be borne by the party concerned in the succession. This Act introduced some amendments to the PIL Code, the Enforcement Act, the Act on Probate Procedure and the Act on Real Estate Registration. In addition to several amendments, Act CXLI of 1997 was supplemented with a new chapter.

4.5. *Legal Assistance (Service of Documents, Taking of Evidence)*

Domestic legal regulation required for the application of the Regulation on the service of documents was incorporated into the national laws in different ways. In Hungary Act

24 The rules relating to the implementation of that Convention in Hungary are still mostly contained in a low-level piece of legislation the content of which has become outdated [Decree No 9/1957 (IX.13.) IM of the Ministry of Justice]. Szőcs, (HVG 2014) 686.

XXX of 2003 amended the Code of Civil Procedure in order to implement the Regulations on the service of documents and on the taking of evidence.

With regard to the service of documents, it may be stated that in the beginning Hungary concentrated the task of designating *transmitting and receiving agencies* in the Ministry of Justice. As a revision of the centralised model, a provision amending Law-Decree No 13 of 1979 on Private International Law entered into force simultaneously with the new Regulation on the service of documents[25], providing for the direct involvement of courts in the mutual provision of legal assistance.[26]

Act XXX of 2008 introduced into the Code of Civil Procedure the institution of agent for service of process, with the aim of avoiding having to apply national or international legislation relating to the service of official documents.[27] This was in conformity with international trends, since individual legal systems typically endeavoured to reduce the number of cross-border cases where they would have to resort to international legal assistance regarding the service of documents. In Hungary, failure to give notification of an agent for service of process results in the domestic service of the document by a notice displayed on public notice boards. According to Szőcs, it was 'necessary to reconsider the regulation in force pertaining to the institution of agent for service of process because in recent times an apparent change has been taking place in the attitude assumed by Union law toward the obligation to announce an agent for service of process.'[28] According to a recent amendment of the Act on Enforcement[29] there is no need to have an agent for service of process in an enforcement procedure under Regulation 861/2007/EC, Regulation 4/2009/EC and Regulation 1215/2012/EU.

With regard to the effect exerted on national procedural laws by the Regulation on the taking of evidence, *one may state the following. In Hungary* no separate Act was passed to promote the application of the Regulation, but instead rules of detail and references were incorporated into the national codes of procedure and into laws relating to private international law either by direct reference to the Regulation or in a more abstract way.

As regards the nature of Regulation (EC) № 1206/2001, it constitutes a technical rule basically. It has not resulted in the genuine unification of the laws relating to the taking of evidence abroad; it merely simplifies the process, unifies its technical aspects and accelerates it Europe-wide.[30] It does not directly regulate the method of carrying out the actual taking of evidence abroad. These questions are governed by the provisions of international treaties and the domestic laws of the Member States or they fall within the

25 Council Regulation (EC) 1393/2007 of the European Parliament and of the Council of 13 November 2007 on the service in the Member States of judicial and extrajudicial documents in civil or commercial matters (service of documents), and repealing Council Regulation (EC) 1348/2000 [2007] OJ L324, 79.

26 Act XXX 2008, §62.

27 Explanatory Memorandum for Act XXX of 2008, detailed comments on §§6–8.

28 Szőcs, (HVG 2014) (n 10) 684.

29 Act LIII 1994, §37/B (4).

30 Christian Berger, 'Die EG-Verordnung über die Zusammenarbeit der Gerichte auf dem Gebiet der Bewiesaufnahme in Zivil- und Handelssachen (EuBVO)' (2001) IPrax 524, 527.

court's discretion.[31] The taking of evidence itself follows the principle of *lex fori* regardless of whether it is carried out by the trial court or the requested court.[32]

As a result of the coming into effect of the Regulation on the taking of evidence, one has been able to observe a shift from the traditional system of cross-border legal assistance toward a *new model of cooperation* in the European Union, where the direct taking of evidence in the national territory of another Member State has also become possible within the frames set by the Regulation. By this partial relinquishment of the exercise of judicial power, the Member States have *given up a small segment of state sovereignty*, which means an essential change compared to the rules contained in either the Hague Convention of 1954 on civil procedure[33] or the Hague Convention of 1970 on Taking of Evidence.[34][35]

A regulation is a norm that is *directly applicable* in the Member States; therefore, it does not require a separate legislative act on the part of the Member States. Nevertheless, some articles of the regulation leave it to national legislation to regulate some questions of detail which are intended to promote the implementability of the regulation (thus, e.g. the appointment of the acting courts and a central body, the determination of the language in which requests addressed to the courts of the Member State may be accepted). The Hungarian legislator laid down these rules among the provisions of the *Law-Decree on International Private Law* and *Decision No. 1147/2002 (IX.4.) Korm. of the Government*.[36]

4.6. *The European Order for Payment Procedure and the European Small Claims Procedure*

Regulation (EC) 1896/2006 is the first one to regulate a (whole) procedure that is uniform at the level of the Community. However, its peculiarity lies in the regulatory technique used by the European legislator, since although the Regulation contains rules relating to the whole procedure, in many cases these rules define only the main elements of the procedure. Therefore, in the European order for payment procedure, practically, a mixture of Community and domestic legal rules is applied. This results from Article 26, which states that concerning questions of procedural law not regulated expressly by the Regulation, national law is applicable. In some articles, the Regulation expressly refers to national law; however, national law may be applied in other cases as well, when the rules

31 Götz Schulze, 'Dialogische Beweisaufnahmen im internationalen Rechtshilfeverkehr' (2001) IPRax 528.

32 For more detail, see: Viktória Harsági, 'Dimensions of Evidence in Hungary.' (Lex Localis 2015, <http://books.lex-localis.press/evidenceincivillaw/hungary/>[online]).

33 Hague Convention 1 March 1954 on Civil Procedure.

34 Hague Convention 18 March 1970 on the Taking of Evidence Abroad in Civil or Commercial Matters.

35 For more detail on this topic, see: Heinrich Nagel, *Nationale und internationale Rechtshilfe im Zivilprozeß; das europäische Modell* (Nomos 1971) 78.

36 Government Decision No. 1147/2002. (IX. 4.) on measures required for the implementation of Community legislation relating to judicial cooperation in civil matters [1147/2002. (IX. 4.) Kormány határozat egyes polgári jogi igazságügyi együttműködési tárgyú európai közösségi jogszabályok végrehajtása érdekében szükséges intézkedésekről.].

of the Regulation do not cover the given field. One could formulate this as: *national law* may be applied in the European order for payment procedure with a *supplementary, gap-filling character.*

For the applicability of the European order for payment procedure in Hungary, some legal instruments had to be modified, which modifications were placed among the rules of the Code of Civil Procedure (§399) and Act Nr 53 of 1994 on Civil Enforcement (Vht.) at the beginning. From 1 June 2010 the rules of Act Nr 50 of 2009 on the order for payment procedure replaced the above-mentioned provisions of the HCCP; consequently, unless the Regulation makes a provision to the contrary, the rules of this Act are duly applicable to the European order for payment procedure.

In Hungary *it falls within the competence of the notary public to issue a European order for payment.* Submissions may exclusively be filed in paper form in writing with the proceeding notary, in the procedure *exclusively paper-based submissions* are applicable, the proceeding notary issues and serves the documents on the party in paper form.[37]

Regulation (EC) No 861/2007 of the European Parliament and of the Council establishes in Europe the *first uniform civil litigation (adversarial) procedure regulated at Community level,* and thereby, it constitutes a significant *milestone* in the history of development of European civil procedure law. The Regulation contains a few uniformly applicable rules not only concerning the litigation process, but also concerning the recognition and enforcement of the judgment delivered during it. The new procedure is heavily criticised by academic literature because the Regulation regulates the course of the legal action only up to the first instance judgment and even that in a rather fragmented way. The first 'work of legislation' regulating adversarial European proceedings undertakes the task of establishing the foundations of a new civil proceeding for the Member States of the European Union in altogether 15 articles (Articles 4–18). The lawmaker of the Regulation remains silent on numerous procedural issues, concerning which the principle of lex fori is applicable. Article 19 provides that the European Small Claims Procedure shall be governed by the procedural law of the Member State in which the procedure is conducted unless the Regulation provides otherwise. This solution acts against uniform application.[38] Although this system of rules is unified in its main features, but nevertheless diverges with regard to the details, therefore we are faced with *twenty-seven kinds of systems of procedural rules.*

4.7. *Legal Aid*

As opposed to regulation by way of regulations, which dominates other areas of European civil procedure, in the case of legal aid the Union legislator considered it more effective

37 Viktória Harsági, 'The notarial order for payment procedure as a Hungarian pecularity' in Reinhold Geimer and Rolf A. Schütze (eds), *Recht ohne Grenzen. Festschrift für Athanassios Kaissis zum 65. Geburtstag.* (Sellier 2012) 351–353.

38 Isabel Jahn, 'Das Europäische Verfahren für geringfügige Forderungen' (2007) *NJW* 2894.; Walter H. Rechberger, 'Die neue Generation. Bemerkungen zu den Verordnungen Nr. 805/2004, Nr. 1896/2006 und Nr. 861/2007 des Europäischen Parlaments und des Rates' in Rolf Stürner et al. (eds), *Festschrift für Dieter Leipold zum 70. Geburtstag.* (Mohr Siebeck 2009) 313.

to realise harmonisation endeavours and, therefore, decided on regulation by directive, thereby allowing Member States a rather wide scope for action and, at the same time, promoting the applicant's access to justice as well. The cause of choosing this form of regulation in the field of legal aid may, on the one hand, be traced back to differences in the social-historical traditions of the individual Member States, and on the other hand, to differences in the economic situation of the Member States, which also constitute a practical obstacle to a unified – less 'soft' Community regulation (e.g. determination of threshold values).

The aim of the Directive is to define the frames of national legal regulation in order to avoid situations where, in the absence of financial means, the poorest people are simply deprived of the possibility of enforcing their rights in the European Judicial Area.[39] The Directive contains such provisions that are designed to promote compatibility between the legal systems of the individual States. The form of regulation by directive allows the Member States to develop their systems (alongside the legal principles contained in the Directive) in accordance with their own legal traditions.

The Member States were obliged to transpose the provisions of the Directive into their national laws by *30 November 2004* (Article 21). The provisions of the Directive do not prevent Member States from defining a set of more favourable conditions for the applicant (Article 19). The task of transposition was solved differently in the different Member States.[40] In Hungary a separate Act was adopted concerning the issue (Act LXXX of 2003),[41] that is applied in cross-border and pure domestic cases.

4.8. *Mediation*

Article 12 of the EU Mediation Directive requires Member States to bring into force laws and other regulations 'necessary to comply with this Directive' by 21 May 2011 at the latest.[42] Hungarian legal regulation (Act LV of 2002) does not make a distinction between national and cross-border mediation, so it should be applied not only in cross-border, but in pure domestic cases, too. 'Hungary is characterised by monistic regulation: there are no separate provisions for domestic and foreign mediation'.[43] In the beginning only

39 Mário Tenreiro and José Alegre Seoane, 'The Creation a European Judicial Area in Civil and Commercial Matters: What Can the EU Do?' in Marcel Storme (ed), *Procedural Laws in Europe. Towards Harmonisation.* (Maklu, 2003), 469.

40 For more detail, see Harsági and Kengyel, (n 7) 217–218.

41 In 2007 the following decree was issued to implement the Act on Legal Aid: Decree No 56/2007 (XII.22.) IRM of the Ministry of Justice and Law Enforcement on the detailed rules relating to recourse to legal aid.

42 Article 10 of the Directive constitutes an exception, pursuant to which the Commission shall make publicly available, by any appropriate means, information on the competent courts or authorities communicated by the Member States. The deadline for Member States to comply with the obligation contained in this Article is 21 November 2010.

43 For more detail: Viktória Harsági and Miklós Kengyel and Zoltán Nemessányi, 'Hungary' in Carlos Esplugues et al. (eds), *Civil and Commercial Mediation in Europe. National Mediation Rules and Procedures.* Volume I. (Intersentia 2013) 217–238; Viktória Harsági, Gergely Czoboly and Zoltán Nemessányi, 'Hungary' in Carlos Esplugues (ed.), *Civil and Commercial Mediation in Europe. Cross-border Mediation.* Volume II. (Intersentia 2014) 201–220.

out-of-court mediation was possible, but in 2012 the institution of court-annexed-mediation was also introduced.

5. Case Law

5.1. *Hungarian Case Law Relating to European Civil Procedure Law*

In the first years following Hungary's accession to the European Union in 2004, decisions of the national courts primarily concerned the preconditions for initiating a preliminary ruling procedure. The following subchapter (4.2.) presents or analyzes these decisions as well as judgments delivered by the Court of Justice of the European Union in cases involving a Hungarian element. In recent years there has been a surge in the number of problems emerging in Hungarian judicial practice concerning the application of some sources of European civil procedural law, which problems have not been referred to the CJEU by the Hungarian courts.

The majority of the relevant judgments of the past years have addressed questions relating to family law and, within it, to parental responsibility and, in particular, matters pertaining to the wrongful removal and retention of children have had a more substantial presence. Besides the decisions relating to this topic, there were judgments that concern questions of jurisdiction contained in the Brussels-I Regulation, the issue of ordre public[44], using one's mother tongue related to Brussels-I Reg. Probably as a consequence of the economic crisis - insolvency proceedings continue to remain in the centre of attention, and apart from these, there is also a decision of the Curia dealing with unfair terms in consumer contracts. In 2014, relating to this topic, the Curia (Kúria) delivered its first decision on the European order for payment procedure.[45]

5.2. *The Impact of the Case Law of the Court of Justice of the European Union on Hungarian Legislation and the Application of Law*

In the first ten years (2004–2013) following Hungary's accession to the Union, out of the Member States joining the Union in 2004, the highest number of procedures (more than

44 See: Miklós Kengyel, Viktória Harsági and Zoltán Nemessányi, Zoltán, 'National Report - Hungary. Study on the Interpretation of Public Policy Exceptions as referred to in EU Instruments of Private International Law' Manuscript, 19.

45 Viktória Harsági, 'Ungarische Rechtsprechung zum Gemeinschaftsprivatrecht' (2010) GPR 170–173; Viktória Harsági, 'Hungarian Case Law Relating to European Private Law (2010–2011)' (2011) GPR 166–168; Viktória Harsági, 'Hungarian Case Law Relating to European Private Law (2011–2012)' (2012) GPR 189–194; Viktória Harsági, 'Hungarian Case Law Relating to European Private Law (2012–2013) '(2013 GPR 203–209; Viktória Harsági, 'Hungarian Case Law Relating to European Private Law (2013–2014)' (2014) GPR 209–214; Viktória Harsági, 'Hungarian Case Law Relating to European Private Law (2014–2015)' (2015) GPR 221–225.

third of the cases) were initiated by the Hungarian courts. Half of these cases were initiated by courts from the territory of the capital.[46]

In cases where, in proceedings conducted before the court of a Member State, a claim deducible from Union law is being asserted, national rules of procedural law are to be applied while having regard to the Union's basic principles presented above.[47] A good example for this principle is constituted by the two legal cases presented below, which have led to the amendment of the Hungarian CCP and the refinement of judicial practice.

The two most important principles of effective judicial protection are the equivalency of procedures and the principle of the actual implementation of Community law. Since 2004, the implementation of these principles has been promoted by several judgments of the European Court of Justice, the opinions of the Supreme Court and amendments of national law. Following the judgment passed in the joined cases C-290/05 and C-333/05, Act CXXX of 2006, which provided for the refund of registration duty incompatible with Community law, ensured a 180-day time limit for right holders to enforce their claims. Applications were to be submitted to the first instance administration authority. This also opened up the possibility to initiate a claim, since the second instance decision could be challenged before a court.[48]

The standing of defendants in consumer protection lawsuits was improved essentially by Act L of 2009, which modified §41 (5) HCCP so that where the choice of forum clause forms part of the general contract terms, the chosen court shall transfer the case – upon the defendant's request presented during the first hearing at the latest – to the court of competent jurisdiction designated by the defendant to hear and decide the case.[49]

An *essential change* in the Hungarian system of legal remedy was caused by the judgment passed in the *Cartesio case*[50] C-210/06. The European Court of Justice held: 'Where rules of national law apply which relate to the right of appeal against a decision making a reference for a preliminary ruling, and under those rules the main proceedings remain pending before the referring court in their entirety, the order for reference alone being the subject of a limited appeal, the second paragraph of Article 234 EC is to be interpreted as meaning that the jurisdiction conferred on any national court or tribunal by that provision of the Treaty to make a reference to the Court for a preliminary ruling cannot be called into question by the application of those rules, where they permit the appellate court to vary the order for reference, to set aside the reference and to order the referring court to resume the domestic law proceedings. [...] Having regard to the scope of review jurisdiction of the second instance court – its power to vary the decision and

46 Róbert Muzsalyi, 'Az előzetes döntéshozatali eljárás kezdeményezésének tapasztalatai a magyar bíróságok gyakorlatában' in Viktória Harsági et al. (eds.), *Az Európai Unió új és megújuló jogforrásainak szerepe a magyar magánjog fejlesztésében.* (Pázmány Press 2014) 159, 162.

47 Kinga Tímár, 'A nemzetközi és európai uniós szabályozók szerepe a Polgári perrendtartás kodifikációjában' in István Varga, *Codificatio processualis civilis. Studia in Honorem Németh János II.* (ELTE Eötvös Kiadó 2013), 414.

48 Kengyel and Harsági (n 15) 343.

49 Ibid p. 343.

50 Judgment of 16 December 2008 delivered in Case C-210/06 Cartesio Oktató és Szolgáltató Bt [2008] ECR I-9641.

the binding force of the second instance decision on the first instance court – the CJEU held that a separate appeal against the court order for reference for a preliminary ruling is in conflict with Union law.'[51] (Paragraphs 88–98.) The consequence of this conclusion was that Act LXVIII of 2009 modified §155/A. (3) HCCP, which had previously permitted a separate appeal against the order for reference for a preliminary ruling. In accordance with the new rule, such an order is *no longer subject to appeal.*[52]

Another change in the national regulation was brought about by the *so-called Pannon case.*[53] The principles stated earlier[54] were supplemented by the CJEU, holding that: the role attributed to the national court by Directive (ECC) No 93/13[55] is not limited to a mere power to rule on the possible unfairness of a contractual term, but also consists of the obligation to examine that issue of its own motion, including when it is assessing whether it has territorial jurisdiction. In carrying out that obligation, the national court is not, however, required under the Directive to exclude the possibility that the term in question may be applicable, if the consumer, after having been informed of it by that court, does not intend to assert its unfair or non-binding status. The HCCP did not contain the required rules relating to this obligation of the court, therefore Parliament adopted Act L of 2009[56] to amend the rules of the HCCP relating to the stipulation of territorial jurisdiction. 'Pursuant to this, if the stipulation of territorial jurisdiction is contained among the general contract terms, the court whose jurisdiction has been stipulated shall, on the application of the defendant submitted at the first hearing at the latest, transfer the proceedings to the court – specified by the defendant and having general or other (elective) jurisdiction as regulated in §§29–40 – to conduct the trial and adjudge the case.'[57] The question did not leave case law intact either. In its opinion No 2/2011. (XII.12.) PK[58], the Supreme Court expounded that, in the case of a consumer contract, right at the stage of preparation for the trial the court shall examine ex officio whether the stipulation on jurisdiction is based on the registered seat or domicile of the party contracting with the consumer and in this case the defendant shall be called upon to state whether he/she wants to refer to the unfairness of that stipulation. The Supreme Court took the position that even without an application to this effect the court has to examine ex officio whether the legal relationship giving rise to the proceedings can be

51 Tímár (n 47) 413–414.

52 Kengyel and Harsági (n 15) 344. In its Joint Opinion No 1/2009 (VI.24) PK-KK, the Supreme Court 'stated that the appellate court cannot set aside the order for reference with regard to such aspects as its necessity, or the content of the questions posed, or the reasons given for it. Therefore, in cases where rules preceding the above amendment of the HCCP were still applicable, the court proceeding at second instance shall uphold the order made relating to reference for a preliminary ruling.' [Joint Opinion No 1/2009 (VI. 24.) PK-KK on the adjudication of appeals against orders relating to reference for a preliminary ruling and the obligation to refer. Bírósági Határozatok [Court Decisions] 2009/9.].

53 C-243/08 *Pannon GSM Zrt. v Erzsébet Sustikné Győrfi* [2009] ECR I-04713.

54 C-240/98 and C-244/98 *Océano Grupo Editorial and Salvat Editores* [2000] ECR I-4941, paras 21–22.

55 Council Directive 93/13/ECC of 5 April 1993 on unfair terms in consumer contracts.

56 Act L 2009 on the order for payment procedure, §62 (1). Pursuant to the Act, the amended provisions are applicable to actions brought after 30 June 2009.

57 Muzsalyi (n 14) 352–353.

58 A Legfelsőbb Bíróság Polgári Kollégiumának 2/2011. (XII.12.) PK véleménye a fogyasztói szerződés érvénytelenségével kapcsolatos egyes kérdésekről. Source: Bírósági Határozatok 2012/3.

classified as a consumer contract or not. However, the court cannot order the taking of evidence ex officio in order to ascertain the nature of the legal relation.[59]

6. Main Tasks to be Carried Out during the Codification of the New Code of Civil Procedure

As it has been demonstrated by the present paper, during the codification work regard must be had to basic principles, codified Union law and the case law of the CJEU as well. As far as specific legislative tasks are concerned, the following problems will have to be remedied. As a result of amendments carried out in the past decade, Hungarian regulation relating to European civil procedure law has by now become rather unclearly organised. It may also be worth revising some rules from the aspect of their content.[60] A reconsideration and systematisation of the present rules is likely to lead to the conclusion that it would be reasonable to collect the present dispersed rules into one chapter of the HCCP (or the PILC respectively) and to render the HCCP more user-friendly.[61] It is problematic that the statements and declarations made concerning the two Union regulations on legal aid are laid down only in government decisions despite the fact that they do not only concern technical questions, but also confer powers on some organs involved in carrying out tasks relating to international legal assistance (the appointment of transmitting and receiving agencies and of the central body). There is still no comprehensive regulation in matters relating to parental responsibility. There is a long line of international and Union acts institutionalising cooperation between central authorities in this field as well; however, the present domestic regulation relating to the performance of these tasks is fragmented and incomplete.[62] It may be raised as a further problem that lest the new HCCP should not contain a small claims procedure, the background rules of the Regulation on the European small claims procedure should be incorporated into some part of it.

59 Muzsalyi (n 14) 353; Lénárd Darázs: 'A 'bíróságválasztás' mint tisztességtelen szerződési kikötés' (2012) Gazdaság és Jog 19–24.

60 Szőcs (n 10) 687.

61 Tímár (n 47) 413–414.

62 Szőcs (n 10) 683, 686.

Bart Krans*

THE IMPACT OF EU LAW ON DUTCH CIVIL PROCEDURE LAW

1. A Growing Interplay

The growing volume of EU law has gradually revealed an intriguing interplay between EU law and national private law. This is also demonstrated by the growing role played by EU law in Dutch private law case law. As a result, the relationship between EU law and national private law has started to draw the attention of Dutch legal scholars.[1]

Aware of the growing importance of EU law to national law in general, the Dutch Ministry of Justice began a project to improve knowledge of European law within the Dutch judiciary.[2] It aimed to improve the accessibility of information sources on European law by using web technology, by improving knowledge of European law in the Dutch judiciary and by setting up and maintaining a network of European law court coordinators.[3] The Hague Institute for the Internationalisation of Law initiated research into the role of national judges as European Union judges. The central aim of that research was to identify how EU law is applied by national courts in the Member States by questioning national judges on their views with regards to the application of EU law. One of its main conclusions was that Dutch (and German)[4] judges want more information

* Full Professor of Private Law and Civil Procedure Law at Leiden University, the Netherlands.

1 For example AS Hartkamp and others (eds), *De invloed van het Europese recht op het Nederlandse privaatrecht* (1st edn, Kluwer 2007, two volumes (in Dutch)). The title of these books can be translated as 'The influence of European law on Dutch private law'. In 2014 an extended and update edition was published (partially in English). Other examples are provided by the PhD thesis of MH Wissink, *Richtlijnconforme interpretatie van burgerlijk recht* (Kluwer 2001) and the PhD thesis of R Meijer, *Staatsaansprakelijkheid wegens schending van gemeenschapsrecht* (Kluwer 2007) (both in Dutch).

2 The project was called 'Eur*infra*'. It was launched under the direction of the Ministry of Justice and transferred to the Council for the Judiciary in 2002, see §1 of the project brochure 'Eur*infra*: Reinforcing the knowledge of European Law within the Dutch judiciary Eur*infra*: Le renforcement de connaissance du droit europēen au sein de la magistrature nėerlandaise', <https://www.rechtspraak.nl/English/International-cooperation/Pages/Eur*infra*.aspx> accessed October 2015. The project was completed in 2004, but that does not mean, as stated in §1 of the brochure, that the activities undertaken within the project's framework were ended as of that date.

3 These court coordinators are supposed to meet regularly and act as focal points for European law issues for their court colleagues (see for more information on that network and the court coordinators, the Eur*infra* brochure (n 3) §3.3).

4 German experiences were also included in this research.

on EU law if it enables them better to recognise possible EU law issues and better to understand how to deal with those issues in the cases they decide.[5]

The growing volume of EU law is not only important for national private law in general, but has also started to be of increasing significance for national civil procedure law. The interplay between EU law and national civil procedure law has gradually been revealing itself as an expanding area. Dutch civil procedure law has come increasingly under the influence of EU law. A vast amount of European Union law can be relevant to questions which can arise in civil proceedings before national courts which nonetheless lack a cross-border element.[6]

The 'Europeanisation of civil procedure' report of the European Parliamentary Research Service addresses sector-specific harmonisation by way of directives as one potential route to the Europeanisation of civil procedure law and refers to it as the 'Europeanisation of EU law through the back door'.[7] That characterisation is correct, at least for the Netherlands: sector-specific EU law can be relevant in several areas of Dutch civil procedure law. European Union law can be relevant in several areas of Dutch national civil procedure law, such as *ex officio* applications, evidential burden, standards of proof, costs of proceedings, the right to free choice of a lawyer, preliminary injunctions, and matters concerning attachment and collective actions. The back door is open, and not just ajar.

The procedural autonomy of the Member States plays a significant role when discussing the relevance of European law for national civil procedure law.[8] Despite the importance of that procedural autonomy and the significance of infringements of that autonomy, it will not be discussed in this paper as such.[9] Nor will I discuss all the individual areas of Dutch civil procedure law with a European dimension. The aim of this paper is to illustrate the relevance and the importance of EU legislation for Dutch civil procedure law by discussing some new questions occasioned by EU case law which have arisen in a classic area (§2), several new legal rules resulting from EU legislation which have greater or lesser impacts on the existing state of Dutch law (§3) and some remarks on spontaneous harmonisation in Dutch civil procedure law (§4).[10]

5 The results of this research were published in 2011: Tobias Nowak, Fabian Amtenbrink, Marc Hertogh and Mark Wissink, *National Judges as European Union Judges* (Eleven International Publishing 2011).

6 Elsewhere I have referred to the subject as an invisible pillar in the Europeanisation of national civil procedure law (HB Krans, 'EU Law and National Civil Procedure Law: an Invisible Pillar' [2015] ERPL 567–587).

7 The European Parliamentary Research Service (author: Rafael Mańko) 'Europeanisation of civil procedure Towards common minimum standards' (June 2015) <www.europarl.europa.eu, §4.1> accessed October 2015.

8 Compare CN Kakouris, 'Do the Member States Possess Judicial Procedural 'Autonomy''? [1197] CMLRev 1389–1412, M Tulibacka, 'Europeanisation of Civil Procedures: In Search of a Coherent Approach' [2009] CMLRev 1527–1565 and T Tridimas, *General Principles of EU Law* (OUP 2006).

9 The principles of effectiveness and equivalence as such, however important, are omitted from this paper.

10 The influence of Art. 6, ECHR and of the EU Charter of Fundamental Rights on national civil procedure law will not be considered in this contribution. Cross-border cases fall outside the scope of this paper as well.

2. New Questions about a Long-running Subject

The vast volume of European case law made by the European Court of Justice (ECJ) on *ex officio* applications by national courts (where courts are required to raise heads of claim available under the law which have not explicitly been pleaded by the applicants) has certainly attracted attention in the Netherlands. The decision of the ECJ in *Faber v Hazet* is a recent development, as one of many European rulings on the subject. This case, arising in the Netherlands, concerned a car which suddenly caught fire while being driven. In the ensuing civil proceedings between Ms Froukje Faber, owner and driver of the car, and the car vendor, the company denied liability for the accident. The court at first instance rejected Ms Faber's claims, considering that (to put it briefly) she was out of time in making her complaint. Ms Faber argued several grounds on appeal, but she did not specify whether she had purchased the car as a consumer. The Dutch Court of Appeal therefore referred several questions to the ECJ, the first on whether the national court is obliged to examine of its own motion whether in relation to a contract, the purchaser is a consumer within the meaning of Directive on consumer sales.[11] The ECJ ruled that the Consumer Sales Directive must be interpreted as meaning that a national court before which an action relating to a contract which may be covered by that Directive has been brought is required to determine whether the purchaser may be classified as a consumer within the meaning of that Directive, even if the purchaser has not relied on that status. The ECJ added a condition for this obligation on national courts: the court must have at its disposal the matters of law and of fact necessary to find that such a determination is necessary, or be able to do so simply by making a request for clarification.[12] Accordingly, within the framework of the Consumer Sales Directive, a national court is obliged to examine *ex officio* whether a purchaser has acted as a consumer.

Protection of the consumer as the weaker party vis-à-vis the commercial other party is the driving force behind the vast majority of ECJ case law on *ex officio* application of EU consumer law by national courts.[13] Certain provisions in European directives have to be applied *ex officio* by national courts.[14] The decision in *Faber v Hazet* can be seen as

11 Council Directive (EC) 99/44 on certain aspects of the sale of consumer goods and associated guarantees [1999] OJ L171 (Consumer Sale Directive or Directive on Consumer Sale).

12 Case C-497/13 *Faber v Hazet* [2015] ECLI:EU:C:2015:357; see on this topic B Krans, European relief for consumers. Procedural challenges to the fairness-test, *forthcoming*.

13 See on this topic B Krans, European relief for consumers. Procedural challenges to the fairness-test, *forthcoming* (n 12), §3.

14 E.g. Cases C-240–244/98 *Océano Grupo Editorial SA v Rocío Murciano Quiontero (C-240/98)* [2000] ECLI:EU:C:2000:346; C-473/00 *Cofidis SA v Jean-Louis Fredout [2002]* ECLI:EU:C:2002:705; C-168/05 *Elisa María Mostaza Claro v Centro M'vil Milenium SL* [2006] ECLI:EU:C:2006:675; C-243/08 *Pannon GSM Zrt. V Erzébet Sustikné Györfi* [2009] ECLI:EU:C:2009:350; C-40/08 *Asturcom Telecomunicaciones SL v Christina Rodrígues Nogueira* [2009] ECLI:EU:C:2009:615; C-137/08 *VB Pénzügyi Lízing Zrt. V Ferenc Scneider* [2010] ECLI:EU:C:2010:659; C-76/10 *Pohotovosťs. r.o. v Iveta Korčkovská* [2010] ECLI:EU:C:2010:685; C-472/10 *Nemzeti Fogyasztóvédelmi Hatózág v Invitel Távlözlési Zrt* [2012] ECLI:EU:C:2012:242; C-453/10 *Jana Perenicova & Vladislav Perenic v SOS Financ, Spol. s r. o.* [2012] ECLI:EU:C:2012:144; C-618/10 *Banco Español de Crédito v Joaquin Calderón Camino* [2012] ECLI:EU:C:2012:349; C-472/11 *Banif Plus Bank Zrt v Csaba Csipai & Viktória Csipai* [2013] ECLI:EU:C:2013:88; C-415/11 *Mohamed Aziz v Caixa d'Estalvis de Catalunya, Tarragona I Manresa*

another step down the path of *ex officio* application. If national courts also have to investigate of their own motion whether the contract at hand was concluded by a consumer, legal rules relating to consumer sale are within the scope of this obligation as well. Consumer protection may be stretched even further.

The arguments the ECJ has provided thus far for its line of reasoning in *ex officio* cases – in particular, that the consumer may not be aware of his rights[15] or may be deterred from enforcing his rights on account of the costs which judicial proceedings would involve[16] – are equally applicable if the consumer does not state that he is a consumer for the purposes of the contract at hand. Considering the rationale that the ECJ has provided, it would have been surprising if it had ruled in *Faber v Hazet* that courts do not have to take an active approach on the question of whether the buyer has acted as a consumer.

The practical consequences of this *ex officio* application of EU law by national courts are not entirely clear.[17] In the Netherlands this topic has brought about many questions and a vast amount of case law.[18] Among those questions are the scope of the topic and the way how courts have to deal with it.[19] The seriousness of the impact of this European case law for Dutch law is, at least to some extent, illustrated by the appearance of a report by a working group of the Council of the Judiciary, containing guidelines for courts in 2010 (updated in 2014)[20] and an important decision of the Dutch Supreme Court in which it examines in detail the topic in an *obiter dictum*.[21]

3. New Rules

European directives have resulted in several new legal rules in Dutch civil procedural law. Several of these new European rules have had some impact on Dutch procedural law,

[2013] ECLI:EU:C:2013:164; C-92/11 *RWE Vertrieb AG v Verbraucherzentrale Nordrhein-Wastfalen e.V.* [2013] ECLU:EU:C:2013:180; C-488/11 *Asbeek Brusse and Katarina de Man Garabito v Jahani BV* [2013] ECLI:EU:C:2013:341; C-32/12 *Soledad Duarte Hueros v Autociba SA and Automóviles Citroën España SA* [2013] ECLI:EU:C:2013:637; C-226/12 *Constructora Principado SA v José Ignacio Menédez Álvarez* [2014] ECLI:EU:C:2014:10; C-26/13 *Árpád Kásler & Hajnalka Káslerné Rábai v OTP Jelzágolbank Zrt* [2014] ECLI:EU:C:2014:282; C-169/14 *Juan Carlos Morcillo & María del Carmen* García v *Banco Bilbao* [2014] ECLI:EU:C:2014:2099; C-567/13 *Nóra Baczó & János István Cizsnyiczai v Raiffeisen Bank zrt* [2015] ECLI:EU:C:2015:88.

15 See e.g. Case C-168/05 *Elisa María Mostaza Claro v Centro M´vil Milenium SL* [2006] ECLI:EU:C:2006:675 para 28 and C-429/05 *Rampion and Godard v. Franfinance* ECJ [2007] ECLI:EU:C:2007:575 para 65.

16 See e.g. Case ?????:015:565a da Silvdo pBrite andt Others v Estado protugues guarantees rinsippet.8 er en hybrid. Objektiv skyld er ikkeCase C-473/00 *Cofidis SA v Jean-Louis Fredout [2002]* ECLI:EU:C:2002:705 para 34 *Mostaza Claro* (n 15), para 29.

17 In addition to consequences for national courts, the subject of *ex officio* application has also attracted attention in arbitration in the Netherlands; see e.g. I Brand [2015] MvV 211–213.

18 See on the impact for Dutch law B Krans ERPL (n 6) 573–576; and B Krans, European relief for consumers. Procedural challenges to the fairness-test, *forthcoming* (n 12). On this subject see e.g. AGF Ancery, *Ambtshalve toepassing van EU-recht* (Kluwer2012) (in Dutch, with a summary in English, pp 215–220).

19 The matter is therefore the subject of many publications, the vast majority of which are in Dutch.

20 The report (LOVCK werkgroep, *'Ambtshalve toetsing II'* (November 2014)) can be found on the website <www.rechtspraak.nl> accessed February 2016.

21 SC 13 September 2013, ECLI:NL:HR:2013:691, NJ 2014/274 (*Heesakkers/Voets*), with case note HB Krans.

while other new rules have had less impact. After considering some examples (section A), I will go into these types of new rules in greater detail (B–D).

3.1. *Some Examples*

The rules on the burden of proof provide us with some examples. At first glance, the burden of proof may appear to be a subject which is solely the domain of national law. The apportionment of the burden of proof in civil cases can be closely related to both matters of procedural law and substantive law. A closer look reveals that several European directives contain prescriptions concerning the burden of proof which can be relevant to Dutch civil procedure law. There are several examples of the European influence on the burden of proof,[22] one of which is provided by the regulations on misleading and comparative advertising.[23] Specific rules on the evidential burden for claims concerning unfair commercial practices have been introduced, with a view to implement the Directive on unfair commercial practices.[24] The same can be said for the prescription on the burden of proof concerning damage, the defect and the causal relationship between defect and damage.[25] This prescription is the subject of many publications in the Netherlands. National laws implementing directives on equal treatment[26] or rules on European competition law are other examples of this trend. Accordingly, several specific rules on the burden of proof have been introduced into Dutch law as a result of EU legislation.[27]

Although the standards of proof can also seem to be the preserve of national law, several rules have been introduced in Dutch law as a result of EU legislation.[28] A clear example can be found in the chapter of the Civil Procedure Code (CPC) on intellectual

22 For example, we can question whether the indicative and non-exhaustive list of terms which may be regarded as unfair (Annex to Council Directive (EEC) 93/13 on unfair terms in consumer contracts [1993] OJ L95 (Directive on unfair terms) can influence the evidential burden on unfair terms. I will not go into that question further because the implementing legislation in the Netherlands states that the appearance of a clause from that list is 'only' an indication of the unfairness of a clause.

23 Council Directive (EC) 97/55 amending Directive 84/450/EEC concerning misleading advertising so as to include comparative advertising [1997] OJ L290 (Directive on misleading advertising).

24 Art. 6:193j CC, seeking to implement Art. 12 Council Directive (EC) 2005/29 of the European Parliament and of the Council of 11 May 2005, concerning unfair business-to-consumer commercial practices in the internal market and amending Council Directive 84/450/EEC, Directives 97/7/EC, 98/27/EC and 2002/65/EC of the European Parliament and of the Council and Regulation (EC) No 2006/2004 of the European Parliament and of the Council [2005] OJ L149/22. See on these rules on burden of proof D.W.F. Verkade, *Oneerlijke handelspraktijken jegens consumenten,* (Deventer: Kluwer 2009) 55–59 (in Dutch).

25 Art. 6:188 CC, seeking to implement Art. 4 Council Directive (EEC) 85/374 on the approximation of the laws, regulations, and administrative provisions of the Member States concerning liability for defective products [1985] OJ L210/29.

26 For example Art. 7:646 CC.

27 See for more detailed information HB Krans, *Nederlands burgerlijk procesrecht en materieel EU-recht* (Kluwer 2010) Chapter 6 (in Dutch).

28 Title 14 Book 4 CPC (Art. 1019 - Art. 1019i CPC).

property rights.[29] The introduction of this chapter was a direct result of the Directive on the enforcement of intellectual property rights.[30] Specific rules for proceedings concerning intellectual property rights were enacted, *including* applications for the presentation of evidence.[31] Dutch law recognises an existing obligation to present evidence (known as the '*exhibitieplicht*').[32] This is a more general requirement for the 'disclosure' of documents. The rules on 'disclosure' in cases concerning intellectual property (IP) under EU law are more generous for the owners of IP rights than existing Dutch law.

The Directive on the enforcement of IP rights has also led to the introduction of a power to request the provisional examination of witnesses in IP cases.[33] The Dutch Civil Procedure Code already provided a general power to request the provisional examination of witnesses.[34] The scope and purpose of these two powers for provisional witness hearings is not identical.[35]

There are further examples of rules on the standards of proof with a European dimension: the rules on electronic signatures and electronic deeds, to mention but two. Since 2004 the Dutch Civil Code (CC) has included a chapter on electronic commerce. Part of that chapter sets out the rules on electronic signatures.[36] If certain conditions are met, an electronic signature can have the same evidential value as a handwritten signature. The Dutch regulations on electronic signatures were drafted and enacted as a result of the Directive on electronic signatures,[37] and include rules on the method of

29 The objective of this directive is to approximate legislative systems so as to ensure a high, equivalent and homogeneous level of protection in the internal market (recital 10, Preamble).

30 Council Directive (EC) 2004/48 on the enforcement of intellectual property rights [2004] OJ L195/16 (Directive on enforcement of IP rights). In a Communication, the European Commission stated it will make proposals to modernise enforcement of IP rights, focusing on commercial-level infringements (the 'follow the money' approach) (Commission, 'A digital single market strategy for Europe' (Communication) (Com (2015) 192 final)).

31 According to Art. 6 Directive on enforcement of IP rights (n 30), Member States must ensure that on application by a party which has presented reasonably available evidence sufficient to support its claims, and has, in substantiating those claims, specified evidence which lies in the control of the opposing party, the competent judicial authorities may order that such evidence be presented by the opposing party, subject to the protection of confidential information.

32 Art. 843a CPC.

33 Art. 1019f CPC, seeking to implement Art. 8 Directive on the enforcement of IP rights (n 30) (which EU rule states: '[...] in response to a justified and proportionate request of the claimant, the competent judicial authorities may order that information on the origin and distribution networks of the goods or services which infringe an intellectual property right be provided by the infringer and/or any other person [...]').

34 See on this power to require the provisional examination of witnesses B Krans, 'Provisional Witness Hearing in The Netherlands' [2015] 40 Revista de Processo 407–423.

35 Krans (fn 27) 83.

36 Art. 3:15a-15c CC.

37 Council Directive (EC) 99/93 on a Community framework for electronic signatures [1999] OJ L013/12 (Directive on electronic signatures). Another part of this special section (Art. 3:15d–3:15f CC) was introduced with a view to implementing the Directive on electronic commerce (Council Directive (EC) 2000/31 on certain legal aspects of information society services, in particular electronic commerce, in the Internal Market [2000] OJ L 178/1 (Directive on electronic commerce). Recital 4 of the Preamble states that it is important to ensure that electronic commerce can fully benefit from the internal market.

authentication. Provided certain conditions are met, the rules provide a rebuttable presumption that the method of authentication is presumed is sufficiently reliable.[38] Since 2010, the Dutch Civil Procedure Code has special rules on electronic deeds.[39] These rules have not found their way into the Dutch Civil Procedure Code as a direct result of EU legislation. Nevertheless, there is a connection between the rules on electronic deeds and on electronic signatures, and the latter are based on EU law.

New national legislation implementing EU legislation can have a greater or lesser impact on national law. The impact of the new rules depends on whether they lead to departures from the status quo.

3.2. *New Rules with Impact*

European directives have led to several new Dutch rules with some impact on an aspect of civil procedure. A well-known example is the legislation resulting from the Consumer> Sales Directive. It can be difficult for a consumer to prove that a non-conformity in goods pre-existed their delivery, especially if the vendor states that the non-conformity was the result of the improper use of the goods by the consumer.[40] The Consumer Sale Directive contains a presumption of non-conformity.[41] According to the Preamble to this Directive, the European legislator desired the introduction of a rebuttable presumption of non-conformity with the contract.[42] This rebuttable presumption affects the evidential burden on a consumer who wants to claim rights resulting from non-conformity of goods bought from a commercial vendor. This presumption of non-conformity is termed an 'all-risk insurance' requiring the vendor to prove that the non-conformity was caused by the buyer.[43]

The European rule was implemented in the Dutch Civil Code.[44] The Dutch regulation presumes that goods delivered in consumer sales did not conform with the contract if the non-conformity becomes apparent within six months of delivery, unless the nature of the goods or the nature of non-conformity preclude this. This European rule departs from what would follow from the general principles of Dutch sales law. The evidential burden of non-conformity is in principle on the purchaser.[45] A textbook on sales contracts law has described this prescription as one of the more spectacular parts of the implementation of the Consumer Sale Directive.[46]

38 Art. 3:15a CC.

39 Art. 156a CPC.

40 Explanatory Memorandum, II 2000/2001, nr. 3, p 19.

41 'Unless proved otherwise, any lack of conformity which becomes apparent within six months of delivery of the goods shall be presumed to have existed at the time of the delivery unless this presumption is incompatible with the nature of the goods or the nature of the lack of conformity.' (Art. 5(3) of the Consumer Sale Directive (n 11)).

42 Recital 8, Consumer Sale Directive (n 11).

43 N Reich, HW Micklitz, P Rott and K Tonner, *European Consumer Law* (Intersentia 2014) 177.

44 Art. 7:18, para 2 CC. There had been no prior rule for consumer sales with the same aim in Dutch law.

45 This follows from Art. 150 CPC.

46 J Hijma 'Asser-Hijma 7-I*' (Kluwer 2013) 332a (Art. 7:18 par 2 CC 'vormt een van de meer spectaculaire onderdelen van de richtlijnimplementatie').

It follows from the Explanatory Memorandum to the inclusion of that provision that the purchaser must assert and, in the event of a dispute, prove that the goods do not conform with the contract and that the non-conformity became apparent within six months of delivery.[47] It is then for the vendor to assert and to prove that the goods did conform with the contract at the time of the delivery.[48]

Dutch first-instance courts have dealt with many cases concerning this presumption of non-conformity.[49] Questions have been raised about the scope of the presumption. This has concerned the exception granted in Article 5(3) Consumer Sales Directive ('unless this presumption is incompatible with the nature of the goods or the nature of the lack of conformity').[50] There is case law on this subject concerning the sale of animals or plants.[51]

If the presumption applies, a dispute on non-conformity will not yet be settled, as the vendor is allowed to rebut that presumption, thereby being offered the opportunity to prove otherwise.[52] There has been debate about what exactly this proof otherwise means. The wording of the Dutch Civil Code does not provide a clear answer, neither do the explanatory documents to the Dutch Civil Code on this point,[53] and the matter is subject to debate among Dutch scholars.[54] Does the presumption mean that the vendor must prove the contrary to rebut the presumption? Or is it enough for the vendor to cast doubt on the presumed non-conformity at the time of the delivery?[55] In a decision argued at great length the Court of Appeal in Arnhem, referring to the Consumer Sales Directive in the English, French and German versions, ruled that the vendor must prove the contrary.[56] Neither the Dutch Supreme Court nor the ECJ have ruled on this point so far.

In a comparative study, Sikorska has concluded that there are remarkable differences between the laws of several Member States concerning this presumption of non-

47 The consumer does not have to prove the cause of non-conformity.

48 *Faber v Hazet* (n 12) para 11.

49 Examples, from many, many cases, include: District Court Haarlem 21 May 2008, ECLI:NL:RBHAA:2008:BD2453 (couch), District Court Groningen 21 December 2005, ECLI:NL:RBGRO:2005:AV2288 (horse), District Court Arnhem 9 January 2012, ECLI:NL:RBARN:2012:BV3827 (mobile phone), Court of Appeal Arnhem Leeuwarden 26 November 2013, ECLI:NL:GHARL:2013:8982 (shipmotor) and Court of Appeal Arnhem-Leeuwarden 10 September 2013, ECLI:NL:GHARL:2013:6714 (Ford Focus).

50 For example District Court Alkmaar 19 August 2009, NJF 2009/442 and District Court Haarlem 12 May 2010, NJF 2010/315.

51 See MBM Loos, *Consumentenkoop* (Kluwer 2004) 25; J Hijma, 'Bewijslastperikelen rond een uitgemergelde parkiet' in CG Breedveld-de Voogd et al (eds), *Signora Senatrice* (BJu 2011) 31–41; and MCP van Dongen and A de Feijter, ''Ontsnappingssprongen' met paard of pony inzake het wettelijke bewijsvermoeden ex Art. 7:18 part 2 BW' [2010] 3 NTBR 11–17 (in Dutch).

52 Art. 5(3) Directive Consumer Sale (n 11): 'Unless proved otherwise [...]'.

53 See Explanatory Memorandum, II 2000/2001, nr. 3, p 19 versus NMvA, I 27 089, nr. 32a, p 3.

54 See WDH Asser, *Bewijslastverdeling* [1992] Mon. BW A24 13 and 15; N Frenk, 'Herziening van de regeling van consumentenkoop'[2003] 12 AA (52) 953–959; and WL Valk, 'Stellen en bewijzen in geval van dwaling en non-conformiteit II (slot)' [2010] 6868 WPNR 949–957 (in Dutch).

55 See KM Sikorska, *The presumption of non-conformity in European consumer sales law* (Eleven international publishing 2015). The comparative approach in this thesis included four legal systems (the Netherlands, Poland, Germany and England & Wales) paras 5.6.4.

56 Court of Appeal Arnhem 2 May 2006, NJF 2006/342; see, with the same conclusion Court of Appeal Amsterdam 23 November 2010, NJF 2010/80; compare Valk, WPNR 2010 (6868) (n 54).

conformity.[57] In the Netherlands, this presumption in European law has introduced a new rule concerning the burden of proof which has led to a vast volume of case law and raised several questions.

In *Faber v Hazet* the referring Dutch court asked the ECJ whether Article 5 Consumer Sales Directive can be regarded as a rule which may be raised by a national court of its own motion in the context of an appeal. The ECJ responded that the apportionment of the burden of proof under Article 5(3) of this Directive is binding on both the parties – who may not derogate from it – and on the Member States. It follows that according to the ECJ, this rule on the burden of proof must be applied even if it has not been expressly relied on by the consumer who may benefit from it.[58] This provision must be regarded as a rule of public policy. Where a national court has under its domestic legal system the discretion to apply such a rule of its own motion, it must nonetheless apply any provision of domestic law which transposes Article 5(3) Consumer Sale Directive of its own motion.[59] This boils down to national courts being compelled to apply a presumption of non-conformity of their own motion. For Dutch law this means that a court can be obliged to apply a European rule on the burden of proof in very common consumer sales contracts, which departs from the general principles on the burden of proof of non-conformity in contract in Dutch law. This is not a trivial instance of Europeanisation.

3.3. *New Rules with Lesser Impact*

Not all the new national rules originating from the EU have a great impact. As a result of Article 7 of the Directive on misleading and comparative advertising, the Dutch Civil Code contains a rule on the burden of proof for certain claims related to misleading and comparative advertising. There are detailed rules on the evidential burden for the unlawfulness of the act[60] and on the evidential burden of the imputability of the unlawful act.[61] The rule on the evidential burden for unlawfulness is held to be more important than the rule on imputability. The reason is simple: as far as the imputability is concerned, the general rules of Dutch law concerning the burden of proof will in most cases yield more or less the same result as this EU rule. In contrast, the Supreme Court has attached importance to the specific rule on unlawfulness in its case law.[62]

3.4. *New Rules: Always at Least Some Impact*

A rule implementing an EU directive does not by definition result in a different procedural outcome than would have been reached before the new rule. The line of reasoning in the EU rule may be similar to the national status quo. Even if this is the case,

57 Sikorska (n 55), e.g. Chapter 6.
58 *Faber v Hazet* (n 12) para 55.
59 Ibid paras 56 and 57.
60 Art. 6:195 para 1 CC.
61 Art. 6:195 para 2 CC.
62 SC 15 January 1999, *NJ* 1999/665 (*Procter and Gamble v Kimberly Clark*).

this does not mean that the European dimension should be neglected. The new national rule following from EU law *does* have a European dimension. That European dimension means *inter alia* that EU case law on the topic must be taken into account. This can be existing EU case law, or possible future EU case law. This case law can originate from the Netherlands or, of course, from another Member State. To mention just one example: at the time the Directive on unfair terms was introduced, it was not well known, let alone anticipated, that this directive would be the basis for a such a large amount of European case law on *ex officio* application.

4. Spontaneous Harmonisation

EU legislation can lead to 'spontaneous harmonisation' at the national level.[63] This can be done by the national legislator, or by the national courts. The Directive on the enforcement of IP rights provides an example for the Netherlands. As a result of that Directive, national judicial authorities may, on application by a party who presents reasonably available evidence to support his claims that his intellectual property right has been infringed or is about to be infringed, order prompt and effective provisional measures to preserve relevant evidence in respect of the alleged infringement, subject to the protection of confidential information.[64] This European rule needed to be implemented in Dutch law. A special rule for this type of seizure in IP cases was introduced in 2007 with the enactment of the Act implementing the Directive on the enforcement of IP rights.[65]

Does Dutch law provide a general power for the seizure of evidence?[66] Surprisingly, the answer to this question was not clear for a long time, both before and after the enactment of the Act implementing the Directive on the enforcement of IP rights. It was clear that there was no specific legal basis for seizure of evidence in general. The Explanatory Memorandum to the Act implementing the Directive on the enforcement of IP rights states that Dutch law does not provide a general legal basis for the seizure of evidence *expressis verbis*. Elsewhere in that Explanatory Memorandum the Minister states that this seizure of evidence is a new form of attachment before judgement (*conservatoir beslag*).[67]

Therefore, the enactment of the Act implementing the Directive on the enforcement of IP rights in 2007 led to a somewhat remarkable situation: on the one hand, seizure of evidence became possible in IP cases, while on the other hand, it was not clear whether this power existed in non-IP cases. Some Dutch scholars had previously advocated for a general power to seize evidence (so also for non-IP cases).[68] The debate centred on

63 See on the topics of this paragraph also Krans ERPL (n 6) para 10 and 12.

64 Art. 7 Directive on the enforcement of intellectual property rights (n 30).

65 Art. 1019b CPC.

66 See for greater detail (in Dutch) on this paragraph my case note on SC 13 September 2013, *NJ* 2014/455, with further references.

67 MvT, TK 2005–2006, 30 392, nr. 3, pp 20 and 22.

68 WA Hoyng, 'Vier procesrechtelijke wensen' in BWM Nieskens-Isphording et al. (eds.), *In het nu wat worden zal* (Kluwer 1991) 108–111; JM Barendrecht and WAJP van den Reek, 'Exhibitieplicht en bewijsbeslag', [1994] 6155 WPNR 739–745; and JBM Vranken, *Asser-Vranken ** (*Kluwer 1995*)* 24.

whether existing legal rules in the Civil Procedure Code could be interpreted in such a way as to permit a general power for the seizure of evidence.[69] The majority of scholars appeared to accept the possibility of this general power,[70] though several argued that there was insufficient legal basis.[71]

Meanwhile, the situation in legal practice was not completely clear and the decisions of the lower courts were divergent.[72] Although it was obvious that legal practice would benefit from clarity on the point, the Dutch legislator did not intervene. On the contrary, an Explanatory Memorandum to another Act (concerning evidence) stated in 2011 that the legislator preferred to await developments in practice (instead of making new rules).[73]

The absence of complete clarity seems to be an important reason for the Amsterdam court having asked in interlocutory proceedings for a preliminary ruling of the Dutch Supreme Court on the topic.[74] This resulted in an extensive ruling from the Supreme Court. In that ruling, before answering the question, the Supreme Court stated that the laws of the countries neighbouring the Netherlands offer various answers to the question of whether a general power for the seizure of evidence exists and if so, what the applicable conditions are. It would therefore have been preferable if the legislator had acted in this area.[75] Consequently, the Supreme Court took it upon itself to decide, at least in part, by approving a general power for the seizure of evidence, provided that adequate and effective safeguards are in place and that arbitrary interference and abuse are prevented.[76] In its relatively long judgment, the Supreme Court went into the relevant conditions and safeguards for this power, including the protection of confidentiality. The Supreme Court virtually acted, almost *nolens volens*, as quasi-legislator. Several references were made in this important decision to the existence of power for the seizure of evidence in IP cases.[77] EU IP legislation therefore played a role in introducing a general power for the seizure of evidence in Dutch civil procedure law.

69 This concerned in particular Art. 730 CPC and Art. 843a CPC.

70 E.g. MML Harreman, *Conservatoire beslagen tot afgifte* (BJu 2007) 43–44; JR Sijmonsma, *Het inzagerecht* (Kluwer 2010) 217; J Ekelmans, *De exhibitieplicht* (Kluwer 2010) §13.2.4; RH de Bock, *Tussen waarheid en onzekerheid: over het vaststellen van feiten in de civiele procedure* (Kluwer 2011) §4.7.1; and WDH Asser, *Procesrecht/Asser 3* (Kluwer 2013) 201 (all in Dutch).

71 JGA Linssen, 'Bewijsbeslag', in A.J. van der Meer et al. (eds), *De reikwijdte van het beslag* (Bju 2009) 24–26 and LP Broekveldt, 'Algemeen bewijsbeslag: tekort in huidig recht (art. 730 jo. art. 843a Rv) én in komend recht' [2013] 15 NTBR 125–126 (in Dutch).

72 Some examples: District Court Den Bosch 27 March 2002, JBPR 2002/10 (positive) and Court of Appeal Leeuwarden 14 August 2009, ECLI:NL:GHLEE:2009:BJ4901 (negative).

73 II 2011/2012, 33 079, nr. 3, p 8.

74 If certain conditions are met, Dutch lower courts may refer questions on a matter of law to the Dutch Supreme Court by way of a preliminary procedure (Art. 392–394 CPC). An answer to the question must be necessary to decide several claims based on the same or similar facts and must derive from the same or similar causes or the answer must be necessary for the adjudication of several disputes arising from similar facts turning on the same question (Art. 392, para 1 CPC). This power to ask preliminary questions of the Supreme Court was enacted in July 2012.

75 SC 13 September 2013, ECLI:NL:HR:2013:BZ9958, NJ 2014/455 (*Molenbeek v Begeer*), sub 3.3.3.

76 SC 13 September 2013, ECLI:NL:HR:2013:BZ9958, NJ 2014/455 (*Molenbeek v Begeer*), sub 3.5.

77 See SC 13 September 2013, ECLI:NL:HR:2013:BZ9958, NJ 2014/455 (*Molenbeek v Begeer*), sub 3.6.1, 3.7.2, 3.7.3.

5. Conclusions

1. The issues I have considered in this paper demonstrate that procedural matters in the Netherlands can have an EU-law dimension in civil cases even if they lack a cross-border element.[78] Courts and lawyers in the Netherlands need to be aware that several areas of procedural law can have an EU-law dimension.[79]

2. What does this EU-law dimension mean for the role of national courts? It remains up to national courts to decide on several issues, even if EU law is involved. For example, it is up to national courts to decide whether a term in a contract can be considered unfair.[80] It is up to national courts to decide how to deal with *ex officio* application, as long as they follow the 'instructions' in EU law. It is up to national courts to decide whether the general obligation to interpret domestic law and acts to conform with directives can be fulfilled.[81] If doubt remains about the interpretation of EU law, the ECJ has the final word, but national courts decide when to refer cases to the Luxembourg Court. The question of when to refer a case was the subject of two recent decisions of the ECJ.[82] In my view the relationship between the Luxemburg Court and national courts is not merely a top-down one, but would appear to be more of a two-way street, a matter of cooperation. The growing EU-law dimension for Dutch civil procedure law means that the two-way street between national courts and the ECJ has broadened the scope of its traffic.

3. European directives and regulations aim to harmonise, at least to a certain degree. Nevertheless, the influence of EU law on national civil procedure law can lead to inconsistency within a national procedural system.[83] National legislators can decide to treat such inconsistencies as inevitable and leave the law as it stands. They can also try to diminish the inconsistency or even remove it. If the national legislator intervenes without the direct need being occasioned by EU legislation, but as a result of inconsistencies at the national level caused by the influence of EU law, this can be referred to as spontaneous harmonisation.[84] Such spontaneous harmonisation can cause other parts of national civil procedure law which do not have an EU-law dimension to change as well. That is a national decision, but a consequence of the Europeanisation of national civil procedure law.

78 For more on the influence of EU law on costs and on the free choice of lawyers see Krans, ERPL 2015 (n 6), §6. For more topics in Dutch procedural law with an EU law dimension see Krans (n 28).

79 As I have set out elsewhere, this dimension can give rise to additional legal uncertainty and differences between Member State jurisdictions; see Krans, ERPL 2015 (fn 6) 567–587.

80 Case C-237/02 *Freiburger Kommunalbaiten GmbH Baugesellchaft & Co. KG v Ludger & Ulrike Hofstetter* [2004] ECLI:EU:C:2004:209.

81 See e.g. Case C-106/89 *Marleasing SA v La Comercial Internacional de Alimentacion SA* [1990] ECLI:EU:1990:395; compare M Wissink, 'Interpretation of Private Law in conformity with EU Directives' in AS Hartkamp et al. (eds), *The influence of EU law on National Private Law* (2 edn Kluwer 2014) 119–158.

82 Case C-72/14 and Case C-197/14 (joined cases) [2015] ECLI:EU:C:2015:564; and Case C-160/14 *Joao Filipe Ferreira da Silva e Brito and Others v Estado Portugues* [2015] ECLI:EU:C:2015:565.

83 See Krans, ERPL (n 6), §10 on Internal Fragmentation; compare M Dougan, *National remedies before the Court of Justice: issues of harmonisation and differentiation* (Hart 2004).

84 See on spontaneous harmonisation Wissink (n 1) nr. 330; R Meijer, 'Betere Europeanisering: made-to-measure' [2001] 12 NTBR 92–95 (in Dutch) and HHB Vedder, 'Spontaneous Harmonisation of National (Competition) Laws in the Wake of the Modernisation of EC Competition Law' [2004] Competition Law Review, 5–21.

Anna Nylund*

NORWAY: AN INSIDER OUTSIDE – OR AN OUTSIDER INSIDE – EUROPEAN CIVIL JUSTICE

1. The EU, the EEA Agreement and Norwegian Law

Norway has stood on the doorsteps of the European Union (then the European Communities (EC)) for more than four decades. In 1960, Norway became one of the seven original members of the European Free Trade Association (EFTA), a trade-bloc-alternative to the European Economic Community (EEC).[1] The Norwegian people voted against EC-membership in 1972 and 1994. In the late 1980's, a plan to create a single market including both EC and EFTA member states was launched. It resulted in the agreement on the European Economic Area (EEA), which extends the single market and the free movement of goods, persons, services and capital to non-EU EEA member states. Since 1995, EEA has only three member states: Iceland, Liechtenstein and Norway.

The EEA Agreement is limited in scope: It does not include inter alia justice and home affairs. For EU legislation to become EEA law, the EEA Joint Committee must unanimously agree on including it to the EEA agreement.[2] The EEA has its own institutions, including the EFTA Court, which has a similar function as the European Court of Justice.[3] National courts in the EEA states can request advisory opinions on the interpretation of the EEA Agreement.[4] The goal of the EEA is homogeneity and effectiveness, meaning equal and effective application of law in the EEA region. Effective application of substantive law often requires changes in the civil justice system.[5]

* Professor of Law, Faculty of Law, University of Tromsø - The Arctic University of Norway.

1 The other members were Austria, Denmark, Portugal, Sweden, Switzerland and the United Kingdom. Finland became an associate member in 1961 and a full member in 1986, Iceland became a member in 1970 and Liechtenstein in 1991. Denmark, Portugal and the United Kingdom left EFTA for EC membership, in 1973 respectively 1986. Austria, Finland and Sweden did so in 1995.

2 Consequently, not all directives and regulations marked as EEA relevant by the Commission are included in the EEA Agreement, and some directives and regulations become part of the EEA Agreement although the Commission has not identified them as EEA relevant.

3 Agreement between the EFTA States on the Establishment of a Surveillance Authority and a Court of Justice (Surveillance and Court Agreement), art. 31–37.

4 Ibid art. 34.

5 Halvard Haukeland Fredriksen, 'The EFTA Court 15 Years On' (2010) 59 International and Comparative Law Quarterly 731; John Temple Lang, 'The Duty of National Courts to Provide Access to Justice in the EEA' in EFTA Court (ed), *Judicial Protection in the European Economic Area* (German Law Publishers

Despite being outside EU, Norway participates in some aspects of judicial cooperation. It is a party of the Lugano Convention[6] on jurisdiction and recognition and enforcement judgments in civil and commercial matters of 1988, revised in 2007[7], and the Schengen Agreement.[8] To enlarge judicial cooperation, the Norwegian government seeks to establish a parallel convention to the regulation on service of documents[9] and the regulation on taking of evidence.[10] The Norwegian civil procedure system is consequently far from unaffected by European law.

Norway, as a rule, rejects EEA relevance of EU legislation based on article 81 TFEU[11], judicial cooperation in civil matters. As a principle, Norway also rejects legislation based on article 114 TFEU on approximation of laws to ensure the functioning of the internal market, if the content is primarily procedural. For instance, the Intellectual Property Rights Enforcement Directive[12] has not been incorporated to EEA law due to Norwegian resistance. However, chapter 28 A on special rules on intellectual property rights was added to the Dispute Act[13] (the Norwegian Civil Procedure Act) in correspondence with the directive. The approach is self-contradictory: the government desires to stress the limited scope of EEA Agreement, yet it in practice recognises the need for approximation of procedural rules and the need for a single judicial area for enforcing the law regulating the single market.

The EFTA Court has an important role of filtering both substantive and procedural law from the EU to the EEA system. The Court achieves this by closely following the case law of the Court of Justice of the European Union (CJEU). The case law of the CJEU is not binding for the EFTA Court, but to obtain homogeneity, the EFTA Court generally applies CJEU case law as if it were binding.[14]

Directives do not have direct effect in the EEA; they have to be transformed to national law to be valid.[15] Regulations are applicable even before they are translated to

2012); Halvard Haukeland Fredriksen and Christian N. K. Franklin, 'Of pragmatism and principles: The EEA Agreement 20 years on' (2015) 52 Common Market Law Review 629.

6 The Convention of Lugano on jurisdiction and the enforcement of judgments in civil and commercial matters, done at Lugano on 16 September 1988 (Lugano Convention 1988) [1988] OJ L319/9.

7 The Convention on jurisdiction and the recognition and enforcement of judgements in civil and commercial matters, done at Lugano on 30 October 2007 (Lugano Convention) [2007] OJ L339/3.

8 The Schengen acquis – Agreement between the Governments of the States of the Benelux Economic Union, the Federal Republic of Germany and the French Republic on the gradual abolition of checks at their common borders [2000] OJ L239/13.

9 Parliament and Council Regulation (EC) 1393/2007 on the service in the Member States of judicial and extrajudicial documents in civil or commercial matters (service of documents) [2007] OJ L324/79.

10 Council Regulation (EC) 1206/2001 on cooperation between the courts of the Member States in the taking of evidence in civil or commercial matters [2001] OJ L174/1.

11 Consolidated versions of the Treaty on European Union and the Treaty on the Functioning of the European Union [2012] OJ C326/1.

12 Parliament and Council Directive 2004/48/EC on the enforcement of intellectual property rights [2004] OJ L195/16.

13 Act of 17 June 2005 no. 90 relating to mediation and procedure in civil disputes (The Dispute Act). It is the Civil Procedure Act of Norway.

14 Halvard Haukeland Fredriksen, 'One Market, Two Courts: Legal Pluralism vs. Homogeneity in the European Economic Area' (2010) 79 Nordic Journal of International Law 481.

15 Agreement of the European Economic Area [1994] OJ L1/572 art 7 (a).

Norwegian.[16] According to the Norwegian EEA Act[17] section 2, Norwegian acts and decrees of law implementing EEA obligations have primacy over other national legislation. Norwegian courts strive to interpret national legislation in conformity with EEA law. The Supreme Court has numerous times stated that EEA case law has decisive weight when interpreting Norwegian law.[18] In *Finanger I*[19], the Supreme Court rejected direct effect in case of inadequate implementation of a directive. Yet in *Finanger II*[20], the Supreme Court ruled for state liability for inadequate implementation of directives, although Norwegian law has no provision for such liability.[21] *Finanger II* illustrates the impact on EEA law on Norwegian law and on Norwegian courts.

This paper disseminates the impact of European law on Norwegian civil procedure by looking at three different topics. The first topic is the role of the Lugano Convention in Norwegian law. The second topic is the role of other EU legislation, soft law and case law on Norwegian civil procedure. The third topic covers the relationship between the Norwegian Supreme Court and the EFTA Court, and the impact of the relationship on development of Norwegian procedural law. The final part of the paper discusses the outlooks.

2. The Lugano Convention

The Lugano Convention, a parallel instrument to the Brussels Convention[22] and its successor the Brussels I Regulation[23], extends the area for jurisdiction and recognition and enforcement of judgments to EFTA states, not including Liechtenstein. According to

16 The Danish version of regulations are already available, and as the languages are quite similar, it is possible to use the Danish versions.

17 Act on implementation to Norwegian Law of the main part in the Agreement of the European Economic Area etc. (EEA-Act) Act no. 109 of 27 November 1992. 'Provisions of Acts of Parliament which serve to fulfil Norway's obligations under the Agreement shall in case of conflict prevail over other provisions which regulate the same matter...' Translation from Henrik Bull, 'The EEA Agreement and Norwegian Law' (1994) European Business Law Review 291, p. 295.

18 See *inter alia Paranova AS v Merck & Co Inc, Merck, Sharp & Dohme B.C. and MSD (Norge) AS* [2004] Rt. (Norsk Retstidende) 2004 p. 904, para. 67; *A v The State by the Justice department* [2005] Rt. 2005 p. 1365, para 51; *Norsk Lotteri- og Automatbransjefrbund v The State by the Norwegian ministry of Church and Culture* [2007] Rt. 2007 p. 1003, para. 79; *Pedicele AS v The State by the Ministry of Health and Care Services* [2009] Rt. 2009 p. 839, para. 7; *STX OSV AS and Others v The State by Tariffnemnda* Rt. 2013 p. 258.

19 *Storebrand Skadeforsikring AS v A* [2000] Rt. 2000 p. 1811, the court was split. The minority of five (out of 15) justices gave direct effect to EEA law.

20 *A v The State by the Justice Department* [2005] Rt. 2005 p. 1365.

21 The EFTA Court President and the CJEU argue that there is direct effect in EEA law, see Carl Baudenbacher, 'The EFTA Court Ten Years On' in Carl Baudenbacher, Per Tresselt and Thorgeir Orlygsson (eds), *The EFTA Court Ten Years On* (Hart Publishing 2005) 24–25; Carl Baudenbacher, 'If Not EEA State Liability, Then What? Reflections Ten Years after the EFTA Court's Sveinbjörnsdóttir Ruling' (2009) 10 Chicago Journal of International Law 333.

22 1968 Brussels Convention on jurisdiction and the enforcement of judgments in civil and commercial matters [1972] OJ L299/32.

23 Council Regulation (EC) 44/2001 on jurisdiction and the recognition and enforcement of judgements in civil and commercial matters [2001] OJ L12/1.

Kohler, it is 'an essential component of the judicial structure of the EEA'.[24] The Regulation and the Convention are parallel, which refers to (almost) identical texts and interpretation of the instruments. When the Brussels regime has been amended, the Lugano Convention has so far been subsequently amended to restore parallelism. The CJEU has a pivotal role in interpreting the instruments, although courts in non-EU member states may not request preliminary rulings. In Norway, the Lugano Convention has the status of law and replaces the national rules on international jurisdiction as lex specialis.

The application and interpretation of the Lugano Convention has become more complex over the years. Firstly, when the Brussels I recast[25] entered into force *parallelism was lost* between the two instruments. The discrepancies are currently limited to a few issues, but subsequent amendments to the Regulation could change the situation if parallelism is not restored. Secondly, *the relationship between the two instruments is complex*. Article 64 of the Lugano Convention includes a disconnection clause, but it is not clear whether the clause should be interpreted narrowly or widely. Eurosceptics tend to advocate a narrow interpretation giving the Convention primacy and emphasising the consequent difficulties. Adrian Briggs has described the combined effect of lack of parallelism and the unclear relationship between the documents as a situation which is trickier than the ideal would be.[26] Thirdly, the *interpretation of the Lugano* Convention is essentially in the hands of the CJEU according to the Protocol 2[27] on interpretation of the Convention. The courts of the Lugano States, including the CJEU, have an obligation to 'pay due account to the principles laid down by any relevant decision' from courts in other states. In practice, both the CJEU and courts in EU member states go directly to the corresponding provision in the Brussels I Regulation.[28] In theory, interpretation should be a two-way street where the CJEU studies Icelandic, Norwegian and Swiss case law, but in practice, it is a one-way street.[29]

24 Christian Kohler, 'Homogeneity or Renationalisation in the European Judicial Area? Comments on a Recent Judgment of the Norwegian Supreme Court' in The EFTA Court (ed), *The EEA and the EFTA Court Decentered Integration* (Hart 2014).

25 European Parliament and Council Regulation (EC) 1215/2012 on jurisdiction and the recognition and enforcement of judgements in civil and commercial matters (recast) (Brussels I bis Regulation) [2012] OJ L351/1.

26 Adrian Briggs, *Civil Jurisdiction and Judgments* (6th edn, Routledge 2015) 25. The earlier stage of lack of parallelism was described as 'a set of jurisdictional rules which, in their combined effect is a legal minefield and a public disgrace' Adrian Briggs, *Civil Jurisdiction and Judgments* (4th edn, Norton Rose 2005) 24.

27 Protocol 2 on the uniform interpretation of the Convention and on the Standing Committee.

28 See Case C-456/11 *Gothaer Allgemenine Versicherung and Others v Samskip GmbH* [2012] ECLI:EU:C:2012:719 and Alegria Borrás, Irene Neophytou and Fausto Pocar, '13th Report on National Case Law Relating to the Lugano Conventions' (May 2012). https://www.bj.admin.ch/dam/data/bj/wirtschaft/privatrecht/lugjurispr-13-e.pdf (accessed 9 March 2016).

29 Cf. Carl Baudenbacher, *Judicial Dimensions of the European Neighbourhood Policy* (College of Europe, Department of EU International Relations and Diplomacy Studies 2013) 7. Domej notes that the CJEU should meet the Lugano-only courts at 'eye level', as equals, see Tanja Domej, 'Das EU-Zivilprozessrecht und die Schweiz' in Christoph Busch, Christina Kopp, Mary R. McGuire and Martin Zimmermann (eds), *Jahrbuch Junger Zivilrechtswissenschaftler 2009: Europäische Methodik: Konvergenz und Diskkrepanz europäischen und nationalen Privatrechts* (Richard Boorberg Verlag 2009).

The CJEU has used the Brussels I Regulation to develop the 'single justice area' and to enforce the policy of mutual trust. The Brussels I Regulation has become a foundational element of the internal market procedure, which forms a self-contained regime[30] with autonomous concepts. From a Norwegian point of view, this development is troublesome, as the EEA Agreement does not cover judicial cooperation. The question is if, and to which extent, Norwegian courts are allowed to depart from CJEU case law in the application of the Lugano Convention. For example, the *absolute* duty of the second court to stay proceedings[31] could be less absolute for Lugano-only states allowing for exceptions in torpedo cases.

The Supreme Court has so far been loyal to CJEU case law when interpreting the Lugano Convention. However, in the periphery of area covered by the Convention, the Supreme Court has taken a more restrictive view than the CJEU. In *Trico Subsea* (Rt. 2012, s. 1951), the defendant was domiciled in Norway, but otherwise the case had no connection to Norway. The question was if the Lugano Convention was applicable as the Convention primarily regulates situations between the contracting states, not the relationship to third states. Referring to the CJEU decisions in *Group Josi*[32] and *Owusu*[33], the minority of two justices found that the Lugano Convention was applicable and Norwegian courts had jurisdiction. The majority of three justices differentiated *Owusu* from the case at hand and concluded that the Lugano Convention was not applicable, as the claimant was not domiciled in a Lugano state, nor had the case any other connection to a Lugano state. The argumentation of the majority of three judges is not very convincing, and has been criticised.[34]

In the *Samsung* case (Rt. 2015, p. 1040), CKT Marine Services, a Netherlands company, was to deliver a helipad and a housing block for an oil platform. In oil contracts, the parties must choose Norwegian law as the law of the contract. Samsung and CKT Marine Services designated Stavanger as the place for arbitration. A Belgian financial undertaking, Nationale, gave a bond on behalf of CKT Marine Services. The choice-of-court clause in the contract between CKT Marine Services and Nationale designated Stavanger District Court as the forum. When CKT Marine Services and Samsung were

30 Cf. Burkhard Hess, *Europäisches Zivilprozessrecht: ein Lehrbuch* (Hüthig Jehle Rehm 2010) 153.

31 Richard Fentiman, 'Section 9: Lis pendens – related actions' in Ulrich Magnus, Peter Mankowski and Alfonso Luis Calvo Caravaca (eds), *Brussesl I regulation* (2 nd. rev. ed. edn, Sellier European Law Publishers 2012). Case 144/86 *Gubisch Maschinenfabrik KG v Giulio Palumbo* [1987] ECR I-4871, paras 14–19; Case C-406/92 *The owners of the cargo lately laden on board the ship 'Tatry' v the owners of the ship 'Maciej Rataj'* [1994] ECR I-5439 paras 42 ff.; Case C-111/01 *Gantner Electronic GmbH v Basch Exploitatie Maatschappij BV* [2003] ECR I-4207, paras 30–32; Case C-39/02 *Mærsk Olie & Gas A/S v Firma M. de Haan en W. de Boer* [2004] ECR I-9657.

32 Case C-412/98 *Group Josi Reinsurance Company SA v Universal General Insurance Company* [2000] ECR I-5925.

33 Case C-281/02 *Andrew Owusu v N.B. Jackson, trading a 'Villa Holidays Bal-Inn Villas' and others* [2005] ECR I-1383.

34 Torstein Frantzen, 'Tvisteloven og Luganokonvensjonen. En duplikk til Skoghøy' [2012] 51 Lov og Rett 573; Kohler [n 24]. There was an intensive Norwegian debate on the issue, see Jens Edvin A. Skoghøy, 'Tvisteloven og Lugano-konvensjonen' [2012] 51 Lov og Rett 193; Torstein Frantzen, 'Tvisteloven og Luganokonvensjonen. En replikk til Skoghøy' [2012] 51 Lov og Rett 379; Jens Edvin A. Skoghøy, 'Tvisteloven og Lugano-konvensjonen – en duplikk til Frantzen' [2012] 51 Lov og Rett 438.

not able to agree on adjustment, Samsung requested that Nationale pay the bond. CKT Marine Service requested interim measures against both Samsung and Nationale in the Oslo District Court. Samsung denied that Norwegian courts have jurisdiction, but Nationale did not. The Supreme Court surprisingly decided the case without any reference to the Lugano Convention, even though Norway has jurisdiction on the main question and Nationale did not oppose Norwegian jurisdiction. By reference to the Dispute Act, section 4–3, requiring 'a sufficiently strong connection to Norway' for Norwegian jurisdiction the Court decided that the threshold was particularly high for interim measures in commercial cases.

These cases illustrate a certain reluctance towards the Lugano Convention. Although the Norwegian Supreme Court as a rule applies the Lugano Convention and actively uses CJEU case law in interpreting the convention, there are signs of the court favouring the Dispute Act in cases on the periphery of the Convention. The Court stresses Norwegian sovereignty, not legal certainty and the need to uniform application of the rules on jurisdiction and enforcement of judgments. Giving preference to Norwegian law and concepts creates a gap between the Lugano Convention and the Brussels I Regulation. Together the loss of parallelism and different interpretation of the rules weaken legal certainty and the role of the Convention.

3. Impact of EEA Law on Norwegian Civil Procedure

EU legislation creating a European civil procedure has received only limited attention in Norway. Particularly laws on creating specific proceedings for certain types of cross-border cases have had no impact on Norwegian civil procedure. The Consumer ADR Directive[35] and the Consumer ODR Regulation[36] are examples of the opposite. Norway is currently implementing them as part of the revision of Norwegian law on consumer dispute resolution, although these have so far not been incorporated in the EEA. Other pieces of EU secondary law could be used as benchmark for improving Norwegian law.[37] While the front door of Norwegian civil procedure remains closed for Europeanisation, the back door is ajar.

Procedural autonomy is the leading principle in EEA law as well as in EU law.[38] Due to the limited scope of the EEA, procedural autonomy is presumably larger for EEA states than EU Member States. However, the requirement of effective application of EEA

35 Directive 2013/11/EU on alternative dispute resolution for consumer disputes and amending Regulation (EC) 2006/2004 and Directive 2009/22/EC [2013] OJ L165/63.

36 Regulation (EC) 524/2013 on online dispute resolution for consumer disputes and amending Regulation (EC) No 2006/2004 and Directive 2009/22/EC [2012] OJ L165/63, p. 1.

37 Anna Nylund, 'Europeanisation of Norwegian Civil Procedure?' in Volker Lipp and Halvard Haukeland Fredriksen (eds), *Reforms of civil procedure in Germany and Norway* (Vol. 83, Mohr Siebeck 2011); Anna Nylund, 'European Integration and Nordic Civil Procedure' in Laura Ervo and Anna Nylund (eds), *The Future of Civil Litigation Access to Courts and Court-annexed Mediation in the Nordic Countries* (Springer 2014).

38 See e.g. Diana-Urania Galetta, *Procedural autonomy of EU Member States: paradise lost?: a study on the' functionalized procedural competence' of EU Member States* (Springer Science & Business Media 2010).

law and the goal of homogeneity have had a significant impact on procedural law. In *Swiss life*, the EFTA Court stated that 'access to justice and effective judicial protection are essential elements in the EEA legal framework' and that EEA nationals and economic operators must 'enjoy equal access to the courts'.[39] National procedural rules must be 'no less favourable than those governing similar domestic actions (principle of equivalence), and they must 'not render practically impossible or excessively difficult the exercise of the rights conferred by EEA law'.[40] The language resembles CJEU case law reducing the procedural autonomy of member states. However, the consequent argumentation of the EFTA Court shows that EFTA member states have more autonomy.[41] The extent of the difference is not manifest.

EEA law influences Norwegian civil procedure in many different ways. Three examples illustrate the development: the rules on *locus standi*, the question of judicial guidance and the question of *ex officio* application of consumer law.[42]

In *Allseas*[43] the Norwegian Supreme Court admitted that EEA law could have an impact on national civil procedure law. The question was if the employees of Allseas had *locus standi* in a case about taxation of the company. According to Norwegian law, they clearly did not, but the Supreme Court discussed if they had so according to EEA law. The Court found against the employees, but it stated *obiter dicta* that the rules on *locus standi* are more lenient in cases where EEA law is applied.

EEA law also has an impact on the right or duty for *judicial guidance* (*materielle Prozessleitung* in German). Norwegian judges have a duty to encourage the parties to clarify factual and legal issues, Dispute Act section 11–5 (3), and to encourage a party to take a position on factual and legal issues that appear to be of importance for the case, Dispute Act section 11–5 (4).[44] To ensure the effectiveness of EEA law – and to contribute to legally 'correct' judgments, judges have a duty, not merely a right, to give guidance to the parties by raising the question of applicability of EEA law. The exact extent of the enhanced duty to give guidance on EEA law remains under debate.[45]

Another important question is if Norwegian courts have a duty to apply EEA law *ex officio* in cases that have a character of *ordre public*, specifically in areas of consumer and competition law. The answer seems to be in the affirmative: *de facto* identical application

39 Case E-11/12 *Beatrix Susanne Koch, Lothar Hummel, and Stefan Müller v Swiss Life (Liechtenstein) AG* [2013] EFTA Ct. Rep. 272, para 117.

40 *Swiss Life* (n 39) para. 121.

41 Cf. Halvard Haukeland Fredriksen, 'Tvisteloven og EØS-avtalen' [2008] 121 Tidskrift for Rettsvitenskap 289, 330–331; Erik Eldjarn, *Materiell prosessledelse* (2015) 222–225.

42 Other areas of civil procedure have also been affected including rules on evidence, time limits and rules on legal costs.

43 *Arie Christian Poot, Frank Bergmann and Pasqual Dozo Gondar v The State by The Central Office for Foreign Tax Affairs* Rt. 2005. p. 597, para 36 et seq.

44 Cf. Anna Nylund, 'Preparatory Proceedings in Norway – Efficiency by Flexibility and Case Management' in Laura Ervo and Anna Nylund (eds), *Current Trends in Pre-Trial Proceedings* (Springer forthcoming).

45 Anne Robberstad, 'Norske dommeres plikt til å veilede om EØS-retten'(2002) Lov og Rett 195; Fredriksen [n 41] 328–333; Eldjarn [n 41] 222–225. For a similar argumentation from a Swedish perspective, see Anna Wallerman, *Om fakultativa regler. En studie av svensk och unionsrättslig reglering av skönsmässigt beslutsfattande i processrättsliga frågor* (Iustus förlag 2015) 165 ff.

of rules is a requisite for homogeneity. Norwegian courts already have a duty to apply national laws in some limited areas *ex officio,* thus extending the duty to corresponding EEA law is natural.[46] Courts have to apply the law in its own motion (*iura novit curia* and *da mihi factum dabo tibi ius)*, Dispute Act section 11–3. The principle of *ne ultra petita* restricts the *ex officio* application of law, Dispute Act section 11–2 (1). The claims made and the main factual basis of the case restricts which provisions the court may base its decision on. However, especially in consumer law, protection of the weaker party permeates Norwegian legal thinking. Although consumer cases as such are classified as contentious, the rules are mandatory and the courts have a stronger duty to ensure that consumer rights are protected and consequently a limited duty to *ex officio* application of EEA law.[47]

In practice, judges are not always aware of the relevance of EEA law. Some judges seemingly believe it is the task of the parties (their legal counsel) to raise the question of EEA law and, when necessary, ask the court to request an advisory opinion form the EFTA Court. In view of the principle of *iura novit curia* and the right (or duty) to provide judicial guidance, this approach is false. The Dispute Act and doctrine stresses the duty of the court to provide for substantially and legally correct judgments by *inter alia* judicial guidance.[48] To raise the question if EEA law is applicable does not make a judge partial. The parties choose whether they want to invoke EEA law, and whether they want to adjust the claims and the facts invoked in the case.

The CJEU has *inter alia* developed a European concept of identity of cases in respect to *lis alibi pendens*[49] and *res judicata.*[50] In the future, the coexistence of European and national concepts of the identity of the case and *res judicata* may 'irritate' national concepts. The project on model 'European Rules of Civil Procedure' may unfold as a trigger for further approximation of national civil procedure both by voluntary national measures and by EU institutions. Norway is not immune to these developments. Thus, the Norwegian legislator, courts and scholars must vigilantly keep track with and participate in the processes creating and developing European law. Norwegian law is not – and should not be – an island. By participating in the European development of law, Norway can advance its civil procedure system, and influence the development of European civil procedure.

46 Cf. Fredriksen [n 41], 324–325; Anne Robberstad, *Sivilprosess* (3 edn, Fagbokforlaget 2015), 311–312; Tore Schei and others, *Tvisteloven. Kommentarutgave Bind I*, vol 1 (2nd edn, Universitetsforlaget 2012) 403–404; Jens Edvin A. Skoghøy, *Tvisteløsning* (2 edn, Universitetsforlaget 2014) 577–580.

47 Fredriksen [n 41] 326–328; Eldjarn [n 41] 208–212.

48 Robberstad [n 46]; Schei and others [n 47] 525 ff.; Skoghøy [n 47] 558–568; Robberstad [n 47] 12–14, 189–192.

49 Fentiman [n 31].

50 *Gothaer Allgemeine Versingerung* [n 28].

4. The Norwegian Supreme Court and the EFTA Court: A Turf War or Dialogue?

Norwegian courts, including the Supreme Court, habitually apply EEA law in a faithful manner and interpret statutory law in light of EEA law and case law from the Luxembourg courts. Nevertheless, the relationship between the Supreme Court and the EFTA Court has been strenuous for many years. There are two main reasons for the disagreements between the courts: different attitudes interpretations of the character of advisory opinions and of the EEA agreement.

4.1. Advisory Opinions

The turf war originates significantly from different views on the character of advisory opinions: is there a duty to request advisory opinions and what is the effect of advisory opinions. Where a question on the interpretation of the EEA Agreement 'is raised before any court or tribunal in an EFTA State, that court or tribunal *may*, if it considers it necessary to enable it to give judgment, request the EFTA Court to give [an advisory] opinion' (emphasis added).[51] The highest courts do not have a duty to request opinions. The EFTA Court continually attempts to establish an obligation for highest courts to refer cases by citing the obligation of loyalty.[52]

Norwegian (and Icelandic) courts reject this view, and they are often reluctant to request opinions. As the EFTA Court opinions are advisory in their nature, courts feel less obliged to refer cases.[53] Since the financial crisis in 2008 Icelandic courts have made a significant number of requests. A comparison of Nordic countries in table 1 shows that Norwegian courts have made very few requests both in absolute numbers and per one million inhabitants.[54] Requests to the EFTA Court are not fully comparable to requests to the CJEU, as the latter has a far wider jurisdiction and making requests is mandatory

51 Surveillance and Court Agreement art. 34.

52 Case E-18/11 *Irish Bank Resolution Corporation Ltd v Kaupþing hf* [2012] EFTA Ct. Rep. 592, para 58 et seq.; Case E-2/12 *HOB-vín and The State Alcohol and Tobacco Company of Iceland* [2013] EFTA Ct. Rep. 816, para 11; Case E-3/12 *The Norwegian State, represented by the Ministry of Labour and Stig Arne Jonsson* [2013] EFTA Ct. Rep. 138, para 60; *Swiss Life* [n 39] para 116.

53 For an overview of Norwegian requests until 2011, see Halvard Haukeland Fredriksen, 'The Two EEA Courts' in EFTA Court (ed), *Judicial Protection in the European Economic Area* (German Law Publishers 2012) 200–201. For an Icelandic perspective, see Páll Hreinsson, 'The Interaction between Iceland Courts and the EFTA Court' in EFTA Court (ed), *Judicial Protection in the European Economic Area* (German Law Publishers 2012); Davíd Thór Björgvinsson, 'Application of Article 34 of the ESA/Court Agreement by Icelandic Courts' in Mario Monti and others (eds), *Economic Law and Justice in Times of Globalisation Festschrift for Carl Baudenbacher* (Nomos Verlag 2007); Thorgeir Örlygsson, 'Iceland and teh EFTA Court: Twelve Years of Experience' in Mario Monti and others (eds), *Economic Law and Justice in Times of Globalisation Festschrift for Carl Baudenbacher* (Nomos Verlag 2007).

54 For figures until 2009, see Halvard Haukeland Fredriksen, *EU/EØS-rett i norske domstoler* (Europautredningen Utvalget for utredningen av Norges avtaler med EU, 2011) 90.

and the answers binding. Establishing what the proper amount of requests is difficult,[55] but an expected number could be set at approximately half of Nordic EU member states. Sweden does not serve as an example as the number of request has been so low that the Commission has interfered.[56] The number of Norwegian requests is half of that of Sweden and a quarter of the number of Denmark and Finland, thus the number is remarkably low.

Table 1. Cases referred to the Luxembourg courts by Nordic courts

	Referred cases total until 2014, ECJ or EFTA-court[57]	Referred cases 2010–2014	Referred per 1 million inhabitants per year in 2010–2014
Denmark	113	40	1.4
Finland	91	33	1.2
Sweden	114	33	0.7
Norway	46	9	0.35
Iceland	27	15	9

The Norwegian Supreme Court has been particularly reluctant to request advisory opinions. Between *Paranova*[58] in 2002 and *Holship*[59] in 2015 the Norwegian Supreme Court did not request a single advisory opinion. The total is three referrals, and a withdrawn referral, in 21 years.[60] The Icelandic Supreme Court has made six requests, but considering the Icelandic population is less than 10% of the Norwegian population, the numbers cannot be directly compared.[61]

Table 2. References to the Luxembourg courts from different Nordic courts

	Supreme Court(s)	Special courts	Other courts and tribunals	Total
Denmark	35 (21%)	6 (4%)	124 (75%)	165
Finland	61 (67%)	11 (12%)	19 (21%)	91
Sweden	49 (43%)	10 (9%)	55 (48%)	114
Norway	2 (4%)	5 (11%)	39 (85%)	46
Iceland	6 (22%)	0	21 (78%)	27

55 Morten Broberg and Niels Fenger, 'Variations in Member States' Preliminary References to the Court of Justice – Are Structural Factors (Part of) the Explanation?' [2013] 19 European Law Journal 488.

56 For more details, see Wallerman in this volume.

57 The table include references to the CJEU by Denmark, Finland and Sweden from 1995 to the end of 2014. For Iceland and Norway, the table includes references to the EFTA Court from 1994 to the end of 2014.

58 Case E-3/02 *Paranova AS v Merck & Co. Inc. and Others* [2003] EFTA Ct. Rep. 101.

59 Case E-14/15 *Holship Norge AS v Norsk Transportarbeiderforbund* (the case is still pending).

60 Case E-1/99 *Storebrand Skadeforsiking AS mot Veronika Finanger* [1999] EFTA Ct. Rep. 119.

61 For criticism of the Icelandic courts, see Hreinsson [n 54].

Justice Bårdsen has cited several grounds for not requesting advisory opinions: the parties must raise the question of application of EEA law; parties do not want the court to make a request; making a request and waiting for the opinion takes time and is costly.[62] Considering the principle of *iura novit curia* and the duty of the judge to promote legally sound judgments, these reasons are neither understandable from the perspective of homogenous application of EEA law, nor from the perspective of Norwegian civil procedure law.[63]

The role of the CJEU as a *de facto,* although not *de jure,* master of the EEA Agreement is a significant factor of low number of requests. The EFTA Court follows CJEU case law closely. When the CJEU has not settled a question, the EFTA Court tries to anticipate how the CJEU would rule.[64] The Norwegian Supreme Court sometimes sidesteps the EFTA Court and interprets directly case law of the CJEU. It does so sometimes even if the content of EU law is not clear and one of the parties want an advisory opinion.[65] The Supreme Court considers itself in the position to do independent evaluations of how the CJEU would solve the case or how the case should be solved in light of CJEU case law.[66] Lower courts follow the example of the Supreme Court.

The *STX* case (Rt. 2013 p. 258) brought the relationship between the Supreme Court and the EFTA Court to a freezing point. The Borgarting Court of Appeal requested an advisory opinion from the EFTA Court if universally applicable, and thus mandatory, terms and conditions of collective employment agreements were compatible with EEA law.[67] The EFTA Court found that requiring the employer to pay certain forms of compensation were not compatible with EEA law. The parties appealed to the Supreme Court. The Supreme Court, citing *Finanger I,* held that it has the right and duty to decide to which extent the advisory opinion is binding. The advisory opinion has significant weight as a legal source.[68] Having analysed recent case law from the CJEU, the Supreme Court found that the opinion of the EFTA Court was wrong. Chief Justice Schei was one of the five judges deciding the case, thus the case could be understood as the Supreme Courts general attitude towards the EFTA Court. The EFTA Court answered rapidly in *Jonsson*[69] by upholding its earlier stance. Instead, the Supreme Court could have requested a new advisory opinion or requested the EFTA Court to clarify its judgment.

62 Arnfinn Bårdsen, 'Noen refleksjoner om Norges Høyesterett og EFTA-domstolen' [2013] 52 Lov og Rett 535.

63 Similarly Fredriksen [n 54].

64 See inter alia Henrik Bull, 'European Law and Norwegian Courts' in Peter-Christian Müller-Graff and Erling Selvig (eds), *The Approach to European Law in Germany and Norway* (Berliner Wissenschafts-Verlag 2004) 105–108; Baudenbacher [n 21]; Vassilios Skouris, 'The ECJ and the EFTA Court under the EEA Agreement: A Paradigm for International Cooperation between Judicial Institutions' in Carl Baudenbacher, Per Tresselt and Thorgeir Örlygsson (eds), *The EFTA Court Ten Years on* (Hart Publishing 2005); Fredriksen [n 5]; Fredriksen [n 14].

65 Fredriksen,[n 55] 91–92; Fredriksen [n 54] 196–199.

66 Cf. Bull [n 65] 111–113; Fredriksen [n 55]. 95–96.

67 Case E-2/11 *STX Norway Offshore AS and Others v The Norwegian State, represented by the Tariff Board* [2012] EFTA Ct. Rep. 4.

68 *STX OSV AS and Others v The State by Tariffnemnda* Rt. 2013, p. 258, para 93 and 94.

69 *Jonsson* (n 52).

In doing so, the EFTA Court would have got an opportunity to back from its earlier position due to subsequent case law from the CJEU.[70]

In 2015, the relationship between the courts has improved. In particular, the request for an advisory opinion in *Holship*[71] has been beneficial. However, should the relationship between the courts have been better, and the Supreme Court requested advisory opinions more often, the incident could be characterised as a mishap, or as an opening of a discussion on balancing workers' rights with free movement. The Supreme Court must recognise that it is the task of the EFTA Court to develop and ensure uniformity in EFTA law. If the Supreme Court takes charge of development of EEA law, homogenous application will be inevitable lost.

4.2. *The Nature of the EEA Agreement – Dynamic or Static?*

Another issue of controversy is the interpretation of the EEA Agreement. The main problem is the widening gap between the EEA Agreement and the EU. The EEA was modelled to fit the European landscape of the 1990's and the Maastricht treaty, not the post-Lisbon European of the 2010's. Thus, the EFTA court (and the CJEU) have had the challenge to interpret the EEA Agreement in congruence with development of EU law. The EFTA Court has managed to side-step delicate issues, such as citizenship and the EU Fundamental Rights Charter, yet it has largely managed to introduce the same concepts through interpretation of other legislation and legal principles or through judge made law.[72] The EFTA Court doctrine on stressing the objective of homogenous interpretation makes in fact the CJEU the master of EEA law.[73] Consequently, concepts from EU law migrate to EEA law.

Although Norwegian courts have so far applied EEA law steadfastly, many Norwegian lawyers complain about the judicial activism and pro-EU stance of the EFTA Court. The pro-EU writings of EFTA Court President Carl Baudenbacher have irritated Norwegian lawyers.[74] Although dynamic interpretation of the EEA Agreement is necessary to keep the Agreement relevant two decades after its conclusion and to bridge the gap between

70 See Carl Baudenbacher, 'EFTA-domstolen og dens samhandling med de norske domstolene' [2013] 52 Lov og Rett 515; Bårdsen [n 63]; Catherine Barnard, 'Reciprocity, Homogeneity and Loyal Cooperation: Dealing with Recalcitrant National Courts?' in The EFTA Court (ed), *The EEA and the EFTA Courts Decentered Integration* (Hart 2014).

71 *Holship* (n 59).

72 Fredriksen and Franklin [n 5].

73 Niels Fenger, Michael Sanchez Rydelski and Titus van Stiphout, *European Free Trade Association (EFTA) and European Economic Area (EEA)* (Wolters Kluwer 2012) 68–69; Fredriksen and Franklin [n 5] 673.

74 Halvard Haukeland Fredriksen, 'Bridging the Widening Gap between the EU Treaties and the Agreement on the European Economic Area' [2012] 18 European Law Journal 868. For an example of controversial ideas see e.g. Carl Baudenbacher, 'Some Thoughts on the EFTA Court's Phases of Life' in EFTA Court (ed), *Judicial Protection in the European Economic Area* (German Law Publishers 2012); Fredrik Sejersted and others, *EØS-rett* (3 edn, Universitetsforlaget 2011), 172–173. Sejersted characterises the EFTA Court as more Catholic than the Pope and the role of the court as highly problematic.

EEA and the EU, the interpretations are sometimes difficult to accept from a Norwegian perspective, where state sovereignty is central. In the opinion of many Norwegian citizens and lawyers, the EFTA Court appears to be too activist.[75]

Judicial dialogue is a current 'hype' and the Supreme Court actively uses case law from the European Court of Human Rights (ECtHR) in its argumentation. The Supreme Court has in controversial judgments made significant changes to the jury system used in criminal justice[76] and introduced a duty for Courts of Appeal to give reasons when they dismiss appeals clearly lacking merit.[77] Compared to other Nordic Supreme Courts, the Norwegian Supreme Court uses case law from the ECtHR more extensively – both as to the number of cases and to the depth of argumentation – in its argumentation.[78] The dialogue with Strasbourg is in sharp contrast with the silent relationship to Luxembourg.

Having a meaningful conversation with the EFTA Court is an art and requires know-how. It takes time to learn to talk to European courts,[79] to recognise cases where EEA law may be relevant and to write good requests for advisory opinions. The answer from the EFTA Court may depend on how the court frames and articulates the question and on which information it supplies to the EFTA Court. Learning the necessary skills is indispensable for participating in a judicial dialogue.

The Supreme Court may feel threatened by the position of the EFTA Court, and by its own role being reduced.[80] The Court may also desire to engage in a dialogue with the CJEU, but it is barred from it. Yet, a constructive dialogue, which naturally does not exclude disagreement, with the EFTA Court is the road to development of EEA law. Elucidation of the extent of the primacy of EEA law, procedural autonomy in EEA law and *ex officio* application of EEA law requires national courts to request advisory opinions. By engaging in a dialogue with the EFTA Court, Norwegian courts can influence the development of EEA law and thus increase foreseeability of EEA law. Norwegian courts are EFTA courts, but their task is not to develop EEA law; it is the task of the EFTA Court.

75 See also Fredriksen and Franklin [n 5] 675–676.

76 *A v The Public Prosecutor* Rt. 2009, p. 773.

77 This applies both to criminal cases (*A v The Public Prosecutor* Rt. 2008, p. 1764) and civil cases (*Avante AS v Finsbråten Eiendom AS* Rt. 2009, p. 1118).

78 Anne Lise Kjær, 'European Legal Concepts in Scandinavian Law and Language' [2011] 80 Nordic Journal of Human Rights 321. The Norwegian Supreme Court made references to ECtHR case law 3.5 times as many as the Swedish Supreme Courts and 4 times as many as the Danish Supreme Court.

79 Michal Bobek, 'Learning to talk: preliminary rulings, the courts of the new member states and the court of justice' [2008] 45 Common Market Law Review 1611. In this context, one could even argue that Icelandic courts are 'shouting' at the EFTA Court in the wake of the financial crisis. See Michal Bobek, 'Talking Now? Preliminary Rulings in and from the New Member States' [2014] 21 Preliminary Rulings in and from the New Member States.

80 Hans Petter Graver, 'Dømmer Høyesterett i siste instans?' [2014] Jussens Venner 265, 267, 279; Fredriksen [n 55] 94–95.

5. Consequences of a Janus-faced Approach to the EU and EEA

Norway faces the challenges of two-speed integration[81] of European civil procedure law; Simultaneously, it is both inside and outside the core of Europe. The tension between the desire to on the one hand participate in the single market and on the other hand stress the sovereignty of the state creates unpredictable, and sometimes contradictory, approaches. The Janus-faced approach of the Supreme Court towards Europeanisation of law and toward the Strasbourg court and the EFTA Court is detrimental. The ambiguity in application of European law, especially when the solution depends on whether the stance is principled or pragmatic, results in less predictability. The interpretation and development of European aspects of Norwegian civil procedure is arbitrary rather than coherent, depending on inter alia which Justices decide a case.

The turf war between the EFTA Court and the Supreme Court is unfortunate. It has been pernicious for the development of the EEA law, but also for the discussion on how EEA law affects Norwegian (civil procedure) law. The line of argumentation stressing state sovereignty blurs the perspective of the parties and the rationale of the EEA Agreement: access to and participation in a single European market. Norwegian businesses and their business partners must be able to trust homogenous and equal application of EEA law. Legal certainty is important for economic prosperity of Norway. Citizens and traders must know which rules are applicable, and that the rules are applied in the same way throughout the EEA area. The promise of homogenous application of EEA law and the promise of parallelism between Brussels I bis Regulation and the Lugano Convention should be taken seriously. The voice of the Norwegian government should not overcome the perspectives of private parties.

In the famous book The Hitch Hikers Guide to the Galaxy by Douglas Adams, we learn why a towel is useful tool: '[you can] wrap it round your head to … avoid the gaze of the Ravenous Bugblatter Beast of Traal (a mindboggingly stupid animal, it assumes that if you can't see it, it can't see you – daft as a brush, but very very ravenous).'.[82] The Norwegian discussion on EEA law, especially voices stressing the sovereignty of the Norwegian state and the wish to keep national law intact, is similar to the Beast of Traal. If you only resist European civil procedure in principle, it will go away and you have no more worries. However, the resistance towards Europeanisation hampers the ability to analyse soberly the emergence and development of European civil procedure. European civil procedure is no longer statutory law equivalent to traditional supranational cooperation: indeed, it is a growing web of increasingly interconnected pieces of European law. European civil procedure is not a candy store where one can pick and choose – instead the pieces are increasingly woven together. In sum, Europeanisation permeates Norwegian civil procedure and will increasingly continue to do so.

81 Burkhard Hess, 'Abgestufte Integration im Europäischen Zivilprozessrecht' in Rolf Stürner and others (eds), *Festschrift für Dieter Leipold zum 70 Geburtstag* (Mohr Siebeck 2009).

82 Douglas Adams, *The Hitchhiker's Guide to the Galaxy* (Orion Publishing 2011 (1979)) 21.

Anna Piszcz*

POLISH CIVIL PROCEEDINGS: HOW MUCH EUROPEANISED?

1. Introductory Ideas

National procedural systems have always played an important role in enforcing European Union (EU) law. The details of these systems have differed substantially in different legal cultures and over time. The common elements that emerge in them are growing in number which can be associated with what is usually called 'Europeanisation'. If a necessary impulse for domestic change is provided to countries by the EU, it is justified, however, to use names 'EU-Europeanisation' or 'Unionisation', as put directly by A. Lenschow.[1] *Largo sensu* Europeanisation, on the other hand, is not limited to the EU-Europeanisation and EU effects on domestic developments. There may be other international impacts from other European fora. The impact of the European Court of Human Rights within European countries can be interpreted as an instance of *largo sensu* Europeanisation. In Poland, the European Convention of Human Rights was incorporated into laws in early 1990s. The influence of the Court interpreting the Convention on Polish laws can be seen in the introduction of the legal framework for the summons for injunctions against delays in proceedings in 2004 and its significant amendment in 2009. However, these changes are not going to be analysed in this chapter.

'The EU represents a set of rules, an arena and a discursive framework for domestic actors,' Lenschow writes, 'in short a point of departure for impulses that flow top-down, horizontally and 'round-about' when impacting on the domestic level'.[2] According to Bulmer and Radaelli, 'Europeanisation is not simply about formal policy rules but about less tangible aspects, such as beliefs and values'.[3] This chapter will focus on the top-down impact of the EU on civil proceedings, ie the penetration of the European dimension into national legal framework for civil proceedings in Poland. It will regard, first of all, the normative (formal) EU-Europeanisation as the process whereby domestic laws and

* Dr. Hab., professor at the University of Białystok (Poland), Faculty of Law.

1 Andrea Lenschow, 'Europeanisation of public policy' in Jeremy John Richardson (ed), *European Union: Power and Policy-making* (Routledge, Abingdon 2006) 59.

2 Ibid.

3 Simon J Bulmer and Claudio M Radaelli, 'The Europeanisation of National Policy?' (2004) 1 Queen's Papers on Europeanisation <https://www.qub.ac.uk/schools/SchoolofPoliticsInternationalStudiesandPhilosophy/FileStore/EuropeanisationFiles/Filetoupload,38405,en.pdf> accessed 7 October 2015, 5.

regulations are adapted to conform to EU rules. The normative EU-Europeanisation refers to procedural laws, substantive laws as well as institutional design of administration of justice but the two latter are beyond the scope of this chapter. National law established by the Polish legislature, which is a part of the Polish legal system of a multi-centre nature (multilevel system), binding in domestic territory along with the directly applicable EU laws,[4] is being Europeanised in a literal sense. It absorbs and adjusts to legal standards created by the EU. The history of Poland's accession to the European Union has been closely tied up with the obligation to approximate Polish laws to that of the EU. However, the Europe Agreement of 16 December 1991 establishing an association between the European Communities and their Member States, of the one part, and the Republic of Poland, of the other part, did not provide for the duty to amend the legal framework for civil proceedings. In Poland the EU-Europeanisation of civil proceedings became more visible in the post-accession period. Interestingly, both 'soft' and 'hard' mechanisms of the EU-Europeanisation of Polish civil proceedings can be identified.

On the other hand, also the application and interpretation of Polish national law is being EU-Europeanised. Courts, as interpreters of law, have begun to perform a pro-EU interpretation, which is characterised as functional (purposive) rather than linguistic, and/or draw inspiration from the jurisprudence of the Court of Justice of the European Union.

2. EU Europeanisation through 'Soft' Measures

A. Lenschow suggested that Europeanisation may take place because the EU had provided an arena for the exchange of ideas and shaped a discourse by identifying general goals or principles, disseminating information and pointing out examples of 'best practice'.[5] She argues that in cases of soft law and merely coordinative policy of the EU the explicit hierarchical pressure on domestic institutions and practices is weak; instead of complying with rules, national actors are expected to widen their ideational horizon due to the exposure to European or neighbour country discourses and to reconsider previously held beliefs, expectations and preferences.[6]

It is worth looking to the interesting example of such 'soft' or spontaneous EU-Europeanisation, in the case of Polish civil proceedings, ie the introduction of collective redress mechanisms. The Polish Act on the Pursuit of Claims in Group Proceedings (in Polish *ustawa o dochodzeniu roszczeń w postępowaniu grupowym*), hereafter referred to as the APC, was adopted on 17 December 2009 and came into force on 19 July 2010.[7] How did we get here? The history of the discussion on collective redress

4 Ewa Łętowska, 'Co-operation of the ECHR with Supreme National Judiciary Bodies (Consultative Opinions) and the Role of Popularising the Case-law of the ECHR' in *Reforming the European Convention on Human Rights: A work in progress: A compilation of publications and documents relevant to the ongoing reform of the ECHR* (Council of Europe Publishing, Strasbourg 2009) 205.

5 Cf Lenschow (n 1) 66.

6 Ibid.

7 More Anna Piszcz, ''Class Actions' in the Court Culture of Eastern Europe' in Laura Ervo and Anna Nylund (eds), *The Future of Civil Litigation – Access to Courts and Court Connected mediation in the Nordic Countries* (Springer International Publishing Switzerland, Cham 2014) 357–79.

in Poland can be traced back to 2005 when the Green Paper – Damages actions for breach of the EC antitrust rules[8] was published by the European Commission. The Commission stated therein as follows:

> 'It will be very unlikely for practical reasons, if not impossible, that consumers and purchasers with small claims will bring an action for damages for breach of antitrust law. Consideration should therefore be given to *ways in which these interests can be better protected by collective actions* [italics added]. Beyond the specific protection of consumer interests, collective actions can serve to consolidate a large number of smaller claims into one action, thereby saving time and money.'

The Polish Government took a position on this suggestion and it can be seen therefrom that in 2005–2006 they were strongly opposed to the introduction of collective actions, even though they supported the introduction of some solutions intended to facilitate 'collective' redress for consumers (eg joint attorneys).[9] The Commission did not stop there in 2005 and in its Communication to the Council, the European Parliament and the European Economic and Social Committee of 13 March 2007 – EU Consumer Policy strategy 2007–2013: Empowering consumers, enhancing their welfare, effectively protecting them,[10] it stated that it would consider action on collective redress mechanisms for consumers both for infringements of consumer protection rules and for breaches of EU antitrust rules (section 5.3). In 2007–2008 this initiative was followed by conferences, brainstorming events, workshops of the Commission and studies produced by outside contractors for the Commission. The Polish Government exposed to this huge debate going on about collective redress did not remain unaffected by it. In 2008 the Government changed its position on collective redress and began working on the draft Bill on the Pursuit of Claims in Group Proceedings.

The initiative was already underway in the Government when the Green Paper of 27 November 2008 on consumer collective redress was published by the European Commission.[11] The Commission presented four policy options (no EC action, cooperation between member states, mix of policy instruments, judicial collective redress procedure). The fourth option was accompanied by the list of issues to be decided including the financing of the procedure, how to prevent unmeritorious claims, standing in court, the question of an opt-in or opt-out procedure and the distribution of compensation. Although this list was known to the Polish government, they remained quite independent in their attitude towards, anyway, this EU-inspired initiative. Not all the issues referred to in the Commission's checklist were resolved in the APC. The Polish collective action model is opt-in. As to standing in court, the APC applies to proceedings in which claims

8 Commission, 'Green Paper – Damages actions for breach of the EC antitrust rules' COM (2005) 672.

9 In Polish available at: <http://ec.europa.eu/competition/antitrust/actionsdamages/files_green_paper_comments/permanent_representation_of_the_republic_of_poland.pdf> accessed 7 October 2015.

10 Commission, 'Communication to the Council, the European Parliament and the European Economic and Social Committee – EU Consumer Policy strategy 2007–2013: Empowering consumers, enhancing their welfare, effectively protecting them' COM (2007) 99 final.

11 Commission, 'Green Paper on consumer collective redress' COM (2008) 794 final.

of a single type arising from common or similar issues of fact are pursued by a group of at least ten persons (Article 1 para 1 APC). The APC does not reserve the benefit of group proceedings exclusively to consumers and thus the group can include businesses. The statement of claim is filed by the group representative (Article 4 para 1 APC). A member of the group (lead claimant) or a regional (municipal) consumer ombudsman[12] can act as the group representative (Article 4 para 2 APC). However, such an important form of protection of market participants as group actions filed by consumer (non-governmental) organisations was seen as dispensable by the Polish Government. The plaintiff (lead claimant or consumer ombudsman) must be represented by a barrister or legal advisor; it is compulsory unless the plaintiff is a barrister or legal advisor herself/himself (Article 4 para 4 APC). Another distinguishing feature is the deposit (Article 8 APC), designed primarily to prevent unmeritorious claims from being brought. The issue of the financing of the procedure was not referred to in the text of the APC. However, in its response of 2 March 2009 to the Green Paper, the Polish Government supported the fourth option and took a position that the EU could issue a directive calling for legislation in an area of collective redress.[13] It also mentioned that in Poland the works on the introduction of the collective redress mechanisms were underway.

On 25 March 2009 the draft Bill was submitted to the Parliament. It is claimed that this decision was not based on an in-depth analysis of the social status quo but on a subjective decision of the decision makers.[14] It is worth noting that the EU support for the collective redress mechanisms was mentioned in some documents accompanying the legislative works. However, the explanatory notes to the draft Bill did not define clearly the sources of inspiration of the Polish Government and did not mention any EU documents. Creators of a bill proposal are required to provide assurance of its compliance with EU law in the explanatory notes (and they did) but not to describe a source of inspiration. Frequently they do not exceed the required minimum.

Interestingly, when responding to the Commission Staff Working Document of 4 February 2011 – Public Consultation: Towards a Coherent European Approach to Collective Redress,[15] the Polish Government not only emphasised that Poland had already introduced the collective redress mechanism but it also offered to the Commission certain Polish solutions as a possible model that could be reproduced in other EU member states.[16]

To sum it up, the soft initiatives of the EU resulted in the adoption of the 'hard' legislation on collective redress in Poland. However, the last EU initiative in the form of inter alia Commission Recommendation (EU) of 11 June 2013 on common principles for

12 In Polish *powiatowy (miejski) rzecznik konsumentów.*

13 In Polish available at: <http://ec.europa.eu/consumers/archive/redress_cons/responses/Polish_Perm_Rep_pl.pdf> accessed 7 October 2015.

14 Marek Niedużak, *Pozwy grupowe – po pierwszym roku funkcjonowania* [*Group actions – after the first year of functioning*] (Helsińska Fundacja Praw Człowieka, Warszawa 2011) 7.

15 Commission, 'Commission Staff Working Document – Public Consultation: Towards a Coherent European Approach to Collective Redress' SEC (2011) 173 final.

16 In Polish available at: <http://ec.europa.eu/competition/consultations/2011_collective_redress/ministry_of_justice_poland_pl.pdf> accessed 7 October 2015.

injunctive and compensatory collective redress mechanisms in the Member States concerning violations of rights granted under Union Law,[17] which recommends that all member states have national collective redress systems with respect to rights granted under Union law based on a number of common European principles implemented till 26 July 2015 at the latest, has not been followed by Poland. Member states' national legislatures have little incentive to undertake reforms in national civil procedural rules in accordance with the mandates incorporated in the soft-law instrument.[18] Non-legally binding recommendations are, however, often implemented by the EU member states pursuant to the principle of loyal or sincere cooperation. The Polish government does not infringe this principle, since it seems to wait for a directive suggested by the European Economic and Social Committee[19] and, thus, avoid double legislative works which may be contradictory and counterproductive if the contents of a directive are different from the contents of the Commission Recommendation (which is not excluded). It may be also believed that this 'standby' time is convenient to the new government formed in November 2015 after the last parliamentary election which is very engaged with other changes to legislation.

In the meantime, Polish courts gain the experience of handling the collective actions. Since the APC came into effect in 2010 to the end of 2014 courts received collective statements of claim in 162 cases, ie civil (156) and commercial (6) cases (2010 – 21, 2011 – 38, 2012 – 39, 2013 – 22, 2014 – 42 cases).[20] Although courts have not developed a significant body of jurisprudence yet concerning collective actions, the Supreme Court, when deciding an appeal for cassation in one of collective cases, considered an allegation that the judicial interpretation of the APC was in breach of the inter alia Commission Recommendation.[21] The decision of the Supreme Court in this case concludes that the mentioned EU documents only encourage member states to introduce collective redress mechanisms and that, if a member state already has them, the applicable legal framework should be interpreted in a way that would promote their effectiveness; such an interpretation, however, is quite obvious and irrespective of the EU recommendations, as corresponding to the principles of functional (purposive) interpretation applied here by the Supreme Court without the necessity of referring to EU law.

17 [2013] OJ L201/60.

18 Zampia Vernadaki, 'Civil Procedure Harmonization in the EU: Unravelling the Policy Considerations' (2013) 9(2) Journal of Contemporary European Research 308.

19 European Economic and Social Committee, 'Opinion on the Communication from the Commission to the European Parliament, the Council, the European Economic and Social Committee and the Committee of the Regions Towards a European Horizontal Framework for Collective Redress' COM (2013) 401 final, [2014] OJ C170/68. See point 3.3 where the Committee states that only a directive would ensure a solid core of harmonisation while at the same time giving the member states enough leeway for accommodating the particularities of their national legal systems.

20 See *Pozwy zbiorowe w latach 2010–2014* (*Collective actions in 2010–2014*), in Polish available at: <http://isws.ms.gov.pl/pl/baza-statystyczna/opracowania-wieloletnie/> accessed 7 October 2015.

21 *Zofia P. v State Treasury* [2015] 7–8 OSNC 97, Case I CSK 533/14.

3. EU Europeanisation through 'Hard' Measures

EU Europeanisation of civil proceedings resulting from the EU 'hard' legislation has not used to occur very often so far.

Regulations, as directly applicable secondary legislation, automatically have legal effect in domestic laws without further enactment. However, member states introduce into their national legal systems such measures of a complementary or supplementary nature as are necessary to apply EU regulations. Poland appears in this instance to be doing the same. In particular, the main body of legal rules regarding Polish civil procedure, that is Civil Procedure Code 1964 (*Kodeks postępowania cywilnego* 1964, hereafter referred to as the CPC), in part I book I ('Contentious proceedings') title VII ('Separate proceedings') division VII ('European proceedings in cross-border cases') contains chapters on the European order for payment procedure (chapter 1) and the European Small Claims procedure (chapter 2). They do not repeat, conflict or overlap with the provisions of EU regulations but only refer to them and complement them. It is worth adding that the domestic order for payment and small claims procedures have not been spontaneously harmonised with the European ones. The decision makers resolved that there was no need of verification of effective domestic procedures.

Furthermore, there were a few amendments to the CPC and some other acts which were described as implementing or transposing provisions of the EU directives. It refers to both sector-specific directives (regarding enforcement of claims arising under a given sector of EU law) and horizontal directives limited to specific aspects of civil procedure ('piecemeal' directives).[22]

These were, among others, rather uncontroversial provisions of the Directive 2011/7/EU of the European Parliament and of the Council of 16 February 2011 on combating late payment in commercial transactions.[23]

Second, it was the Directive 2004/48/EC of the European Parliament and of the Council of 29 April 2004 on the enforcement of intellectual property rights.[24] Interestingly, the legal basis employed for the purpose of this harmonisation concerns the functioning of the internal market. Therefore, this sector-specific Directive applies to any infringement of an intellectual property right, even one of a purely national character[25] (whilst the legal basis concerning judicial cooperation in civil matters would limit the scope of the Directive to cross-border matters). The amendments to the couple of Polish acts, including the CPC, entered into force on 20 June 2007. Since then, Polish courts have struggled with questions of how to interpret national provisions on the right of information at least a few times. In the case of discrepancies between Article 8

22 Rafał Mańko, 'Europeanisation of civil procedure: Towards common minimum standards?' (2015) European Parliament <www.europarl.europa.eu/RegData/etudes/IDAN/2015/559499/EPRS_IDA(2015)559499_EN.pdf> accessed 7 October 2015, 4.

23 [2011] OJ L48/1.

24 Corrigendum to directive (EC) 48/2004 on the enforcement of intellectual property rights [2004] OJ L195/16.

25 Magdalena Tulibacka, 'Europeanization of civil procedures: In search of a coherent approach' (2009) 46 Common Market Law Review, 1528.

of the Directive ('Right of information') and Polish provisions, the Polish courts of appeals (in Białystok,[26] in Warsaw[27]) interpreted the latter to mean that the right of information under national provisions must cover substantially the same elements as under Article 8 of the Directive, however, subject to fundamental rights protected by the EU legal order and the other general principles of EU law, such as the principle of proportionality. The courts supported their conclusions with citations to judgments of the Court of Justice.[28]

Third, a vast area of civil procedural law Europeanised by means of a directive is alternative dispute resolution (ADR). In Poland rules on mediation in civil cases were adopted in 2005;[29] at the same time, revised provisions on arbitration were reintroduced. Although the Acts amending the CPC emphasised that mediation and arbitration were not within the scope of the EU rules, it was stressed that the main objectives of amendments were essential for the assessment of the compliance of the Polish legal system with European solutions. At the same time, two soft law instruments specifically designed for alternative dispute resolution already existed at European level, ie Commission Recommendation 98/257/EC on the principles applicable to the bodies responsible for the out-of-court settlement of consumer disputes[30] and Commission Recommendation 2001/310/EC on the principles for out-of-court bodies involved in the consensual resolution of consumer ADR.[31]

The reform of the Polish legal framework for mediation in civil cases was triggered by the Directive 2008/52/EC of the European Parliament and of the Council of 21 May 2008 on certain aspects of mediation in civil and commercial matters.[32] At all events, it may be said that, although the Directive required to harmonise certain rules applicable to resolving cross-border disputes, identical provisions were introduced to deal with purely internal proceedings. The decision makers did not opted for the work of 'separation' of the two categories of disputes from each other.

As sort of a continuation of the reform, Directive 2013/11/EU of the European Parliament and of the Council of 21 May 2013 on alternative dispute resolution for consumer disputes and amending Regulation (EC) No 2006/2004 and Directive 2009/22/EC (Directive on consumer ADR)[33] is going to be transposed by way of the Act on the alternative resolution of consumer disputes. However, the works which started in the beginning of 2015 will need to be conducted for the second time due to the parliamentary election in October 2015.

26 *V.L. v N.S. J.S. partnership* [2013] Case I ACz 114/13, 1 OSAB 36; *Centrum Informatyki 'Z.' S.A. v State Treasury* [2012] Case I ACz 1379/12, 4 OSAB 47.

27 *X. v Telekomunikacja Polska S.A.* [2012] Case VI ACz 2212/11, 1 Apel.-W-wa 7.

28 *Productores de Musica de España (Promusicae) v Telefonica de España SAU* [2008] Case C-275/06, I-00271; *LSG* v *Tele2* [2009] Case C-557/07, I-01227.

29 More Marta Janina Skrodzka, 'Civil law mediation and the culture of pre-trial litigation: A mediator's perspective' in Anna Piszcz (ed) *Court culture: Contemporary Problems. Białystok Volumes on Law & Culture, vol. 2* (Temida 2, Białystok 2014) 170–81.

30 [1998] OJ L115/31.

31 [2001] OJ L109/56.

32 [2008] OJ L136/3.

33 [2013] OJ L165/63.

Interestingly, in parallel with these works, the legislative works on the draft Bill amending the CPC and some other acts with regard to the promotion of alternative dispute resolution (ADR) methods were conducted. The Act was adopted on 10 September 2015 and came into force from 2016. The explanatory notes to the draft Bill clarify that it develops the framework for the obligation of Poland as a EU member state to ensure the availability of mediation services and their promotion resulting from the already-transposed Directive 2008/52/EC. The explanatory notes refer also to the European Parliament resolution of 13 September 2011 on the implementation of the directive on mediation in the Member States, its impact on mediation and its take-up by the courts.[34] It introduces inter alia the following solutions:

- permanent mediators;
- the principle of culpability for negligent refusal to be referred to mediation;
- the obligation of the mediator to use various methods aimed at amicable resolution of disputes, including the support for the parties determining their settlement offers and – if required by all parties – the presentation of ways to resolve the dispute that are not binding on the parties;
- the possibility to conduct the information meeting regarding ADR methods, in particular, mediation.

Furthermore, the Act of 2001 – Law on Common Courts Organisation changes. Among others, coordinators for mediation are established in courts.

Fourth, legislative works on the transposition of the Directive 2014/104/EU of the European Parliament and of the Council of 26 November 2014 on certain rules governing actions for damages under national law for infringements of the competition law provisions of the Member States and of the European Union,[35] regarding private enforcement of competition law, are underway. The Damages Directive contains both rules of substantive civil law and rules of civil procedural law, eg on evidence, effect of decisions of national competition authorities on court proceedings regarding damages actions, consensual resolution of disputes.[36] It seems slightly misleading to speak of 'the competition law provisions of the Member States' in the title of the Damages Directive. In the definition contained in Article 2(3), national competition law is limited to provisions of national law that are applied to the same case and in parallel to EU competition law pursuant to Article 3(1) of Council Regulation 1/2003 of 16 December 2002 on the implementation of the rules on competition laid down in Articles 81 and 82

34 2011/2026 (INI).

35 [2014] OJ L349/1.

36 More: Sofia Oliveira Pais and Anna Piszcz, 'Package on Actions for Damages Based on Breaches of EU Competition Rules: Can One Size Fit All?' (2014) 7(10) Yearbook of Antitrust and Regulatory Studies 223–34; Aleš Galič, 'Disclosure of Documents in Private Antitrust Enforcement Litigation' (2015) 8(12) Yearbook of Antitrust and Regulatory Studies 99ff; Vlatka Butorac Malnar, 'Access to Documents in Antitrust Litigation – EU and Croatian Perspective' (2015) 8(12) Yearbook of Antitrust and Regulatory Studies 127ff; Raimundas Moisejevas, 'The Damages Directive and Consensual Approach to Antitrust Enforcement' (2015) 8(12) Yearbook of Antitrust and Regulatory Studies 181ff.

of the Treaty.[37] The Damages Directive should not affect actions for damages with respect to infringements of national competition law which do not affect trade between member states within the meaning of Article 101 or 102 TFEU (last sentence of Recital 10 of the Preamble). It is thus justified to say that for these matters the Damages Directive does not require member states to model their legal frameworks on the Damages Directive; albeit they are free to do so.

This sector-specific (sectoral) legislation in the form of the Damages Directive may be used here as an example of how the use of minimum harmonisation clauses can be a critical factor in the scope that Europeanisation takes. The Directive uses phrases such as 'at least' (with regard to the effect of national decisions and limitation periods) and 'wider' (with regard to the disclosure of evidence). They allow for different national solutions. If individual member states choose the minimal solution or the highest standard solution or one of the options in-between, the impact of the EU initiative on the particular area of civil procedure will not be uniform. Therefore, hypothetically speaking, to some extent the Damages Directive may have implications taking form of the phenomenon of forum shopping.

It is still difficult to predict precisely what the shape of the Polish act implementing the Directive will be. The assumptions underlying the draft Bill were published in early December 2015 on the webpage of the Civil Law Codification Commission at the Ministry of Justice (hereafter referred to as the CLCC).[38] However, the CLCC's members were dismissed in mid-December 2015. The Minister of Justice announced plans to create the new Codification Commission of the Republic of Poland.

First, the assumptions state the cause for the legislative action. They also attempt to explain why the impact of the Damages Directive to the system of private enforcement of competition law is going to be far more widespread than the title suggests, by pointing out, that having double standards with respect to the two different types of infringements (those with and those without EU effect) would make private enforcement of competition law even more difficult for courts and parties. National rules governing actions for damages are going to be modelled on the Damages Directive not only with regard to infringements of EU competition rules (and national rules applied in parallel) but also with regard to violations of national competition law which do not affect EU trade (infringements of a purely national scope). As expected, the Damages Directive will influence the latter through the 'back door'.[39]

The respectable part of the assumptions sets out the plans for the amendments of the substantive law to reflect the rules laid down in the Damages Directive. They continue, addressing issues of civil proceedings, those resolved by the Damages Directive and those left to the discretion of member states. The CLCC is of the opinion that a regional court (in Polish *sąd okręgowy*) – and not a district court (in Polish *sąd rejonowy*) – as a

37 [2003] OJ L1/1.

38 In Polish available at: <https://bip.ms.gov.pl/pl/dzialalnosc/komisje-kodyfikacyjne/komisja-kodyfikacyjna-prawa-cywilnego/> accessed 17 December 2015.

39 Anna Piszcz, 'Piecemeal Harmonisation Through the Damages Directive? Remarks on What Received Too Little Attention in Relation to Private Enforcement of EU Competition Law' (2015) 8(12) Yearbook of Antitrust and Regulatory Studies 91.

court of first instance should have authority over actions for antitrust damages (as it already is with unfair competition claims and all collective redress actions). Jurisdiction of regional courts means that such cases will be decided by a panel of three professional judges. Their superior experience and expertise are likely to allow them to handle such complex cases better than a single professional judge at a district court. Although this falls outside the scope of the Directive, in the CLCC's opinion, associations of undertakings and consumer organisations should have legal standing to initiate representative actions for antitrust damages. Furthermore, the CLCC takes an opportunity to reflect on the disclosure of evidence, effect of national decisions, actions for damages by claimants from different levels in the supply chain, quantification of harm as well as suspensive and other effects of consensual dispute resolution with regard to those parties that are or that were involved or represented in the consensual dispute resolution. By-the-bye, it is evident that in the case of minimum harmonisation clauses the CLCC does not recommend to exceed the required minimum. The assumptions should be carefully examined and debated upon before being used as a point of departure for the continuation of the scheme of legislative works, more precisely composing the draft Bill.

4. Judicial EU Europeanisation

The role of the judiciary was quite limited in the pre-accession phase, but already then Polish courts began to develop the pro-EU interpretation of laws[40] which can also be considered as a method of the approximation of laws.[41] As a result of Poland's accession to the European Union, Polish judges found themselves under an obligation to adapt to the different conditions of dispute resolution. Since then they face the obligation to ensure supremacy and direct effect of EU law as well as the obligation to ensure equivalence and effectiveness of EU law. They are also obliged to interpret national laws in harmony (conformity) with EU law. This obligation is known as the directive of conforming interpretation (consistent interpretation, indirect effect); it has its roots in the principle of solidarity, and is strictly bound with the supremacy, efficiency and procedural autonomy principles.[42]

National civil judges became obliged to function as EU law judges. Very soon, the limitations of this function of judges were beginning to be evident. A socio-legal study by U. Jaremba provides empirical – quantitative and qualitative – data concerning how Polish civil judges establish their own understanding of EU law and the new requirements it has imposed upon them.[43]

40 Eg *Polish Confederation of Private Employers* [2003] Case K 2/02, 24 Dz.U. 202 [4.4].

41 Adam Lazowski, 'Adaptation of the Polish legal system to European Union law: Selected aspects' (2001) Sussex European Institute Working Papers <https://www.sussex.ac.uk/webteam/gateway/file.php?name=sei-working-paper-no-45.pdf&site=266> accessed 7 October 2015, 21.

42 Aleksandra Wentkowska, 'A 'Secret Garden' of Conforming Interpretation – European Union Law in Polish Courts Five Years after Accession' (2009) 12 Yearbook of Polish European Studies 128.

43 Urszula Jaremba, *National Judges as EU Law Judges: The Polish Civil Law System* (Martinus Nijhoff Publishers, Leiden – Boston 2014) 11.

First, it is emphasised that the Polish judges function in the realm of a very positivistic, highly formalised and legalistic legal culture in which a strictly literal (textual) interpretation of law is the main and often the only interpretation method commonly practiced by Polish judges; this seems to be in contrast to what the Court of Justice has expected from national judges.[44] They have been expected to be more flexible in their attitude to interpretation of law, more responsive and adaptable. As it is argued in the literature, European civil procedure is in fact increasingly fond of procedural flexibility and judicial discretion.[45]

Second, judges have contrary views regarding whether EU law should be applied *ex officio*.[46] It needs adding that the Polish Supreme Court is of opinion that if a party failed to raise a point of EU law in the cassation complaint, the Supreme Court does not scrutinise an infringement of EU law, unless there is a need to send a preliminary question to the Court of Justice.[47] The provisions of EU law should be taken into account, according to the Supreme Court, when it is obvious that they regulate the same subject as is regulated by the national law whose violation has been raised in the cassation complaint, and there is a possibility of direct application of EU law or the need to interpret the provisions of national law in accordance with EU law. This may result from the fact that the Polish system is based on the *iura novit curia* principle which means that the court knows and applies the law on its own motion.[48]

Third, the daily operational context was taken into account by Jaremba.[49] Many judges rarely have enough time to either broaden their knowledge of EU law or to engage *ex officio* within any EU law discourse going beyond what is considered absolutely necessary to resolve a dispute.

Fourth, the application of EU law is not considered easy and straightforward. Both EU law and preliminary ruling mechanism are deemed unclear by most judges.[50] The issue of the precedential value of judgments of the Court of Justice generates doubts in Poland. The number of preliminary questions sent to the Court of Justice by Polish civil courts is modest. For instance, the Supreme Court reported in its last report[51] that in 2014 it sent two preliminary questions to the Court of Justice.[52] This is the first case where the Supreme Court revoked the preliminary procedure and the questions regard civil matters (the interpretation of EU secondary legislation).

44 Ibid 161, 171.

45 Aleš Galič, 'The Aversion to Judicial Discretion in Civil Procedure in Post-Communist Countries: Can the Influence of EU Law Change it?' in Michal Bobek, *Central European Judges Under the European Influence: The Transformative Power of the EU Revisited* (Bloomsbury Publishing, Oxford – Portland 2015) 102.

46 Ibid 215.

47 *Ryszard G. v Fundusz Gwarantowanych Świadczeń Pracowniczych* [2008] case II PK 17/06, 1–2 OSNP 8.

48 Maciej Zieliński, 'Iura novit curia a wykładnia prawa' ['Iura novit curia and the interpretation of law'] in Sławomir Lewandowski, Hanna Machińska and Jacek Petzl (eds), *Prawo, język, logika. Księga jubileuszowa profesora Andrzeja Malinowskiego* [*Law, language, logic. The jubillee book of Professor Andrzej Malinowski*] (LexisNexis, Warszawa 2013) 287.

49 Cf Jaremba (n 45) 218.

50 Ibid 223, 231.

51 In Polish available at: <www.sn.pl/osadzienajwyzszym/Dzialalnosc_SN/Dzialalnosc_SN_2014.pdf> accessed 17 December 2015.

52 *Emmanuel Lebek v Janusz Domino*, [2015] case C-70/15, OJ C171/13.

However, preliminary rulings in cases involving a Polish element should not be underestimated. The *Adler* case[53] resulted in the amendment of the CPC provisions on cross-border service considered by the Court of Justice as conflicting with Article 18 TFEU. In the succeeding passages of the adopted judgment, the Court of Justice narrated the various detailed propositions of interpretation of Article 18 TFEU and applicable secondary legislation advanced in support of the contention that legislation of a member state which 'provides that judicial documents addressed to a party whose place of residence or habitual abode is in another Member State are placed in the case file, and deemed to have been effectively served, if that party has failed to appoint a representative who is authorised to accept service and is resident in the first Member State, in which the judicial proceedings are taking place' is precluded. Another important question awaiting for the decision of the Court of Justice was asked by the Court of Appeals in Warsaw and is related to unlawful standard contract terms.[54] In short, a matter for reflection and consideration is whether the use of standard contract terms with content identical to that of terms which have been declared unlawful by a judicial decision having the force of law and which have been entered in the register of unlawful standard contract terms can be regarded, 'in relation to another undertaking which was not a party to the proceedings culminating in the entry in the register of unlawful standard contract terms, as an unlawful act which, under national law, constitutes a practice which harms the collective interests of consumers and for that reason forms the basis for imposing a fine in national administrative proceedings'.

The results of the above-mentioned research under social sciences do not seem to support the assumption that the potential of Polish judges for judicial EU-Europeanisation of Polish law, including civil procedural law, is significant. However, the view is reflected in jurisprudence that the national courts must refuse to apply any provision of national law contrary to EU law, irrespective of whether it is a national rule adopted before or after the adoption of the EU rule and regardless of whether it is a national rule contained in the legislation or administrative act or the court practice.[55] The jurisprudence shows that in principle there is a development from an 'EU-passive' to an 'EU-active' court.

There are even examples of judgments which prove that Polish courts – even if not obliged to apply EU law – draw intellectual inspiration from its sources. One of the examples thereof is the widely discussed judgment of the Supreme Court in case *TPPD S.A. v. State Treasury* regarding the effect of decisions of national competition authorities on civil proceedings.[56] The main difficulty is that, although Article 16(1) of Regulation 1/2003 states the principle of the binding effect of decisions adopted by the European Commission, there is no such principle embodied in Polish statutes in relation to decisions adopted by the Polish competition authority (non-cross-border effect of decisions) or national competition authorities of other EU member states (cross-border effect of decisions). The

[53] *Alder & Alder v Orłowska & Orłowski* [2012] case C-325/11, ECLI:EU:C:2012:824.

[54] *Biuro Podróży 'Partner' v Prezes Urzędu Ochrony Konkurencji i Konsumentów* [2015] case 119/15, OJ C198/24.

[55] See judgment of the Court of Appeals in Poznań of 5 February 2009, *A AG v M sp. z o.o.* [2010] case I ACa 13/09, 5 OSA 36. It refers to the judgment of the Court of Justice of 9 March 1978 in *Amministrazione delle Finanze dello Stato v Simmenthal SpA* [1978] case 106/77, ECR 00629.

[56] *TPPD S.A. v. State Treasury* [2009] case III CZP 52/08, 7–8 OSP 86.

first, general, line of cases resolved by the Supreme Courts considers administrative decisions as only evidence which may be assessed in civil proceedings along with any other material brought by the parties.[57] On the other hand, more surprisingly, in some decisions the Supreme Court established the principle that a decision by the competition authority was the precondition of proceedings before an ordinary court ('prejudiciality').[58] The line represented by the already-mentioned case *TPPD S.A. v. State Treasury* provides for the (non-cross-border) binding effect of national final infringement decisions.[59]

The Supreme Court arrived at such conclusion after the analysis of the solutions contained in EU law (Article 16 of Regulation 1/2003) which were viewed by the Court as a 'strong argument' in favour of the adopted resolution. According to the Court, different interpretation of Polish procedural law would be contrary to the principle of effectiveness of EU law.

As it has been already said, the resolution fills in a kind of lacuna left by the national legislature. Judicial freedom in evaluating evidence provided for in Article 233 CPC can be limited on specific legal grounds only;[60] under the CPC this is possible exclusively in relation to the binding effect of a judgment of a criminal court finding that a crime was committed. This rule is provided for in Article 11 CPC that refers to a 'criminal court' but does not precise which criminal courts are within the scope of this purely procedural provision – only Polish criminal courts or also foreign criminal courts. Also this provision was subject to the functional and to some extent systemic interpretation in one of the judgments of the Supreme Court of 2013 in the context of EU law.[61] The judgment states that Article 11 CPC is applicable also to final judgments of criminal courts of other EU member states. The notes (justification) to the judgment demonstrate that the basis for this conclusion was the pro-EU interpretation of Article 11 CPC. The conclusion was based on the assumption that Polish criminal courts are bound by judgments of criminal courts of other EU member states finding that a crime was committed, so that in the case of such a judgment the criminal proceedings in Poland cannot be initiated (*res iudicata*). In Polish literature this judgment was discredited.[62] K. Piasecki believes that the link between the obligation to interpret national law in harmony with EU law and the

57 *Danuta K. v Commune K., Alicja G., Tomasz S. and Katarzyna S.* [2008] case III CZP 46/07, 3 OSNC 30.

58 Eg *Housing Cooperative in S. v Energy Company S.A. in Ł. and Commune S.* [1996] case III CZP 135/95, 6 OSP 112.

59 See also Agata Jurkowska-Gomułka, 'W stronę umocnienia prywatnoprawnego wdrażania zakazów praktyk ograniczających konkurencję – glosa do uchwały SN z 23.07.2008 r. (III CZP 52/08)' ['Towards strengthening the private enforcement of prohibitions of pratices restricting competition – commentary to the resolution of the Supreme Court of 23.07.2008 (III CZP 52/08)'] (2010) 5 Europejski Przegląd Sądowy 43–48. The newest line suggests that the very commencement of antitrust proceedings precludes courts from independently examining the anti-competitiveness of a given market conduct (the effect of national antitrust proceedings); *M.N. v (...) general partnership in liquidation in W.* [2009] case VI ACa 422/09, LEX 1120262.

60 See also Ewelina Rumak and Piotr Sitarek, 'Polish Leniency Programme and its Intersection with Private Enforcement of Competition Law' (2009) 2(2) Yearbook of Antitrust and Regulatory Studies 115–16.

61 *D.R. v R.G., Insurance Company (...)S.A. and PZU na Życie S.A.* [2014] case V CSK 185/12, 3 OSP 30.

62 Kazimierz Piasecki, 'Glosa do wyroku SN z dnia 27 marca 2013 r., V CSK 185/12' ['Commentary to the judgment of the Supreme Court of 27 March 2013, V CSK 185/12'] (2014) 3 OSP 30c.

principle of 'procedural autonomy' of the EU member states is unmistakeable; the former cannot lead to the change in the legal rule of the national law. This implies the limited scope of the Article 11 CPC involving only judgments of Polish criminal courts. Procedural rules are seen as of territorial nature unless otherwise permitted directly by the legislation. *De lege ferenda* the Polish legislature should be expected to respond to the need for broadening the scope of Article 11 CPC.

Even though the above examples refer to the narrative for the pro-EU interpretation of laws by Polish courts, it is not always the case. Sometimes courts place limits on the pro-EU 'flexibility' and functional interpretation preferring the literal interpretation supported by the systemic interpretation. The decision of the Supreme Court regarding the resumption of civil proceedings is significant in this respect.[63] Under Article 403 CPC one of the basis for the resumption of civil proceedings is a detection of such facts or evidence which could affect the outcome of the case and on which the party could not rely in the previous proceedings. The Supreme Court's decision states that the contradiction of a final national judgment with EU law or subsequent judgment of the Court of Justice does not provide a basis for the resumption of civil proceedings, in particular it is not a fact or evidence in the meaning of Article 403 CPC. The Court referred to the judgment of the Court of First Instance in case *Rosmarie Kapferer*,[64] in which it is stated that 'Community law does not require a national court to *disapply domestic rules of procedure conferring finality on a decision* [italics added], even if to do so would enable it to remedy an infringement of Community law by the decision at issue (...)'. Commenting the judgment in *Rosmarie Kapferer* the Polish literature articulated that the flexible interpretation of the CPC provisions on the resumption of civil proceedings would be advised in the light of this judgment but the status quo inducing such interpretation is not beneficial in the context of the principle of legal certainty and the interests of individuals seeking legal protection of rights derived from EU law.[65] The Supreme Court decided, however, that the Polish legal system had sufficient measures that ensured the effectiveness of the protection of individual rights in cases where either a final or non-final decision was contrary to EU law. In other words, there is no need to strengthen them with the flexible interpretation of the CPC provisions on the resumption of civil proceedings. The Court emphasised that the lack of possibility of the resumption of civil proceedings in the case of the contradiction of a final national judgment with EU law or subsequent judgment of the Court of Justice did not violate the principle of effectiveness.

5. Concluding Remarks

The EU-Europeanisation has taken place so far in Poland in both previously unregulated (eg collective actions, mediation) and regulated (some other examples) elements of civil procedure, through both 'soft' and 'hard' EU measures. The number of sector-specific or

63 *Anna K. v ZUS* [2011] case I UZ 64/09, 13–14 OSNP 194.

64 *Rosmarie Kapferer v Schlank & Schick GmbH* [2006] case C-234/04, ECR I-02585.

65 Maciej Taborowski, 'Glosa do wyroku TS z dnia 16 marca 2006 r., C-234/04' ['Commentary to the judgment of the Court of Justice of 16 March 2006, C-234/04'] (2007) 3 Europejski Przegląd Sądowy 58.

horizontal initiatives touching civil procedure that need to be followed by the Polish legislature is increasing. In most instances there is too early, however, for a 'mature' assessment thereof.

First, EU regulations introducing European civil procedures, although directly applicable, make Polish legislature introduce into the national legal system some measures of a complementary or supplementary nature that are necessary to apply EU regulations. Remarkably, similar domestic procedures are not harmonised with the European ones. Consequently, procedures in place become more and more fragmented.

Second, civil proceedings change as a result of the transposition of EU directives. However, as a rule the transposition influences not only proceedings with EU element but also ones of a purely national character.

Moreover, as it has been stressed earlier, courts, by way of functional pro-EU interpretation, fill in 'lacunae' left by the national legislature and, thus, 'improve' the national provisions. The resistance of courts to such flexible interpretation is much less frequent. There are, however, some controversies regarding in particular on how the obligation to interpret national law in harmony with EU law and the principle of 'procedural autonomy' of the EU member states are reconciled.

The question of the attitude of national judges is also very important in this context. A socio-legal study quoted above provides reliable albeit worrisome to some extent insight into the judicial practice. Therefore, it remains to be seen how the discussed phenomena will develop.

Aleš Galič*

SLOVENIAN CIVIL PROCEDURE AND THE TRANSFORMATIVE POWER OF THE EU

1. Introduction

After the downfall of communist regimes in the early 1990s Slovenia embarked on the path towards a parliamentary democracy and rebuilding of its legal system. The early era of transition was particularly turbulent as it was linked also to calls for independence. Slovenia became an independent state in 1991, whereby a full international recognition followed in 1992. Slovenia joined the European Union in 2004. The transition of civil justice in Slovenia is a difficult and onerous process, which is far from over yet. There exists a great public dissatisfaction with the functioning of civil justice due to excessive duration of proceedings and backlogs in courts. This still seriously undermines the trust in the judiciary in public opinion. The 'EU justice scoreboard' shows that the situation in both respects is, as the EU Commission keeps pointing out[1], worrying. Nevertheless, at least there is a distinct positive trend as backlogs have been gradually decreasing, the disposition time shortened and the 'clearance rate'is slightly more than 100 per cent, which means that the situation is stable.'[2]

When Slovenia joined the EU, optimistic expectations arose that the increased contact with the EU law as well as increasing familiarity with the case law of the CJEU, its judicial methods and reasoning will substantially affect the national legal system and serve as a source of inspiration for a more fundamental legal reform. It was expected that the impact of EU law would go far beyond areas where this was formally required by EU law itself. In addition, it was aspired that the so called transformative power of EU (law) would also result in a fresh impetus for a transition of the judiciary as well and that working methods and judicial mentality of judges and overall legal culture in Slovenia would be gradually improved.

Since it is more than ten years after Slovenia's accession to the EU it is time to critically assess whether these expectations were perhaps too optimistic. European civil

* Professor of Civil Procedure and International Private Law, University of Ljubljana, Slovenia.

1 Assessment of the 2013 national reform programme and stability programme for Slovenia – Commission Staff Working Document, Brussels, 29.5.2013, (SWD (2013) 374 final) 30; The functioning of judicial systems and the situation of the economy in the European Union Member States, Strasbourg, 15 January 2013 (Report prepared for the European Commission (DG Justice)) 516.

2 Ibid.

procedure is certainly rapidly expanding and developing on the European level, in particular (but not limited to) the cross-border procedural instruments in the field of judicial co-operation in civil and commercial matters. The question, which this paper tries to shad some light on, however is, whether European civil procedure managed to make a substantial impact on Slovenia's national legal system and functioning of civil justice.

2. European Civil Procedure and Changes in National Legislation

2.1. *The 'Minimalistic Approach'*

Since Slovenia's accession to the EU, or more precisely since the accession negotiations started in the late nineties, European civil procedure received much scholarly attention in Slovenia. In addition judicial cooperation in civil matters is extensively included in curricula of judicial training programmes. Comparisons between EU law and national law are frequently discussed and examples from EU law often invoked as an argument in favour of possible reform of corresponding legal instruments in national law.

The legislature failed to follow this trend. There were very few legislative changes influenced by the development of European civil procedure in areas which fall outside of the scope of immediate applicability of EU law. This is not surprising as the Slovenian legislature remains passive even in areas of law, where intervention would be necessary in order to ensure effective transposition of EU directives and smooth application of EU regulations. The Slovenian legislature adopted a 'minimalistic approach'. Directives are (too) often transposed in a copy-paste manner, which in most instances cannot ensure effective application of EU law. On the other hand, there had almost never been any kind of transpositive measures regarding EU regulations (reaching beyond the mere notification of competent courts). Perhaps lessons as to how regulations, unlike directives, are directly applicable, 'backfired'. Namely they arose assumptions that the direct applicability means that no action of member states is required whatsoever. This assumption is however false; often, legislative interventions in national law are a necessary precondition for ensuring a smooth application of EU regulations. The passivity of Slovenian legislature caused numerous uncertainties and problems in regard to application of European civil procedure law. This paper doesn't aim to discuss the interface between national law and European civil procedure concerning application of cross-border regulations. The aspect is mentioned solely as an indication that European civil procedure remains seriously neglected by the Slovenian legislature.

2.2. *Cross-border Regulations as a 'Model Law' for National Legislation?*

As the EU law did not trigger a significant reform of national law in Slovenia even in areas where the intervention was immediately required, it could not be realistically expected that it would trigger such reform in areas where no such immediate reaction was required. For example, payment order procedure in national law remained unaffected by the EU Payment order regulation[3], although some of its features were invoked as appropriate model which could be implemented for a purely national payment order procedure. It was proposed, for example, that the extremely short time-limit for the defendant to raise an objection in the national payment order procedure (8 days[4]) should be prolonged. The Payment order Regulation, which provides for a time limit of 30 days, was reffered to as a model for an adequate solution.[5] The rule in Slovenian national law is particularly burdensome for the defendant, as the objection must be reasoned – it must include facts and evidence supporting it. Again, this was contrasted to the EU payment order regulation, where merely a non-reasoned objection is sufficient.

Regrettably, the legislator did not find much inspiration in the EU Small Claims Regulation[6] either and did not use the opportunity to extend (at least some) positive innovations from the European small claims procedure to domestic cases as well. True, the EU Small claims regulation, it must be openly admitted, was a failure. Nevertheless, certain rules of procedure in this regulation are an expression of general trends of reshaping small claims procedure and could be valuably used in purely national proceedings (e.g. flexibility of taking of evidence, strong reliance on principle of proportionality with appropriate focus on saving time and cost, possibility to depart from a strict application of 'loser pays' rule of cost reimbursement in case of disproportionate costs etc.). On the contrary, the small claims procedure under the Slovenian Civil Procedure Act (hereinafter CPA[7]) does not significantly differ from the procedure for regular cases.[8] Interestingly, the Slovenian legislature found an inspiration in the EU small claims directive merely in a point, where it probably should not have: concerning the monetary threshold for what constitutes small claim (2.000 EUR under the 2007 EU Small claims procedure Regulation). Not only because the appropriate level for what constitutes small claims depend on economic circumstances, but foremost because what should be considered a 'small claims' dispute in a cross-border legal relationship is not necessarily the same in purely domestic cases as well. Similarly, it is probably admissible, from the viewpoint of Art. 6 ECHR to restrict the parties' absolute right to have an oral hearing in cases of cross-border small claim proceedings (because it can result in disproportionate costs for a party residing abroad to either come to the oral hearing in another state or engage a lawyer there). Written small claims proceedings can be promoted in cross-border cases, but it is questionable whether the same logic can

3 Council Regulation (EC) 1896/2006 of the *European* Parliament and of the creating a European order for payment procedure [2006] OJ L399/1.

4 Art. 435 CPA and (concerning the similar instrument of 'enforcement on the basis of a trustworthy document', which is a kind of combination of payment order procedure and authorisation of enforcement, the same rule is set out in Art. 9 of the Enforcement of Judgments and Protective Measures Act.

5 E.g. Aleš Galič and Nina Betetto, *Evropsko civilno procesno pravo* I (GV Založba 2011) 187.

6 Council Regulation 861/2007 of the European Parliament and of the Council establishing a European small claims procedure [2007] OJ L199/1.

7 *Zakon o pravdnem postopku*, Official Gazette No. 73/07 (consolidated version).

8 For a short overview of small claims proceedings in Slovenia see Aleš Galič and Christopher Hodges, 'Slovenia' in Christopher Hodges, Iris Benöhr and Naomi Creutzfeldt-Banda (eds), *Consumer ADR in Europe* (Hart Publishing 2012) 205.

apply to purely domestic cases.[9] These examples show that an uncritical extension of applicability of legal instruments, intended for cross border cases, to purely domestic cases is not always the preferred solution. In some instances, no such caveats exist and instruments, intended for cross-border cases, can be a 'model law' for purely domestic cases. The EU Mediation directive is one such instrument.[10] It applies to cross-border cases, but the Commission aspired to achieve a more general approximation of mediation laws of member states, hoping that when transposing the directive, would not limit the applicability of corresponding legislation to cross border cases. Slovenia fulfilled this expectation with the adoption of the 2008 Mediation Act

2.3. *Effects of the CJEU's Understanding of Indirect Discrimination*

Changes in national legislation, having broader implications, can also be caused by the case law of the CJEU. For example in *Mund & Fester*[11], the Court stated that a national provision of civil procedure which, in the case of a judgment to be enforced in another Member State, authorises seizure simply on the ground that enforcement is to take place abroad, whereas for a judgment to be enforced within the national territory, the provision authorises seizure only if if there exists *periculum in mora*, is a covert form of discrimination which is not justified by objective circumstances. The Court held that such a rule more often adversely affects foreigners than nationals (as it will be foreigners who will more often have assets abroad and thus enforcement abroad shall be necessary). The court added, somewhat idealistically, that with the EU-wide system of enforcement and recognition, the need to have a judgment enforced abroad, puts the creditor in no bigger risk than in cases, where the debtor's property is located in the country where the judgment was rendered.[12] Art. 258 of the Slovenian Enforcement of Judgments and Protective Measures Act (1998) contained the same rule as the German law, which the ECJ scrutinised in *Mund & Fester*. As a direct consequence of the judgment, the Slovenian law was changed.[13] However the ECJ's broad understanding of 'indirect discrimination' when it comes to procedural norms (plus the idealistic perception that due to the

9 The ECtHR holds that in proceedings before a court of first and only instance the right to a 'public hearing' under Article 6 §1 entails an entitlement to an 'oral hearing' unless there are exceptional circumstances that justify dispensing with such a hearing requirements. Demands of efficiency and economy can be considered in this regard. Nevertheless the Court applied this standard solely in social security and similar disputes (e.g. *Miller v Sweden*, App no 55853/00 (EctHR, 8 February 2005) whereas in 'pure' civil cases the position is rigid. If a (1) party requires an oral hearing, and (2) facts, not merely questions of law, are in dispute, he is entitled to have an oral hearing (3) at least on one instance. Council of Europe, Guide on Article 6: Right to a Fair Trial (civil limb) (Council of Europe/European Court of Human Rights 2013) 47–48.

10 Council Directive (EC) 2008/52/EC on certain aspects of mediation in civil and commercial matters [2008] OJ L136/3.

11 Case C-389/92 *Mund & Fester v. Firma Hatrex International Trasport* [1994] ECR 1–467.

12 Ibid.

13 Zakon o spremembah in dopolnitvah Zakona o izvršbi in zavarovanju (ZIZ-C), Official Gazette No. 17/2006. See also the Explanatory memorandum (Predlog Zakona, prva obravnava, 24.11.2005, EVA 2005–2011–0008).

successful judicial co-operation in civil matters it is no longer a valid point of distinguishing, whether the case contains cross-border elements) could have further and more far reaching consequences for national procedural law in the future. It would not be so difficult to argue that e.g. a lack of video-link technology for conducting hearings on average negatively affects foreigners more than own nationals (because on average, they have a longer distance to travel to the hearing). Turning to another point, national rules, requiring litigants residing abroad to appoint representatives for service within the jurisdiction, might constitute a case of indirect discrimination as well. Such rules, in practical consequence, affect foreign nationals far more often than own nationals. It was expected that the CJEU would address this issue in the *Alder* case, where it was asked whether rules the national law, requiring appointment of such representatives, is compatible with EU law (both the TFEU[14] as well as the Cross border service of documents Regulation).[15] Nevertheless, since the CJEU found that the national law (*in casu*: Polish) is already incompatible with Art. 1 of the 1393/2007 Regulation (and contravenes fundamental procedural guarantees), it did not need to examine whether it was also incompatible with the prohibition of discrimination based on nationality (Art. 18 TFEU).

3. European Civil Procedure and Changes in National Case Law

3.1. General Considerations

Rules of European civil procedure have sometimes resulted in changes in case law with broader implications, not merely limited to cross-border cases. For example 18 CPA provides that in case of lack of international jurisdiction the court shall strike out the claim. This has traditionally been understood - and not limited to cases where another court has exclusive jurisdiction - in sense that the court should strike out the claim immediately, before serving it on the defendant. Understandably, when such practice prevailed, it was impossible to make the instrument of jurisdiction by submission (tacit jurisdiction agreement) effective - the defendant simply never got the chance to submit to a Slovenian court lacking jurisdiction. It took some time before the courts realised that immediate striking out of the claim for lack of jurisdiction is incompatible with the rules on tacit jurisdiction agreements in the Brussels I Regulation and that (except in cases, where it is established that courts of another member state have exclusive jurisdiction) the claim must first be served on the defendant. It was equally difficult to change practice of the courts, which automatically insisted that the claimant should, in cases of cross-border service, immediately ensure for a proper translation (which is incompatible with Art. 7 of the 1393/2007 Regulation on cross-border service of judicial documents[16]). Important changes in courts' practice, relevant also for purely domestic

14 The Treaty on the Functioning of the European Union.

15 Case C-325/11 *Krystyna Alder and Ewald Alder v. Sabina Orlowska and Czeslaw Orlowski* [2012] ECR I-0000.

16 Council Regulation (EC) 1393/2007 on the service in the Member States of judicial and extrajudicial documents in civil or commercial matters [2007] OJ L324.

cases, were also triggered by the European Enforcement Order Regulation.[17] Since pursuant to this Regulation a European Enforcement Order may only be issued if the defaulting defendant was given proper information (about interest claimed, about exercising the right of defense, about whether or not he may defend himself in person etc.) the standard letters which courts serve on the defendant simultaneously with serving the claim, have been substantially changed and additional information included therein.

Whereas the above findings relate to international jurisdiction clauses, even more important changes in operation of national law are required concerning territorial jurisdiction and arbitration clauses. This goes on account of the EU consumer protection law – the Unfair contract terms Directive. Following the CJEU's decisions in *Pénzügyi Lízing*[18], *Elisa María Mostaza Claro*[19] *and Asturcom*[20], in case of pre-formulated territorial jurisdiction and arbitration clauses in consumer contracts, their validity, from the viewpoint of unfair contract clauses, should be examined *ex officio*. Thus, in such cases, arbitration tribunal cannot acquire jurisdiction by virtue of a consumer's entering an appearance without invoking invalidity of arbitration agreement. This is a fundamental change that hopefully will not remain unnoticed by Slovenian arbitration tribunals and state courts. True, the Slovenian Arbitration Act already prohibits pre-dispute arbitration clauses in consumer contracts (Art. 44), but it has been left to the consumer, who entered appearance in arbitration, to invoke the invalidity of the arbitration clause.

Concerning the language of proceedings an important change in the change law was triggered by the CJEU's position on the use of minority languages in court proceedings. The Slovenian law has since long permitted Italian or Hungarian language to be used in court proceedings in officially bilingual areas.[21] It has however remained controversial whether only members of the minority could avail themselves to this right or also nationals of Italy or Hungary (or, in fact, any EU citizens speaking these languages). After the CJEU's judgment in *Rüffer*[22], the question is settled: since the EU law guarantees non-discrimination on grounds of nationality, every EU citizen of EU can avail himself to the rights concerning language of civil proceedings, although these rights were originally intended only to protect the Italian and Hungarian minority in Slovenia.

3.2. *Fictitious Domestic Service instead of Service Abroad*

Numerous legal systems have successfully invented ways of avoiding service abroad by providing for different – essentially fictitious – methods of service within their own

17 Council Regulation 805/2004 creating a European enforcement order for uncontested claims [2004] OJ L143.

18 Case C-137/08 *Pénzügyi Lízing Zrt v. Ferenc Schneider* (CJEU,, 9 November 2010).

19 Case C-168/05 *Elisa María Mostaza Claro v. Centro Móvil Milenium SL* [2006] ECR I-10421.

20 Case C-40/08 *Asturcom Telecomunicaciones SL v. Cristina Rodríguez Nogueira* [2009] ECR I-9579.

21 See e.g. Lojze Ude in Lojze Ude et al., *Pravdni postopek – zakon s komentarjem* (Vol 1, GV Založba, Uradni list, 2005) 62–63.

22 Case C-322/13 *Ulrike Elfriede Grauel Rüffer v. Katerina Pokorná* [2014] ECLI:EU:C:2014:189.

jurisdiction. In Slovenia Art. 146 CPA provides that a foreign party must appoint in Slovenia a representative, authorised to accept service. If a party complies with this obligation, service abroad is no longer necessary and if it doesn't, the court will appoint a special curator authorised to accept service on her behalf and serve documents on him. The question arose whether rules of domestic law, which enable for avoiding service in another member state, are compatible with the Regulation No. 1393/2007, in other words whether methods of cross-border service contained in the regulation (e.g. direct service, service through transmitting and receiving authority, service by registered post with acknowledgment of receipt) are mandatory or merely optional. The CJEU has answered this question in the *Alder* case.[23] The CJEU chose not to follow the patterns established in the framework of the 1965 Hague Convention, but rather relied on the opinion of the AG *Bot* who held that 'far-reaching developments in the matter since it acquired a Community dimension entail a re-assessment of the relationship between the rules evolved from Regulation No 1393/2007 and national laws of civil procedure'.[24] The Court concluded that except in situations, explicitely foreseen in the Regulation, if the person to be served with the judicial document resides abroad, the service of that document necessarily comes within the scope of Regulation No 1393/2007 and must, therefore, be carried out by the means put in place by the regulation to that end, as provided for by Article 1(1) thereof. The regulation thus precludes a procedure for notional service such as that (*in casu*) of the Polish national law.

Following the CJEU's decision in the Alder case, the prevailing case law in Slovenia changed and courts no more require litigants from other EU member states to appoint such representatives in Slovenia. It is not entirely sure whether the *Alder* case really requires that change. It should be noted that in *Alder*, the CJEU scrutinised the Polish system, where the sanction for the party's failure to appoint a representative for service was draconic – all further documents were simply left in court's file and the service was deemed to be therewith effected). In Slovenia, courts proceeded in a different manner – it had to appoint a special guardian to a foreign litigant and serve documents on him (with expectation that such guardian would then send the documents to the foreign party or otherwise establish contact with it). Thus, this was not a genuinely fictitious service. Since in *Alder* the CJEU based its findings on inadmissibility of the Polish system on balancing procedural guarantees of the parties concernend, it is not sure that the outcome would be the same if the Slovenian system – where the sanction for non-compliance is milder and does not necessarily lead to purely fictitious service – had been scrutinised. It is however true that the Slovenian system as well enabled for avoiding another important guarantee enshrined in the EU Service of Documents Regulation – the need to ensure that the party receives the document in the language he or she understands. In any case, the Slovenian courts chose the 'safe way' and stopped requiring litigants from other EU member states to appoint representatives for service in Slovenia. Unlike in Austria, no change in the CPA was implemented.

23 Case C-325/11 *Krystyna Alder and Ewald Alder v. Sabina Orlowska and Czeslaw Orlowski* [2012] ECR I-0000.

24 Opinion of AG Bot of 20 September 2012 in Case C-325/11 para. 31.

Although based (*inter alia*) on concerns for an effective protection of fundamental rights, the CJEU Alder judgment (and consequently the change in the case law of Slovenian courts) is not immune to criticism. The CJEU is right in holding that methods of fictitious (deemed) service jeopardise the fundamental right to be heard. Therefore they may only be implemented as the last resort, when absolutely necessary. Thereby competing values (right of effective access to court on the one hand and the right to be heard on the other hand) need to be carefully balanced. But what CJEU failed to sufficiently take into account is that the fictitious domestic service was not implemented automatically (unlike the French system of *remise au parquet* or the US system of 'piercing the veil' for the purpose of service to a foreign company). Rather, it was a sanction for the claimants' failure to follow the court's instruction to nominate a representative authorised to accept service. Had the parties complied with that court order, there would have been no fictitious service at all. In such procedural situation it is, in order to assess compatibility with fundamental rights, wrong to take into account just the consequence (the sanction); one should in the first place examine whether the initial court order was such that it put an unnecessary burden upon the parties, whether it was unreasonably difficult for the parties to comply with it and what the overall consequence for the functioning of the justice system of such rule are. The obligation to nominate a representative authorised to accept service in the country where court proceedings are pending, is not too burdensome and difficult to comply with. Especially when this concerns not the defendants but the claimants (like in *Alder*), it is not unreasonable to expect that they shall first consider and the comply with the law of the country, where they themselves chose to bring proceedings. For example, a party can – instead of appointing such a representative, simply appoint a local attorney (with full powers of representation). After all, numerous procedural systems of the EU member states adhere to the obligatory representation by lawyers in civil procedure meaning that there can be no litigants in person. This inevitably means that a party will in any case need to nominate a member of the local bar (more precisely: authorised to appear in the courts of the given member state) where proceedings are pending and this – in consequence – also means that all documents are be served to the (local) attorney. This is a domestic service, without any need of translations. It is difficult to see how it can be incompatible with the fundamental rights if the party must nominate a representative, authorised to accept service, in the country of proceedings, though it is perfectly acceptable if the party must appoint a fully authorised representative there (which also results in a disappearance of the need for cross-border service). It seems unfair to conclude that legal systems of those member states, which provide for an obligation for foreign resident parties to appoint representatives for service within jurisdiction *per se* violate fundamental rights of (foreign) parties, whereas legal systems of those member states, which provide for an obligation of full representation by a qualified attorney do not. True, the mandatory representation by attorneys does not apply only to parties residing abroad but also to domestic parties. On the contrary, the obligation to appoint a representative, authorised to accept service, affects only parties residing abroad (who will be in most cases foreign citizens). However, this differentiation is no more an issue from the viewpoint of fundamental rights (right to be heard) but merely from the viewpoint of indirect discrimination. This should be examined solely on the basis of Art. 18 TFEU. The test in this regard should be whether there exist any justified grounds for such an – what it undoubtedly is – indirect discrimination.

In any case, the developments after *Alder* show another trend which goes hand-in-hand with the 'Europeanisation' of civil procedure – namely its 'constitutionalisation'. Albeit in Slovenia the constitutionalisation has affected the national civil procedure even before the Europeanisation. This goes on account of the Constitutional Court and its decisions which impacted both the legislation (numerous norms of civil procedure acts have been invalidated by the constitutional courts) as well as case law of regular courts. In Slovenia, the Constitutional Court has (*inter alia*) jurisdiction to examine constitutional complaints against the judgments of regular (ordinary) courts for alleged breaches of fundamental (constitutional) rights.[25] After the exhaustion of all available remedies, individual litigants can have the judgment reached in their case reassessed by the Constitutional Court. The Constitutional Court may only look into 'constitutional matters', leaving the interpretation of ordinary law to the general courts.[26] Nevertheless, in case of very activist constitutional court, a relation between the constitutional court and the ordinary courts, particularly the supreme court, can be very conflict-ridden. In this regard, the Slovenian Constitutional Court has not been as activist and confrontational in relation to the regular judiciary as some other constitutional courts in the region.

4. European Civil Procedure beyond the Judicial Co-operation in Civil Matters: Disclosure of Evidence in the Antitrust Damages Directive

Important EU instruments which directly affect national civil procedure, perhaps even to a greater extent than the 'judicial co-operation in civil matters' can be found in those areas of EU law, which are primarily concerned with substantive, not procedural law. EU consumer protection law in regard to unfair contract terms, has already been mentioned. Other such fields are, e.g. alternative dispute resolution of consumer disputes, protection of collective interests (both in the field of consumer law as well as competition law), effective protection of IP rights and private enforcement of antitrust.

Procedural tools aimed at access to information in general and disclosure of documents in particular are crucial for effectiveness of private antitrust enforcement litigation and for ensuring a more genuine equality of arms. It is therefore not surprising that in the new Antitrust Damages Directive[27] precisely the rules on disclosure of evidence are of central importance (Arts. 5–6). The impact of this new instrument and

25 See e.g. Study on Individual Access to Constitutional Justice – Adopted by the Venice Commission at its 85th Plenary Session in Venice (17–18 December 2010, Strasbourg, 27 January 2011) Study N° 538/2009. www.venice.coe.int/webforms/documents/default.aspx?pdffile=CDL-AD(2010)039rev-e (accessed 10 January 2016), see also *Zdenek* Kühn, *The Judiciary in Central and Eastern Europe: Mechanical Jurisprudence in Transformation* (Martinus Nijhof 2011) 196.

26 See Study on Individual Access to Constitutional Justice (n 25) 55.

27 Council Directive (EC) 2014/104/EU on certain rules governing actions for damages under national law for infringements of the competition law provisions of the Member States and of the European Union [2014] OJ L349.

its underlying policy will not remain isolated to the specific area of antitrust litigation. Neither does the transposition of the requirements of the Directive concerning disclosure of evidence require merely a technical adjustment of the member states' procedural laws. On the contrary, a re-evaluation of the very fundamental principles governing administration of justice in civil and commercial cases will be required at least in certain member states. Such developments on the EU level, at least to a certain extent inspired by the well-settled rules in common law jurisdictions, although restricted to specific types of legal disputes, might trigger a move towards a more general recognition of the duty to disclose and produce documents in national legislations.[28]

The existing principles of Slovenian civil procedure, relating to disclosure of evidence, are very restrictive[29] and partially based on erroneous premise, typical for the traditional civil law approach, namely that the privilege against self-incrimination applies in civil cases in the same manner as in the criminal cases.[30] Based on a German and Austrian heritage of civil procedure, the principle that no one was obliged to help his adversary win the case *(nemo tenetur edere contra se)* or 'to put weapons in the hand of its opponent' applied, perhaps due to a serious misconception that principles of criminal procedure, notably the privilege against self-incrimination, are easily and automatically transferable to civil cases.[31] On the contrary, the principle '*nemo contra se edere tenetur*' is explicitly rejected in the Antitrust Damages Directive: Art. 5(5) stipulates that 'the interest of undertakings to avoid damages actions following an infringement of the competition rules does not constitute an interest that warrants protection.' Experience and recent developments abroad – also in civil law systems and on a level of academic attempts to harmonise civil procedure[32] – show that this restrictive approach to disclosure of documents needs to be re-examined. Extensive rules on disclosure of evidence in the new Antitrust Damages Directive will inevitably support this trend.

The required transposition of the Directive's requirements should therefore be perceived as a positive step. This step will however be successful only if a general reassessment of the disclosure of evidence in Slovenian civil procedure law follows. It

28 Gerhard Wagner, 'Harmonisation of Civil Procedure: Policy Perspectives' in X Kramer and R van Rhee (eds), *Civil Litigation in a Globalising World (*Springer, 2012) 105.

29 The first key difference between the Slovenian system and the common law concept of disclosure is that in Slovenia a party has no duty to disclose unfavourable documents in its possession on its own motion. The second major difference is that in Slovenia the party seeking disclosure must sufficiently identify the document he or she is requesting. A request for production of a document can only be successful if the party is able to describe the content of the requested document in sufficient detail so as to clearly identify it. The regulation is hence merely proper to avoid the concealing of the documents, the existence of which is already known, but not the documents, for which the seeking party does not know to a quite concrete degree what their contents are or that the other party even possesses them.

30 The structure of a civil case differs from a criminal one as it inevitably involves the need to strike a proper balance in the conflict of rights between two equal parties. When striving to protect the constitutional rights or legitimate expectations of one party in a civil case, the court should take into account equally important constitutional rights and legitimate interests of the other party in dispute.

31 Cf: SinišaTriva, Velimir Belajec and Mihaljo Dika, *Građansko parnično procesno pravo* (Školska knjiga 1986) 425: '*Nobody is obliged to testify against himself and to offer evidence, unfavourable to him.*'

32 See Article 16.2 of the ALI / UNIDROIT Principles of Transnational Civil Procedure of 2004.

would be naïve to expect that such move could be achieved if it remained isolated to the very specific area of private enforcement of antitrust. The new disclosure system cannot be effectively applied by judges, who in all other cases, perceive the scope and the purpose of disclosure in an entirely different manner and still adhere to the perception that a party cannot be required to disclose evidence which harms his case. The role of practicing attorneys should not be underestimated either. Preparing requests for disclosure of evidence requires a great amount of diligent and time-consuming work. This can hardly be expected from those lawyers who even find it difficult to engage in a diligent and timely search for information and documents in possession of their own clients. Currently there are merely a handful of law firms in Slovenia, which are realistically capable of properly applying the disclosure mechanism set out in the Directive.

5. The Right to Have a Matter Submitted to the CJEU for a Preliminary Ruling as a Part of the Guarantee of Access to a Court, Established by Law

There is no lack of opportunity for national judges to have contacts with EU law and to respond correctly to challenges that it posed to them. In accordance with Art. 3a of the Constitution EU law must be, as the Constitutional Court recalls[33], applied *ex officio*. More importanty, already a long time before a similar requirement has been adopted by the ECtHR[34], the Constitutional Court established a requirement that regular courts must give reasons for rejection of the party's motion for referral to the CJEU for a preliminary ruling. The Constitutional Court holds that the CJEU must be considered a court, established by law, for purposes of Art. 23 of the Slovenian Constitution, which guarantees access to court. Rules concerning jurisdiction and composition of the court are a part of a precondition of a court being established by law. Hence, if a party is unlawfully deprived by the Supreme Court, as the highest court of the regular judiciary, to have her case brought to the CJEU for a preliminary ruling, this can constitute a breach of constitutional guarantees (the so called 'right to a natural judge'). The Constitutional court can examine such breach in proceedings on constitutional complaint against the Supreme Court's judgment. This does not mean that the Constitutional Court will exercise a full review of a 'fourth instance'. Howbeit it is required that the Supreme Court, if it rejects the party's (sufficiently substantiated) request to have a matter submitted for a preliminary ruling to the CJEU, it must provide sufficient reasons for this rejection.[35] Thus, it must either explain why the question of EU law is not relevant for the case or that it has already been clarified by the CJEU or, as added in another case, that the matter can be considered an *acte clair*.[36] If the latter applies, the Supreme Court must closely apply the CJEU's standards as to when a matter can be considered an *acte clair*. In principle, the positions of the Slovenian Constitutional

33 E.g. the Constitutional Court, Nr. Up-1056/11 of 4 December 2012.

34 *Schipani v Italy* App no 38369/09 (ECtHR, 21 July 2015).

35 The Constitutional Court, Nr. Up-1056/11 of 4 December 2012.

36 The Constitutional Court, Nr. Up-797/14 of 12 March 2015.

Court emphasising on the requirement of referrals to the CJEU for preliminary ruling are in accord with those of the CJEU in e.g. *Köbler*.[37] Yet the practical problem in Slovenia, which is a persistent legacy from the communist era, is that lawyers representing parties to proceedings still too rarely engage in serious legal analyisis, insufficiently argue legal aspects of the case and abstain from case-based reasoning, even when there is no EU law dimension. It can thus hardly be expected that they will adequately be able to argue issues of EU law and engage in case-based reasoning relying on the case law of the CJEU.

6. The Impact of the European Civil Procedure on the Legal Method and Mentality of National Judges

The last sentence of preceding paragraph already brings us to another point. Reform of codified law is important, but what is more crucial is whether one decade of application of EU law has resulted in any positive changes in legal culture and in particular, whether it affected judicial mentality and working methods of judges and lawyers.

Many authors contend that there exists a deep continuity in the methods of legal reasoning employed by judges in the post-communist countries originating from the communist era.[38] For example, legal communities in these countries have difficulties in embracing the idea of judicial flexibility and judicial discretion. The majority of judges and lawyers still prefer a rigid procedural regime with detailed rules, frowns upon the use of open-ended terms in procedural legislation any rejects attempts to provide more room for the judge to adapt the unfolding of proceedings to the characteristics of each particular case. In addition, a preference to formalistic or downright bureaucratic approach to adjudication is still present, which in the same is inevitably linked to lack of appropriate skills and experience of case management, particularly in a complex litigation.[39] Furthermore, judges are insufficiently used of applying the principle of proportionality, for example, when it comes to striking a proper balance between the goal of reaching adequate results on the merits, on the one hand, and the need to control cost and time, on the other.

Does European civil procedure have a potential to produce positive effects here? I believe that – on the long term – it does. The trend of an emphasised reliance on judicial discretion and the judge's reliance on general principles is not only characteristic for contemporary reforms of 'national civil procedure'. It is increasingly characteristic also for the 'European civil procedure'. The affirmation of flexibility in European civil procedure started with the the adoption of so called 'second generation regulations' (European Enforcement order for uncontested claims, European order for payment, European small claims procedure), when European civil procedure has slowly started to detach itself from traditional domains of international private law. In addition to measures adopted in the field of judicial cooperation in civil matters (Art. 81 TFEU) the increased use of open ended terms and reliance on judicial discretion also is typical for

37 Case C-224/01 *Gerhard Kobler v Austria* [2003] ECR I-10239.
38 Kühn (n 25) 165–166.
39 Kühn (n 25) XV and 165.

the sector specific legislation, adopted on the internatl market legal basis (Art. 114 TFEU), e.g. in areas of consumer protection, enforcement of antitrust and intellectual property rights.[40] In these procedural instruments the idea of procedural flexibility, use of open-ended norms and judicial discretion is deeply rooted (e.g. concerning conduct of small claims procedure, including fundamental issues such as scheduling an oral hearing, taking evidence, deciding on reimbursement of costs…).[41] What should also be mentioned in this regard is the growing influence of the Charter of Fundamental Rights of the European Union (hereinafter: the Charter) on the European civil procedure. We are currently in the middle of the process of a genuine 'constitutionalisation of European civil procedure'. In this context especially the principle of proportionality is increasingly referred to in the case law of the CJEU.

So, will the increased contact of Slovenian judges and practicing lawyers with the EU law as well as increasing familiarity with the case law of the CJEU cause the resentment towards judicial discretion and procedural flexibility in Slovenian judiciary to fade away? I am not entirely optimistic. Firstly, an unfortunate fact is that many Slovenian judges still perceive European law as 'foreign law'. And just like they are not very keen on accepting arguments based in comparative law and learning examples from foreign laws (considering it a 'waste of time'), they are not very enthusiastic about the 'EU law argument' either. Although this field of law is rapidly expanding, the fact is that an average Slovenian judge still very rarely deals with a case involving a cross-border element, which is a prerequisite for triggering application of instruments adopted in the field of judicial cooperation. For most judges it is almost a 'once in a life-time' situation. If the presence of European civil procedure does not penetrate into a day-to-day work of judges, the influence of this law to the legal method of the Slovenian judiciary will remain low.

Most importantly, the building of a mutual trust, the cornerstone of the judicial co-operation in civil matters, has so far not concerned genuine, real trust, but rather a required, imposed trust. Moreover it has often been repeated – but without any convincing evidence – that in order to increase mutual trust there should be more uniform law, thus more EU legislative intervention.[42] Why exactly more uniform legislation would necessarily result in more mutual trust concerning the functioning of national judiciaries however remains unanswered. How then are there such deficiencies and delays in application of uniform EU law in certain member states although full harmonisation has already been achieved in the given area (e.g. concerning communication between the requested and the requesting court pursuant

40 See in detail Rafal Manko, 'Europeanisation of Civil Procedure: Towards Common Minimum Standards?' [2015] (European Parliamentary Research service) 20 ff.

41 E.g. pursuant to Art. 20 of the European Payment Order Regulation (similarly, Art. 18 of the European Small Claims Regulation). *the defendant may* apply for an extraordinary review of the European Order for Payment (*inter alia*) where the *defendant was prevented from objecting to the claim … due to force majeure or extraordinary circumstances* without any fault on his part, provided that he acts *promptly*. Not just a Slovenian judge would expect more precise grounds for an extraordinary review of a final judicial decision, but foremost would expect at least a specific time-limit for filing of such a review.

42 Typically Rafal Manko (n 40) 4.

the Service of documents regulation)? Are the malfunctions in certain national judiciaries really a result of an inadequate legislation – so they can be cured by creating new legislation – either on national or on EU level? Even on the national level, it is relatively easy to change the legislation, but changing the working habits, judicial mentality, work ethics, quality of the bar etc. is a much more difficult task. The situation in former communist countries of Central and Eastern Europe proves that merely the change of legislation cannot be a proper cure for dysfunctional judiciaries and that the potential to change the judicial mentality by legislative reform is very limited.[43] If reform of the national legislation cannot cure such problems, why then to expect that the EU legislation could fulfill that task? The mutual trust however will – if one speaks of a genuine and well deserved trust – only grow if the functioning of judiciaries is improved. Yet, irronically, the principle of mutual trust, as promoted in EU legislation, is inevitably linked to the 'dogma' that the judiciaries of individual member states are all equally fit and trustworthy concerning expectation that they will correctly apply the law and safeguard fundamental rights. The main objective on the Commission's agenda concerning European civil procedure is to achieve a genuine 'free movement of judgments', without any hindrances in form of review in exequatur proceedings in the country of enforcement. Logically, it is difficult to push for introduction of such system and in the same time openly admit that there are serious deficiencies in functioning of civil justice in certain member states. Thus, although it seems paradoxical on the face of it, it is in fact not surprising that this push for more integration inevitably resulted in the EU bodies turning 'a blind eye' on existing problems in functioning of national judiciaries. Yet a long term efficiency of the policy of mutual trust would require much more action than (rapid) drafting of new legislation[44] (and much more than undisputed creativity in finding legal bases for extended legislative competences). What is needed is a clear message that where functioning of judiciary is still defective – be it concerning quality on merits, procedural fairness or concerning delays – action is needed to improve it.

The EU 'action' suggested in the preceding paragraph is not predominantly a legislative one though.[45] Rather, a more critical oversight of national judiciaries by EU institutions would be required in order to achieve that they will gradually genuinely be on a more equal footing concerning quality and integrity. It there exists a rule of law crisis in one or more member states, this should be openly admitted. The problem should

43 See e.g. Alan Uzelac, 'Survival of the third legal tradition?' (2010) 49 SCLR 377, 390; Kühn (n 25) 155 ff.

44 Paul Oberhammer, 'Abolition of Exequatur' (2010) 3 IPrax 197, 203.

45 This is not to suggest that 'legal isolationism' is advocated here. Particularly for small countries, such as Slovenia, there is one very positive effect of EU-wide harmonisation of law, which is often neglected. In small countries it is inevitable that domestic case law develops slowly as it simply takes more time before sufficient relevant issues reach courts. In addition, there is less critical dialectic confrontation of ideas on the academic level. It happens all too often that certain legal issues are not debated in the legal writing at all or that there is merely one author who discusses a certain topic. As these two important limbs of development of law – case law and doctrine – can not sufficiently fulfil their role, the result is an aggravated lack of legal certainty and predictability. In case of broad harmonisation of law however, case law of foreign courts and positions of foreign legal scolars can be used as a valuable persuasive authority.

be seriously approached either by formal (including sanctions) or informal means in order to remedy the shortcomings and to address systemic threats to the rule of law. Only in this manner can the genuine – and objectively well founded – mutual trust gradually grow. Such approach would – at least on the long term – serve the idea of a genuine European integration – for the benefit of its citizen and companies – in the field of judicial cooperation and European civil procedure in general much better. Promoting the mutual trust should not result in an unwarranted complacency within certain national judiciaries. This is not to suggest that there was no such scrutiny resulting in positive reforms in the member states so far. But more should be done. It sounds paradoxical but promoting instruments which imply 'less trust' (such as a closer and more critical oversight of functioning of national judiciaries by the EU institutions) will bring about 'more trust' on the long term.

Anna Wallerman*

THE CURIOUS INCIDENT OF THE DOG IN THE NIGHT-TIME: EUROPEANISATION OF CIVIL PROCEDURE IN SWEDEN

'Is there any point to which you would wish to draw my attention?'
'To the curious incident of the dog in the night-time.'
'The dog did nothing in the night-time.'
'That was the curious incident,' remarked Sherlock Holmes.[1]

1. Introduction

In the political discussion preceding Sweden's entry into the EU, and earlier that into the EEA, procedural law was largely left aside. No procedural consequences of EU membership appears to have been foreseen by the legislator.[2] With the exception of a brief statement to the effect that Union law should be enforced in accordance with national procedural law, possible implications for domestic procedural rules were not even commented upon in the *travaux préparatoires*.[3]

As it is now firmly established that where substantive EU law rights are concerned, the so-called procedural autonomy of the Member States does not exclude EU law impact even on core issues of civil procedure in purely domestic disputes,[4] it would be gratifying to be able to say that during the 20 years that Sweden has been a member of the Union, there has been an increased awareness of the procedural implications of EU law. Unfortunately, however, this does not appear to be the case. Instead, the depiction of the Europeanisation of civil procedure in Sweden is a story of a process halted before it

* LL.D., Associate Senior Lecturer, Department of Law, University of Gothenburg.
1 Sir Arthur Conan Doyle, *The Memoirs of Sherlock Holmes: The Adventure of Silver Blaze.*
2 Per Henrik Lindblom, 'EG-rättslig påverkan och forskningsuppgifter på enskilda rättsområden – 3.3.5 Civilprocessrätt och exekutionsrätt' in Ulf Göranson (ed) *Europagemenskap och rättsvetenskap* (Iustus 1992) 122 noted in 1992 that civil procedure 'does not belong to the topics that come to mind first when discussing the content and impact of EU law on Swedish law' (122), but nevertheless predicted that the EU accession would entail significant changes for civil procedure and for the judicial organisation (128–135).
3 Government bill 1994/95:19, 525; cf government bill 1991/92:170, appendix 2, 8 concerning the EEA accession.
4 Eg Verica Trstenjak and Erwin Beysen, 'European consumer protection law: *Curia semper dabit remedium?*' [2011] 48 CMLR 95, 98–99 with references.

started: of what might have happened, but did not; of what ought to have been done, but was omitted.

The Swedish approach to implementation of EU law in the field of procedures and remedies is mostly a restrictive one. Clear obligations are complied with, but there is little evidence of loyalty going beyond the minimum requirements. European legal acts are typically implemented, but not considered as possible models for national reform beyond their immediate scope of application. Spillovers are rare; as are legislative and judicial attempts at proactivity or avoidance of fragmentation. The case law of the Court of Justice for the European Union (ECJ) is often overlooked or interpreted narrowly, and courts only occasionally consider the need for harmonious interpretation or setting aside of national procedural rules. In procedural law textbooks, the subject is treated with little interest; the most widely used textbook, a six-volume series originally authored by the late professor Per Olof Ekelöf, discusses the principles of effectiveness and equivalence in one small-print paragraph and otherwise briefly mentions the preliminary ruling institute and the Brussels and Rome regimes,[5] whereas its two main (and more modern) competitors each devote 3–4 pages to EU law aspects.[6] As one of these textbooks remarks, many 'still to this day appear to be of the opinion that EU law only rarely has any more profond impact on Swedish civil procedure.'[7]

This chapter will begin with a brief survey of how the legislator and the judiciary have responded to EU law developments (section 2), excluding measures only affecting cross-border cases. It will then proceed to discuss the reception of the preliminary ruling institute (section 3), the interpretation and effects of some Swedish references to the ECJ (section 4) and the compatibility of Swedish civil procedure with the ECJ case law on *ex officio* powers of the court (section 5). It will argue that while the Swedish approach ensures a certain minimum EU law compliance, it fails to connect EU law with ongoing domestic procedural debates and does not appear to appreciate the importance of ECJ jurisprudence as a source of law. The chapter will, however, end on a cautiously optimistic note, outlining a current development which may signal increased interest in and awareness of EU law matters (section 6) before summarising the conclusions (section 7).

2. EU-induced Legal Developments

EU influence on Swedish civil procedure is perhaps most noticeable in alternative dispute resolution (ADR). The implementation of the Mediation Directive[8] not only led to the introduction of an act on mediation – a matter until then largely unregulated in

5 Per Olof Ekelöf, Henrik Edelstam and Mikael Pauli, *Rättegång II* (9th edn, Norstedts 2015) 143; Ekelöf and Edelstam, *Rättegång I* (8th edn, Norstedts 2002) 76–78; Lars Welamson and Johan Munck, *Processen i hovrätt och Högsta domstolen: Rättegång VI* (4th edn, Norstedts 2011) 151.

6 Bengt Lindell, *Civilprocessen* (3rd edn, Iustus 2012) 58–60; Peter Westberg, *Civilrättskipning* (2nd edn, Norstedts 2013) 123–126.

7 Westberg (n 6) 125. All quotations are originally in Swedish and translated by the author.

8 Directive 2008/52/EC on certain aspects of mediation in civil and commercial matters [2008] OJ L 136/3.

Sweden – but also to a general strenghtening of the courts' role in promoting mediation and amicable settlements.[9] The mediation act also represents one of relatively few spillovers from EU to Swedish law, in that the act, unlike the directive, is applicable to both national and cross-border mediations.[10] Furthermore, the EU legal acts on consumer alternative[11] and online dispute resolution (ODR)[12] have been implemented by the enactment of a new act on consumer ADR, which entered into force in January 2016.

In both these cases, the legislator considered a new, specialised act to be the most appropriate form of implementation.[13] In many other cases, however, the Swedish legislator has instead chosen to incorporate procedural rules in substantive legal acts. The Directive on the enforcement of intellectual property rights,[14] for instance, was implemented into Swedish law by changes in a number of acts covering diverse types of intellectual property rights, such as trademarks, patents, literary and artistic works, and industrial design; it has largely failed to attract the attention of procedural lawyers. Similarly, both the Consumer Sales Directive[15] and previously the Unfair Terms Directive[16] were implemented as substantive provisions with little regard, both at the time of implementation and in subsequent legal development, of the procedural implications of those acts. While this approach can be seen as an extension of the EU's legislative strategy relying on substantive competences for procedural harmonisation, it arguably has the effect of obscuring the procedural importance of EU law.

In another legislative development, Sweden in 2007 – following a Commission infringement procedure alleging a breach of Art 267(3) TFEU consisting in Swedish last instance courts not requesting a sufficient number of preliminary rulings[17] – adopted an act with certain rules concerning preliminary rulings. Somewhat surprisingly, this act does not restate the national courts' general right/obligation to request such rulings; instead it obliges courts adjudicating at last instance to reason their decision *not* to refer a question to the ECJ, if a party has requested a such referral. The effect of the act has however been limited, as the reasoning provided by the courts is generally kept brief and highly standardised.[18]

9 Government bill 2010/11:128, 19–20.

10 Ibid 48.

11 Directive 2013/11/EU on alternative dispute resolution for consumer disputes and amending Regulation (EC) No 2006/2004 and Directive 2009/22/EC (Directive on consumer ADR) [2013] OJ L165/63.

12 Regulation (EU) No 524/2013 on online dispute resolution for consumer disputes and amending Regulation (EC) No 2006/2004 and Directive 2009/22/EC (Regulation on consumer ODR) [2013] OJ L165/1.

13 Government bill 2010/11:128, 38; government bill 2014/15:128, 25.

14 Directive 2004/48/EC on the enforcement of intellectual property rights [2004] OJ L195/16.

15 Directive 1999/44/EC on certain aspects of the ale of consumer goods and associated guarantees [1999] OJ L171/12.

16 Directive 93/13/EEC on unfair terms in consumer contracts [1993] OJ L095/29.

17 Com 2003/2161 Procedure against the Kingdom of Sweden, C(2004) 3899, 13 October 2004.

18 Martin Johansson and Sara Ahmed, 'De högsta domstolsinstansernas motiveringsskyldighet vid beslut att inte inhämta förhandsavgörande från EG-domstolen – en papperstiger?' [2009] Europarättslig tidskrift (ERT) 783.

When it comes to the judiciary, there are a handful of cases where courts appear to make concessions to accommodate for EU law requirements. To give but a few examples, mention can be made of the Supreme Court's acknowledgement of the courts' duty to raise possible violations of EU competition law *ex officio,* and that an arbitral award contrary to EU competition law is to be considered contrary to public policy and therefore declared void;[19] only the latter conclusion can, however, properly be construed as an example of Europeanisation, as the former had previously been arrived at in legal writing already on the basis of domestic law.[20] EU law oriented reasoning can also be found on appellate level. For instance, one appellate court recently drew extensively on EU law in the interpretation of a time limit laid down in national public procurement law.[21] Another court of appeal has ruled that the Stockholm district court, which has exclusive jurisdiction over community design cases, should be considered a 'special court', rather than a 'certain court', within the meaning of section 10:19 of the Code of Judicial Procedure (CJP),[22] with the consequence that the appellate court achieved a mandate to raise the jurisdiction question *ex officio*, and thereby could ensure that the EU requirement of concentrated jurisdiction was complied with *in casu*.[23] Far from being hailed as a model of harmonious interpretation, however, the latter judgment has been termed 'peculiar' by one influential commentator.[24]

Furthermore, the Supreme Court has on occasion considered the EU law compatibility of Swedish rules of civil procedure and found them to surpass the threshold. It has, for instance, found that the ruling in *Eco Swiss*[25] does not render inapplicable section 4 of the Arbitration Act,[26] which holds that an arbitral tribunal is competent to arbitrate in competition law disputes, and that an arbitration agreement to that effect consequently is valid, as long as the dispute only concerns private law aspects of competition law.[27] It has also held that EU law does not require that a subsequent ruling of the ECJ be considered a reason to grant an application for a *de novo* trial, if the judgment in the first proceedings has gained the force of *res judicata*.[28] Both of these conclusions appear to be in line with ECJ case law.

19 *GDL Transport Öst AB v Sandås Transport Kalmar Aktiebolag* [2013] NJA 2013 p 1017 and *Finants Collect OÜ v ATB Tjänst* [2015] NJA 2015 p 433. In both cases the Supreme Court cited *Eco Swiss* [n 25] in support for its conclusion.

20 Torbjörn Andersson, *Dispositionsprinicpen och EG:s konkurrensregler: En studie i snittet av svensk civilprocess och EG-rätten* (Iustus 1999) 121; Torbjörn Andersson, 'Svensk skiljedomsrätt och EG:s konkurrensrätt – reflektioner i anledning av EG-domstolens avgörande i Eco Swiss-målet' [1999/00] Juridisk tidskrift (JT) 446, 466–467.

21 Hovrätten för Västra Sverige, case T-3349/15, judgment of 16 Dec 2015 (nyr).

22 Rättegångsbalken, 1942:740.

23 *Svensk Export Vodka AB v F.Y.* [2010] RH 2010:67.

24 Peter Fitger *et al,* Kommentar till rättegångsbalken, at 10:17 <www.zeteo.se> last updated October 2015, accessed 3 January 2016.

25 Case C-126/97 *Eco Swiss China Tima Ltd v Benetton International NV* [1999] ECLI:EU:C:1999:269.

26 Lag (1999:116) om skiljeförfarande.

27 *Danska staten genom BornholmsTrafikken v Ystad Hamn Logistik Aktiebolag* [2008] NJA 2008 p 120.

28 *J.A et al* [2013] NJA 2013 p 42.

3. 'There Appears to Be No Need for Special Rules'

With the exception of the above-mentioned obligation to provide reasons for non-referrals, the preliminary ruling institute is unregulated in Swedish law. Although the first draft EEA Act included a section on the, as was then of relevance, advisory opinions of the EFTA Court,[29] that provision was struck out of the bill by the government as it was deemed 'unnecessary'.[30] At the accession to the EU, the legislator took a similar position. It argued that the referral of a question to the ECJ in accordance with the preliminary ruling procedure was a 'case management decision', and as the courts were already accustomed to make (other) case management decisions, it was argued that there 'appeared to be no need for special rules' concerning the forms for or consequences of such decisions.[31] This position was again upheld ten years into the Swedish Union membership.[32] Consequently, Swedish courts rely directly on the Treaty when requesting preliminary rulings from the ECJ.

In this author's opinion, the government stance is regrettable. A provision on preliminary rulings of the ECJ in the CJP could have had at least two positive effects. Firstly, it would have had a pedagogical value. It is submitted that the preparedness of Swedish courts to make use of the preliminary ruling procedure may have been greater if a provision granting them the competence to do so had been incorporated directly in the CJP.[33] Secondly, if the matter had been regulated nationally, those rules could also have addressed certain accessory questions.[34] For instance, the lack of specific regulation on the right of appeal most likely means that a court's decision to refer a case to the ECJ can be appealed.[35] This in turn exposes Sweden to the inconveniences following from the ECJ's *Cartesio* judgment,[36] which have hitherto been acknowledged only in literature.[37]

29 See departmental promemoria Ds 1992:14, 9 (section 18 of the proposed Act), 47. Also Lindblom (n 2) 133 expressed as his opinion that national rules must be issued regarding the preliminary ruling procedure.

30 Government bill 1991/92:170, appendix 1, 147–148.

31 Government bill 1994/95:19, 528.

32 Government bill 2005/06:157, 17.

33 Cf however Morten Broberg and Niels Fenger, 'Förhandsavgöranden från svenska domstolar. Är svenska domstolar väsentligt mindre benägna att begära förhandsavgöranden än domstolar i andra medlemsstater?' [2015] ERT 769, who claim that Swedish courts are no less prone to request preliminary rulings than the courts in other Member States.

34 Cf Per Henrik Lindblom, who notes that Art 267 TFEU gives rise to 'many intricate and purely procedural questions' at the national level ('Harmony of the legal spheres: A Swedish view on the construction of a unified European procedural law' [1997] ERPL 11, 13).

35 49:7 CJP; cf Henrik Matz, 'Arbetsdomstolen undanröjer tingsrätts beslut om förhandsavgörande – några EG-processrättsliga synpunkter' [2002] ERT 313, 316.

36 Case C-210/06 *Cartesio Oktató és Szolgáltó bt* [2008] ECLI:EU:C:2008:723. The procedural aspects of the case have been thoroughly explored by Michal Bobek, '*Cartesio* – Appeals Against an Order to Refer under Article 234(2) of the EC Treaty Revisited' [2010] CJQ 307.

37 Anna Wallerman, 'Överklagande av beslut att begära förhandsavgörande: Några reflektioner med anledning av EFTA-domstolens avgörande i *Irish Bank*' [2013] ERT 308, 313.

However, the choice not to regulate the Swedish courts' referrals to first the EFTA and subsequently the EU Court is all the more remarkable if put into the context of a then recent reform of the CJP: the introduction of a domestic preliminary ruling procedure. In 1989, in an effort to aid the establishment of precedent in certain areas of private law, rules were introduced to allow a court of first instance (tingsrätt) to refer a question on the interpretation of points of law to the Supreme Court (Högsta domstolen), whose ruling would then become the basis on which the first instance court would decide the case before it, as well as a precedent to be adhered to in future cases.[38]

The Swedish preliminary ruling system or the 'Supreme Court lift', as it is commonly nicknamed, is in several respects more restrictive than that stipulated in what is now Art 267 TFEU. A referral is only possible if the parties agree to it and if the case is amenable to out-of-court settlement.[39] Furthermore, the referred questions are subject to the appeal admissibility system in the Supreme Court, and are only admitted if a ruling on the matter is needed in order to provide guidance to the courts on an unclear matter of law; this is a limitation rather more strict than the *acte clair* doctrine of the ECJ.[40]

Nevertheless, the kinship between the two procedures is so obvious that it seems quite incredible that it was not taken into consideration in the legislative procedure, particularly given that the reforms were introduced – at least in the time perception of conservative procedural lawyers – virtually simultaneously. Yet there is no reference to or comparison with the EU mechanism to be found in the *travaux préparatoires* of the CJP reform, and as we have seen the matter was not even mentioned in those of the EEA/EU accession.[41] If the parallel had been established, special rules concerning a court's referral to the Supreme Court – such as for instance the prohibition to appeal against such decisions (CJP 49:8) – could have been extended also to the EU preliminary ruling procedure. The failure to make the connection between the two is a striking illustration of how far apart EU law and civil procedure were in the mind of the legislator.

4. Swedish References for Preliminary Rulings

There are relatively few cases where the ECJ directly addresses Swedish civil procedure; this appears to be a natural consequence of the abovementioned disinclination in Sweden to make the connection between procedural issues and EU law. Nevertheless, a couple of more significant ECJ rulings in the field of procedures and remedies have been handed down in response to references from Swedish courts. One such case is the *Unibet* judgment,[42] which concerned the right to bring an action for judicial review as well as

38 Sections 42:17 a and 56:13–15 CJP.

39 A requirement of an agreement between the parties not to appeal against the district court judgment was removed in 1999.

40 The appeal admissibility system will be discussed further in section 4 below.

41 The similarities were, however, pointed out in scholarly writing, see Lindblom (n 2) 133.

42 Case C-432/05 *Unibet (London) Ltd and Unibet (International) Ltd v Justitiekanslern* [2007] ECLI:EU:C:2007:163.

an accessory question of interim relief. Unibet sought to challenge the Swedish law on lotteries as being contrary to EU law, and it sought to do so by bringing a self-standing action for a declaratory judgment on that compatibility question before Swedish civil courts. This claim was however declared, by courts in all three instances, inadmissible under Swedish law, which only permits actions for declaratory judgments if there is a(n alleged) concrete legal relationship by which one of the parties is entitled to a specific private law remedy (13:2 CJP).[43] Merely being bound by law to undertake or refrain from certain operations does not constitute a legal relationship within the meaning of section 13:2 CJP.[44]

Failing to gain admittance to the courts based on Swedish rules on standing, Unibet claimed that a right to bring a free-standing action for judicial review followed from EU law. Had it been successful in this claim, it would undoubtedly have been a landmark decision for Swedish civil procedure, which not only does not provide for such actions but is also by tradition sceptical of judicial review as such and at the time permitted courts to disapply acts of the government or parliament only if they were manifestly in conflict with higher-ranking rules – a requirement which had already had to be set aside in EU law cases to accommodate for the principle of supremacy. The ECJ however held that EU law does not of itself require such an action to be available before domestic courts.[45] This appears to have been interpreted to the effect that the question lacked EU relevance; where *Unibet* is mentioned in commentaries to the CJP, it is mentioned only as a Supreme Court case reinforcing the previous interpretation of the rule.[46] The referral to the ECJ is left out.

However, it is worth pointing out that *Unibet* was in fact a closer call than may have been fully appreciated. The response of the ECJ was conditioned on there being another avenue for the claimant to instigate judicial review, at least as a preliminary issue, without having to expose itself to administrative or criminal sanctions.[47] In the case at hand, there were at least two such possibilities available to the applicant. However, should a case arise where no such avenues are available – which is perhaps unlikely, but hardly inconceivable – the conclusion of *Unibet* appears to be that a way to admit a free-standing

43 Fitger *et al* (n 24) at 13:2; Ekelöf, Edelstam and Pauli (n 5) 127.

44 Sweden's unwillingness to accept actions brought by parties not personally involved in the legal relationship was also an issue in Case C-263/08 *Djurgården-Lilla Värtans Miljöskyddförening v Stockholms kommun genom dess marknämnd* [2009] ECLI:EU:C:2009:631, where a rule of Swedish environmental procedure substantially circumscribing the right of non-governmental organisations to bring appeals against certain environmental law decisions was declared contrary to EU law. The rule was subsequently amended, providing for increased access to court for such organisations. As the case concerned public law aspects of environmental law and does not appear to have entailed any consequences beyond this field, it will not be discussed further in this contribution.

45 *Unibet* (n 42) paras 40, 71.

46 Fitger *et al* (n 24) at 13:2; Christer Thornefors, Rättegångsbalk (1942:740) 13 kap. 2 §, Lexino 2012-07-01 <www.karnovgroup.se> last updated 1 July 2012, accessed 3 January 2016.

47 *Unibet* (n 42) paras 41, 65.

judicial review action before Swedish courts must be found.[48] As we have seen, this would require either legislative intervention or judicial creativity.

Another Swedish reference to the ECJ resulted in the *Lyckeskog* judgment,[49] in which the ECJ established that the mandatory referral in Art 267(3) TFEU does not apply to appellate courts, even if access to the Supreme Court is significantly limited and dependent on a declaration of admissibility. While this ruling essentially conforms to prior views on the relationship between different levels in the court hierarchy and does not appear to have had any direct implications for the workings of civil procedure in Sweden, the ECJ also stated that the Supreme Court's duty to request a preliminary ruling must be carried out either before deciding on the admissibility of the appeal, or at a 'later stage', ie when admission has been granted.[50]

According to Swedish law, an appeal to the Supreme Court may be declared admissible *inter alia* if the case raises a question of law and it is important for the guidance of the application of law that the appeal be considered by the Supreme Court (CJP 54:10). However, in a ruling from 2004 the Supreme Court has held that the rule on admissibility of appeals must be read in conjunction with Art 267 TFEU.[51] It went on to state, with reference to the ruling in *Lyckeskog*, that where an obligation to refer to the ECJ exists, the conditions for admissibility of the appeal should be considered fulfilled. On the face of the judgment, this would seem to amount to substituting the admissibility criteria in the CJP for the Art 267(3) criteria on the obligation to request preliminary rulings; if the latter criteria are met, the Supreme Court is obliged to refer the case to the ECJ, and thus the criteria for a declaration of admissibility should be deemed fulfilled.[52]

In light of the restrictive *CILFIT*[53] exceptions to the Art 267(3) obligation, it cannot be doubted that such a development would amount to a significant relief for parties seeking to bring an appeal to the Supreme Court. While the two regimes essentially share the *acte éclairé* criterion, allowing for failure to refer (in the case of the ECJ) and for a refusal to consider the appeal (in the case of the Supreme Court) if the point of law has already been decided, the *acte clair* doctrine of *CILFIT* declares that a court of last instance must refer to the ECJ unless the answer to the question of law is obvious.[54] The equivalent criterion in CJP 54:10 – that of 'importance for the guidance of the application of law' – is significantly narrower, allowing for a declaration of admissibility mainly in order to overrule previous precedents or where there is a real risk of

48 See Magnus Schmauch, 'EG-domstolens dom i Unibet-målet – ett nationellt perspektiv' [2007] ERT 691, 702–703; Xavier Groussot and Henrik Wenander, 'Self-standing actions for judicial review and the Swedish Factortame' [2007] CJQ 376, 382.

49 Case C-99/00 *Kenny Roland Lyckeskog* [2002], ECLI:EU:C:2002:329.

50 Ibid para 18.

51 *Luftfartsverket* [2004] NJA 2004 p 735.

52 On a perhaps mostly academical note, it can be noted that the issuing of a declaration of admissibility is optional. This means that the Supreme Court may refuse a declaration, even though the admissibility criteria are fulfilled. To exercise that discretion in a case where the fulfillment of the criteria is presumed pursuant to the *Lyckeskog*-inspired reasoning above would seem, however, to beat the point.

53 Case 283/81 *CILFIT and Others v Ministry of Health* [1982] ECLI:EU:C:1982:335.

54 Ibid para 16.

contradictory judgments in the lower courts, and only if the public interest requires it.[55]

However, it is highly doubtful if this is what the Supreme Court really intended. If so, the judgment should have entailed a significant increase in the number of appeals admitted, which cannot be discerned.[56] A recent judgment may serve to explain this continuously restrictive practise. In this ruling, the Supreme Court remarked that 'if a question concerning the interpretation of the Treaties and the validity and interpretation of Union legal acts arises before the Supreme Court and *the Court considers a preliminary ruling necessary to rule on the matter*, the Court is obliged to request that the ECJ delivers such a preliminary ruling'.[57] The reasoning seems to imply that the Supreme Court has interpreted the necessity criterion in Art 267(3) as relating to the necessity of a preliminary ruling as perceived by the Supreme Court itself, rather than to the necessity of a decision on the matter, which should then be made by the ECJ unless the *CILFIT* exceptions are applicable. Such an interpretation of Art 267 TFEU may account for both the sparseness of ECJ references from the Supreme Court and the lack of significant impact of *Lyckeskog* and of the 2004 ruling on the admissibility of appeals from the appellate level to the Supreme Court.[58]

To summarise, while in both cases there have been attempts to accommodate the rulings of the ECJ, the reception appears to have been relatively superficial. More systemic nuances of the judgments tend to be overlooked, and the interpretation of even fundamental primary rules such as Art 267 TFEU is not free from misconceptions. This shortsightedness becomes all the more noticeable when, in the next section, we move on to consider ECJ case law stemming from other Member States.

5. *Ex Officio* Powers of the Courts

There remain several civil procedural issues where serious doubts must be entertained as to the EU compatibility of Swedish civil procedure. This section will look into one of the most apparent problems, which relate to consumer procedures and different manifestations of the party autonomy principle.

55 See government bill 1971:45, p 88.

56 Statistics provided by the central administrative body for the judiciary (Domstolsverket) show that although the relative number of appeals admitted to the Supreme Court was at a low in 2003, the subsequent rise has not brought the proportion of admitted appeals above the level of 2001, and it remains on average lower than it was in the 1990s.

57 *Finants Collect* NJA 2015 p 433 (emphasis added). A similar statement can be found in *K.H* [2008] NJA 2008 p 259. This can be compared to the ECJ's description of the Art 267 TFEU criteria laid out eg in C-160/14 *João Filipe Ferreira da Silva e Brito and Others v Estado Português* [2015] ECLI:EU:C:2015:565, paras 38–39.

58 This is not the first time that the interpretation of Art 267 TFEU has given rise to difficulties in the Swedish context. One commentator has remarked that the difference between the optional referral of subsection 2 and the mandatory referral of subsection 3 is difficult to grasp, as, 'if a decision is necessary, then surely a preliminary ruling should always be requested?' (Lindell (n 6) 59). This understanding of the Article fails to notice the difference consisting in that lower courts are mandated to make the necessary decision themselves, whereas courts of last instance are not.

The ECJ has established that in consumer law disputes, a national court must *inter alia* be empowered to 1) decline territorial jurisdiction of its own motion, where jurisdiction has been conferred on it by an unfair term;[59] 2) investigate of its own motion whether a clause possesses certain attributes (such as not having been individually negociated) which would entail its being deemed unfair;[60] 3) award other remedies than those sought by the claimant, unless an amendment of the application or the bringing of a new action is allowed;[61] and 4), in the case of an unfair arbitration agreement, annul an arbitration award even if the consumer failed to rely on the unfairness of the agreement before the arbitral tribunal and, if national law provides for the annulment or nullity of arbitration awards contrary to public policy, even if the consumer subsequently failed to challenge the award before the court.[62]

Swedish civil procedure does not provide for any express exception to the party autonomy principle in consumer disputes and indeed only contains quite negligible consumer protection mechanisms.[63] Most of the abovementioned requirements are contrary to established interpretations. As for 1), prorogation agreements can be disapplied for unfairness, but only following the request of a party, and if the party enters an appearance in substance this amounts to a binding acceptance of the jurisdiction of the court.[64] As for 2), courts are not allowed to disapply a prorogation clause unless one of the parties has requested it, and are then restricted to the grounds relied on by that party.[65] As for 3), although the main rule states that an action, once filed, cannot be amended, there are a number of circumstances under which claimants could change their original request for relief (CJP 13:3). However, such changes will be precluded at certain stages of the proceedings and it is unclear if the possibilities afforded to claimants in this regard will be sufficient to constitute an effective remedy. Lastly, as for 4), although an arbitration clause in a consumer contract would normally not be binding, consumers would nevertheless have to file an objection to this effect with the arbitral tribunal and failure to do so would prevent them from later relying on the invalidity of the clause in a challenge against the award.[66]

59 Joined Cases C-240/98 to C-244/98 *Océano Grupo Editorial SA v Rocío Murciano Quintero and Salvat Editores SA v José Luis Copano Badillo and Others* [2000] ECLI:EU:C:2000:346; Case C-243/08 *Pannon GSM Zrt. v Erzsébet Sustikné Győrfi* [2009] ECLI:EU:C:2009:350.

60 Case C-137/08 *VB Pénzügyi Lízing Zrt. v Ferenc Schneider* [2010] ECLI:EU:C:2010:659.

61 Case C-32/12 *Soledad Duartes Hueros v Autobica SA and Automóviles Citroën España SA* [2013] ECLI:EU:C:2013:637. One wonders, however, if even the possibility to bring a new action unhindered by the principle of *res judicata* would surpass the effectiveness bar; few consumer claims are substantial enough to warrant one set of court proceedings, let alone two (cf. Case C-268/06 *Impact v Minister for Agriculture and Food and Others* [2008] ECLI:EU:C:2008:223 para 53).

62 Case C-168/05 *Elisa María Mostaza Claro v Centro Móvil Milenium SL* [2006] ECLI:EU:C:2006:675; Case C-40/08 *Asturcom Telecomunicaciones SL v Christina Rodríguez Nogueira* [2009] ECLI:EU:C:2009:615.

63 The only provision specifically addressing consumers is section 10:8 a CJP, which allows consumers to bring action before their own court of domicile. Furthermore, many consumer disputes are presumably covered by section 18:8 a, which limits the amount of recoverable costs in small claims cases.

64 CJP 10:16, 18.

65 CJP 10:18, 17:3; Fitger *et al* (n 24) at 17:12.

66 Arbitration Act §§ 6, 34.

Some of these difficulties could well be avoided by a quick-witted judge or overcome by harmonious interpretation or other means available to the judiciary and not necessarily amounting to *contra legem* application of law. This pragmatic approach would, however, hardly contribute to legal clarity and foreseeability. Furthermore, these issues probably go deeper than to mere technicalities of consumer procedure. The common denominator for the situations mentioned above is the tension between on the one hand the principle of party autonomy heralded by Swedish civil procedure and actually strenghtened in the most recent major reform in 2005,[67] and on the other hand the effectiveness imperative of EU law, which tends to put a stronger emphasis on the substantive outcome. At least as regards the relief to be awarded, the legal and factual grounds, and the evidence supporting it, the *ex officio* powers of the courts have mostly remained constant since the enactment of the CJP in 1942. Recent developments have, if anything, lessened them; for instance, the courts no longer have power to order any *ex officio* taking of evidence.[68] This tension represents possibly the gravest EU induced challenge of Swedish civil procedure, and it is one that neither the Supreme Court nor the legislator seem keen to take on. While the issues discussed above have on occasion been brought forward by legal scholars,[69] no legislative action has been taken and case law of the Supreme or appellate courts provides little guidance on how Swedish consumer procedure can be rendered compatible with EU law requirements.

6. Grass Root Harmonisation: The Way Forward?

Perhaps the way forward in the Europeanisation of civil procedure lies not with the legislator, or even with the Supreme Court. If change is to be had, it may perhaps sooner arise from the lower levels of the judicial hierarchy.

The development that eventually led up to the ECJ's *Fransson*[70] ruling may, even though the ruling itself mainly concerned criminal and administrative procedure and the legal discussion leading up to it was concerned more with the European Convention on Human Rights (ECHR) than the EU Charter of Fundamental Rights (EUCFR), be illustrative of a tendency; we will be less concerned with the procedural details than with the actions and attitudes of the actors.

The Swedish system prescribing both administrative and criminal sanctions for certain acts of tax fraud, and offering no coordination between the procedures, was accepted by the European Court of Human Rights in *Rosenquist*, handed down in 2004, but had been questioned in legal writing following the *Zolotukhin* ruling of the same

67 SFS 2005:683; see government bill 2004/05:131 p 1, where one of the aims of the proposal is said to be to 'stress the parties' responsibility for the progress of the proceedings.'

68 CJP 35:6 as amended in 2005.

69 Torbjörn Andersson, 'EG-domstolens avgörande i Océano-målet samt konsumenträtt och forumregler i Sverige' [2001] ERT 565; Jori Munukka, 'Oskälighet måste alltid prövas ex officio – men konsumenten kan avstå från detta' [2010] ERT 353, 362–365; Martin Sunnqvist, 'Allmän domstols officialprövning, materiella processledning och upplysande verksamhet i konsumenttvister' [2011/12] JT 164.

70 Case C-617/10 *Åklagaren v Hans Åkerberg Fransson* [2013] ECLI:EU:C:2013:105.

court in 2009.[71] In 2009 and 2010 respectively the Supreme Adminstrative Court and the Supreme Court both considered the matter, and both concluded that the Swedish system was compatible, or at least not manifestly incompatible, with the European *ne bis in idem* regime, and thus to be upheld.[72] These judgments, which may be considered typical for a judiciary highly loyal to the legislator and markedly reluctant to embark on judicial review, were themselves subject to extensive scholarly criticism,[73] but it is the conduct (or lack thereof) of two other main actors that will interest us here.

First, that of the legislator. Two of the five Supreme Court Justices in the 2010 decision explicitly urged the legislator to take action to resolve the unclear question of compatibility between European and domestic law;[74] the Supreme Court later held that the 2010 decision must be seen as 'expressing the view that it would be most natural to let the changed interpretation of the ECHR [brought on by *Zolotukhin*] be assessed and handled by the legislator', rather than by judicial law-making.[75] This call, however, remained unanswered; no legislative action was taken. It is indicative of its level of vexation that the Supreme Court, in its first judgment on the issue following the ECJ's rejection of the Swedish system in *Fransson*, pointed to the legislative inertia as a reason to set aside domestic rules deemed incompatible with the EUCFR and itself take on the law-making role from which the legislator appeared to have abdicated.[76]

Secondly, the rulings of 2009 and 2010 triggered a series of decisions which has been described as a 'rebellion'[77] among courts of first and second instance, in which courts declined to hear cases of tax fraud where the accused had priorly been subject to administrative proceedings, citing European law and explicitly rejecting the reasoning of the Supreme Court. This 'rebellion' attracted much attention in legal and scholarly discussion, but the Supreme Court declined to neither confirm nor overrule its previous decision. It is against this backdrop that the decision of a northern district court to refer the *Fransson* case to the ECJ should be considered. As the position of the Supreme Court was clear and as, as a district court, it was under no obligation to request a preliminary ruling, it is difficult not to interpret the referral as an attempt to circumvent or even overthrow the case law of the Supreme Court; this is all the more so as the discussion

71 *Rosenquist v Sweden*, App no 60619/00 (ECtHR, 14 September 2004); *Sergey Zolotukhin v Russia*, App no 14939/03 (ECtHR, 10 February 2009).

72 *B.H v Skatteverket* [2009] RÅ 2009 ref 94; *The Prosecutor v M.J* [2010] NJA 2010 p 168.

73 See Ola Zetterquist, 'Högsta domstolens och Regeringsrättens bedömning av förenligheten av det svenska skattetillägget/skattebrottet med dubbelbestraffningsförbudet i Europakonventionen' [2010] ERT 592, 593 with references.

74 *M.J* [2010] NJA 2010 p 168: dissenting opinion of Justice Lindskog, para 9; concurring opinion of Justice Lambertz, para 7.

75 *The Prosecutor v P.-M.P* [2013] NJA 2013 p 502 (Grand Chamber), para 57.

76 Ibid para 58.

77 See eg Fredrik Stenhammar 'Internationell anarki i svenska domstolar? Ett folkrättsligt perspektiv på 'HD-upproret' om skattetilläggen' [2011/12] JT 477; Katarina Fast, 'Tusen skäl att förekomma istället för att förekommas – en kommentar till dubbelbestraffningsfallen i EU-domstolen och Högsta domstolen 2013' [2013/14] JT 24, 25 and 35.

until that point had been centered on the ECHR, and it was not obvious that the case had a sufficient EU law component to come within the scope of the EUCFR.[78]

Seen from this perspective, the judicial[79] and legislative[80] actions taken in the wake of *Fransson* can be considered the result of Europeanisation prompted from the judicial grass roots, which may prove to be the most effective way of europeanising Swedish civil procedure. This is especially so as the civil procedure reforms of the latest decades have resulted in an empowerment of (lower-instance) courts, whose discretionary case management powers have increased significantly.[81] Among those discretionary powers is that to request preliminary rulings from the ECJ; a tool at the disposal of even the smallest and remotest first-instance court, which guarantees that bottom-up Europeanisation does not have to be slower or less efficient than a top-down approach originating with the legislator or the Supreme Court. As the tendency – if it really is one – is still in its infancy, it would however be premature to issue any predictions in this regard without serious reserve.

7. Of Barking and Biting

It is perhaps as it is said, that barking dogs seldom bite. The bark itself is certainly of very little value, even though it could be argued that the mere acknowledgement that a rule has European origins may affect its application. Loyal implementation of EU law and harmonious interpretation of national law, which in the end makes direct reliance on Union legal rules redundant, is fully compatible with the doctrine of decentralised enforcement, could well ensure full EU law effectiveness, and is clearly to be preferred over loudly-payed lip service to Union legal principles.

However, the lack of bark in this case does not appear to signify an effective bite. Not unlike the watchdog encountered by Sherlock Holmes, the Swedish legislator in particular, but also the judiciary, appear to react to clearly defined requirements and unambiguous violations of Union law, but to fail to identify problems of a more complex nature and indeed to lack a holistic understanding of EU law in this regard. It seems that EU law impact on civil procedure is regarded as a surprising exception, rather than as a recurring or ongoing development.

As we have seen in the foregoing, there are serious compatibility issues with EU law, which have not been satisfactorily addressed by neither the legislator nor the judiciary. These issues can hardly be resolved by anything less than a thorough overhaul at least of the principle of party autonomy and court passivity, and quite possibly of other areas of

78 This interpretation would be in line with the inter-court competition theory advocated by Karen Alter, 'Explaining National Court Acceptance of European Court Jurisprudence: A Critical Evaluation of Theories of Legal Integration' in Anne-Marie Slaughter, Alec Stone Sweet and J. H. H. Weiler (eds), *The European Court and National Courts – Doctrine and Jurisprudence* (Hart 1998) 227, 241–247.

79 Above-mentioned (n 75) *P.-M.P* [2013] NJA 2013 p 502 and several subsequent rulings.

80 Government bill 2014/2015:131 proposes changes in criminal and procedural aspects of tax law to prevent double trials.

81 See Anna Wallerman, *Om fakultativa regler: En studie av svensk och unionsrättslig reglering av skönsmässigt beslutsfattande i processrättsliga frågor* (2015, Iustus) 70–78.

procedural law as well. It remains to be seen if and when then most authoritative law-making bodies – the legislator and the Supreme Court – are prepared to take up this challenge – and if in the meanwhile judges at the lower levels of the judiciary will be willing to drive the development forward.

Bart Krans and
Anna Nylund*

CONCLUSIONS AND OUTLOOK

1. Impact, in Various Ways

The first and clear conclusion from the papers in this book is far from surprising: law of the European Union has impact on national civil procedure. This might concern primary EU law, secondary EU law, case law, fundamental legal principles or soft law instruments. At the same time, there seems to be significant variation on several aspects of the impact of EU law on national civil procedure law. It appears that there is variation in the level of influence and in the way EU law has impact on national procedural systems. The various countries display considerable variation as to the extent of the influence both in terms of width and depth of the impact. In some countries, many different areas of civil procedure have undergone some change, while in others change is more limited in scope, or on certain areas even absent. Some national civil procedure systems have faced profound impact in some areas. While change in other systems has, at least so far, been limited to a much lower level of just concerns peripheral areas. In some of the countries studied, Europeanisation of EU law has met more resistance than in others. In this concluding chapter, we go into some general conclusions by analysing and comparing the various contributions.

All of the papers are of course limited in length and scope. The particular viewpoint of contributors may perhaps be of influence on the various contributions. The scope of the book does not allow for a full picture of each of the countries. Within the boundaries of the limited scope of the findings of the various papers, some general conclusions and observations can be made.

2. General Conclusions from the Papers

a. Variety in impact. The first conclusion, already stated, is clear and not unexpected: the impact of varies by Member State. In section 4 of this chapter, we will go into this.

b. Diminishing procedural autonomy. As a starting point, national civil procedure law is up to the Member States. It follows from the procedural autonomy that, in absence of

* Bart Krans is Full Professor of Private Law and Civil Procedure Law at Leiden University, the Netherlands. Anna Nylund is Professor of Law at the Faculty of Law, University of Tromsø – The Arctic University of Norway.

EU law Member States are free to construct there procedural system as they deem fit. It is, in the words of the CJEU, for the national legal order of each Member State to establish them in accordance with the principle of procedural autonomy, provided, however, that those rules are not less favourable than those governing similar domestic situations (principle of equivalence) and that they do not make it excessively difficult or impossible in practice to exercise the rights conferred by EU law (principle of effectiveness).[1] Result of the growing influence of EU-law is that the procedural autonomy of Member States is diminishing.[2] The growing amount EU case law and EU rules have impact on the national procedural systems, at least up to a certain level.

It is widely known that EU law is relevant for procedural cross border issues.[3] The EU Treaty refers to 'judicial cooperation in civil matters having cross-border implications'.[4] However, EU law can be relevant for purely domestic cases. The case law on *ex officio* application of consumer law serves as an example for several Member States. The Directive on enforcement of intellectual property rights offers several examples.[5] In several Member States European case law is followed by a discussion addressing the question to what extent national law is compliant with the requirements formulated by the ECJ.[6] Some the contributions demonstrate that, at least in some Member States, there is also attention for Europeanisation through 'soft-measures'.[7]

c. Differences in approaches. At the EU level, there seems to be a more sectoral approach than at the national level. EU legislation concerns for example IP-rights or consumer sale. The new elements introduced by EU mechanisms need to find a decent place in the several national procedural systems.[8] The different way of law making at the EU level and at the national level may lead to questions on the national level. *Ex officio* application of EU consumer law, as resulted from the case law, may serve as an example.

1 See inter alia Case C-439/08 *Vlaamse federatie van verenigingen van Brood- en Banketbakkers, Ijsbereiders en Chocoladebewerkers (VEBIC) VZW* [2010] ECLI:EU:C:2010:739), para 63; Case C-310/14 *Nike European Operations Netherlands BV vs Sportland Oy* [2015] ECLI:EU:C:2015:690, para 28; and recently Case C-74/14 *'Eturas' UAB m.fl. mot Lietuvos Respublikos konkurencijos taryba* [2016] ECLI:EU:C:2016:42, para 32. See on procedural autonomy in general *inter alia* W. van Gerven, 'Of Rights, Remedies and Procedures' [2000] CMLR 2000, 501, John McKendrick, 'Modifying Procedural Autonomy: Better Protection for Community Rights' [2000] ERPL 565, Leo Flynn, 'When National Procedural Autonomy Meets the Effectiveness of Community law, Can it Survive the Impact [2008] 8 ERA Forum 245; and Anne-Marie Van den Bossche, 'Private Enforcement, Procedural Autonomy and Article 19(1) TEU: Two's Company, Three's a Crowd [2014] 33 Yearbook of European Law 41.

2 Some commentators argue there is no longer any procedural autonomy, just residual competencies. See Michael Bobek, 'Why there is no Principle of 'Procedural Autonomy' of the Member States, in B de Witte and Hans Micklitz (eds.) *The European Court of Justice and the Autonomy of Member States* (Intersentia 2011).

3 See on the Brussels I Regulation, European enforcement order cross etc. in Harsági this volume, section 3.

4 Art. 65 TFEU.

5 See Taelman in this volume, section 2 and Petersen in this volume, sections 2.2 and 2.3.

6 Hau in this volume, section 3.1 and Piszcz in this volume, section 4; compare Krans in this volume, section 3.3.

7 Piszcz in this volume, section 2.

8 See Bart Krans, 'EU Law and National Civil Procedure Law: An Invisible Pillar' 23 European Review of Private Law 567, 582–584.

The scope of EU instruments, such the Directive on IP-rights, may also lead to questions. The doctrine touches upon central concepts and ideas in civil procedure, including the role of judges and the division of labour between the court and the parties, thus it has spurred numerous requests for preliminary rulings and much discussion.[9]

d. Spontaneous harmonisation. As a result of the differences in approach in several Member Sates questions has arisen concerning spontaneous harmonisation.[10] In some Member States, it has been discussed if collective redress should be extended beyond consumer rights and competition cases. The Danish paper deals *inter alia* with the question how sectoral harmonisation can affect the coherence by requiring Member States to adopt rules for a particular type of dispute that do not affect the general values and principles of its national civil justice system.[11]

e. Uncertainty. New EU rules may be cause for a certain level of judicial uncertainty. For example, in the chapter on Germany it is mentioned that certain CJEU decisions are usually followed immediately by a discussion addressing the question to what extent the German law is compliant with requirements formulated by the CJEU.[12]

f. Lack of knowledge of EU law. Despite the ongoing training efforts through the European Judicial Training Network, many judges – and legal counsel – seems to have insufficient knowledge of EU law and policies on civil justice. The situation seems to be ubiquitous regardless of the length of membership. The rapid development of all three pillars of EU civil procedure contributes to inadequate awareness of the role of European law for national civil procedure. The result of deficient understanding of Europeanisation may be displayed in numerous ways, including lack of references to EU law and as treating EU law as foreign law.[13]

3. Differences between Member States

The variety in level and way of influence of EU law on national law is up to a certain level not surprising. There were differences between the procedural systems in the various Member States. The pre-existing situation was not equal. It explains why the influence of EU law varies.

At least five types of legal system are represented in the EU: civil law, common law, Nordic – or Scandinavian – law[14], former communist or socialist legal systems[15] and mixed legal systems.[16] Although Nordic and former communist systems can be

9 See inter alia Després in this volume, section 3; Wallerman in this volume, section 5; Krans in this volume, section 2; Taelman in this volume, section 2; Harsági this volume, section 4.2; Piszcz in this volume, section 4.

10 For example Petersen in this volume, section 3; Piszcz in this volume, section 2; and Krans in this volume, section 4.

11 Petersen in this volume, section 2.

12 Hau in this volume, section 3.1.

13 See Galič in this volume, section 2.1.

14 See e.g. Ulf Bernitz, 'What is Scandinavian law? Concept, characteristics, future' 50 Scand Stud Law 13.

15 Alan Uzelac, 'The Survival of the Third Tradition?' 49 Supreme Court Law Review 377.

16 Anna Nylund, 'Introduction to preparatory proceedings' in Laura Ervo and Anna Nylund (eds), *Current Trends in Preparatory Proceedings* (Springer forth coming).

considered as legal families in their own right, they have an affinity with civil law, sharing many fundamental structures and concepts with civil law. The legal system of the EU draws on elements from major European legal families: precedent and court made law comes from common law; the structure and organisation of courts from Romanic (or French) civil law; many legal concepts such as proportionality are transplants from Germanic (or German) civil law; and the principle of transparency from Nordic law. Former communist law has so far had a limited impact on EU law. Yet some elements of EU law are inherently foreign for some legal systems.

English civil procedure seems to be at odds with the views of the CJEU.[17]

In France, courts and case law had have a limited role in development of law and the legal system. Since the French revolution, the courts have had the role to be the mouth that speaks the law, not a law-maker. The French Supreme Court writes only scarce reasons for its decisions. The European courts, particularly the European Court of Human Rights (ECtHR), provide more extensive reasoning for their decisions. The reasoning of national courts sometimes influence the outcome in European courts. The French debate on whether the Supreme Courts should provide more extensive grounds for its decisions, illustrates how EU law may trigger far-reaching changes.[18]

German civil procedural thinking seems to have some traits that resonate with EU civil justice. This has resulted in a positive attitude towards European civil procedure.[19]

Slovenia and Poland seem to struggle with the question of judicial discretion and (excessive) formalism. The European courts seem to expect national court to have discretion and to use their discretionary powers. Literal interpretation gives little room for weighing and balancing legal principles and arguments pro and contra, contrary to the style of European courts. The different approach to legal methods and the role of courts, results in problems when national courts acts as EU courts applying EU law.[20]

However, attributing changes to the underlying legal system is not always fruitful. There are considerable differences between countries having a similar legal culture, structure of civil procedure or same legal institution. Some countries face rapid changes, while a neighbouring country may not do so.

Ex officio application of aspects of consumer and competition law has raised many questions in Sweden and the Netherlands, but does not seem to have spurred the same amount of interest in Belgium and Germany.[21] In Norway, *ex officio* application of EU law seems to cause less problems than in the Netherlands and Sweden.[22] The reason may be the court structure. Because Norway does not have administrative courts, general courts are used to mandatory, indispositive cases and balancing between public interest and public policy on the one hand, and individual interests on the other hand.

17 Andrews in this volume, section 5.
18 Després in this volume, section 4.
19 See Hau in this volume, section 2.2.2.
20 Galič in this volume, section 6 and Piszcz in this volume, section 4.
21 See Krans in this volume, section 2; and Wallerman in this volume, section 5.
22 Nylund in this volume, section 3.

Thirty years ago, Scandinavian Supreme Courts were reluctant towards judicial review, today the Danish and Norwegian Supreme Courts perceive their role differently, and act – at least to some extent – as genuinely European courts. The Swedish Supreme Courts are still desultory to acting as European courts and performing judicial review. Yet, Norwegian courts display the same reluctance towards direct dialogue with the Luxembourg courts as the Swedish courts, whereas the Danish courts are more open.[23]

The impact of Europeanisation on national civil procedure may also depend on specific features of the national civil procedure. The texts on Poland, Hungary and Slovenia indicate that these countries are still in the process of transforming their respective civil procedure systems from communist systems to 'western' civil procedure systems.[24]

Interestingly, the impact Europeanisation on Norwegian civil procedure does not seem to be radically smaller than in the other states, despite the fact that Norway is not a Member State. Europeanisation of civil procedure seems to permeate the law of EEA/ EFTA Member States.

4. Level of Knowledge and Understanding of EU Law amongst Judges

Another probable cause for differences between Member States are differences between knowledge of EU law and its methods and differences between knowledge of impact on national civil procedure.

Many of the contributions mention the lack of knowledge of EU law, and in particular, procedural dimensions of EU law, among judges (and lawyers in general). National judges must have sufficient knowledge of EU primary and secondary law and case law, and they must understand the method employed by the European courts.[25] Some Slovenian judges tend to treat EU law as foreign law.[26] Judges must also learn how to write references for preliminary rulings to actively contribute to clarification (and development) of European procedural law.[27]

The chapters on Poland and Slovenia, both former communist legal systems, discuss if difference in legal thinking and understanding of the role of courts could be a barrier to using European law. Both authors discuss the rendezvous of a legalistic national legal culture with an EU legal culture stressing flexibility and discretion.[28] Knowledge of EU civil procedure law – both legislation and case law – is not sufficient, national courts must also understand their role as European courts.[29] Hungarian courts – on the other hand – have been far more active in making requests for preliminary rulings.[30] By

23 See Nylund in this volume, section 4 and Wallerman in this volume, sections 3 and 4.

24 Galič in this volume,section 1; Piszcz in this volume, sections 1–3; and Harsági this volume, section introduction.

25 See chapter on Dutch law, section 1 and Piszcz in this volume, section 4.

26 Galič in this volume, section 6.

27 See Nylund in this volume, section 3.

28 See Piszcz in this volume, section 4 and Galič in this volume, section 5.

29 See Piszcz in this volume, section 4, and Galič in this volume, section 6. The same seems to be true for Norway, see Nylund in this volume, sections 4.1 and 5.

30 See Harsági this volume, section 4.2.

embracing European civil procedure as a field of study early, German academics have made information more easily accessible to practitioners.[31] In France, European civil procedure has mainly been seen as part of international private law and consumer law, thus many questions have received little attention in literature on civil procedure.[32]

5. Attitudes towards Europeanisation

The attitude towards the EU on the national level may influence the level and methods of EU scepticism. Countries with most widespread scepticism towards EU have either chosen not to become members at all, such as Norway, or they are not fully participating in cooperation in civil justice, such as Denmark and England. However, limited participation in the area of freedom, justice and security applies only to certain legal instruments. Procedural rules in legislation having their legal basis in the functioning of the internal market are either directly or indirectly applicable in these countries. Harmonisation through the invisible pillar[33] of both through general EU law principles, such as non-discrimination and effective application of EU law, and through procedural rules in directives applies fully to these countries. Thus, EU law has a significant impact on national civil procedure in these countries as well.

Although one can discern some resistance towards European law from English and Norwegian courts, Danish courts do not seem to be particularly reluctant to EU law. The Janus-faced approach towards Europeanisation of the Norwegian Supreme Courts is partly a result from a hesitance to the EFTA Court and strong national opposition towards EU membership, not resistance to Europeanisation in and of itself. Despite widespread Euroscepticism, Danish courts are the most active Scandinavian court having dialogue with the CJEU, with the highest frequency of request for preliminary rulings both in absolute numbers and per capita.[34]

In Sweden, the influence on EU law on national civil procedure and EU law on civil procedure in general has received limited attention. The legislator has sparsely explored the need for and possibilities of harmonisation of national rules with similar European rules. Most academics show little interest in Europeanisation of civil procedure and the Swedish courts, in particular the Swedish Supreme Court, have made very few references for preliminary rulings.[35]

German and Dutch lawyers and academics have shown a particular interest in Europeanisation of civil procedure law. The courts in both countries have taken an active role in developing EU law by making many references for preliminary rulings. The style and content of European procedural legislation follows the German style, yet German law has retained some of its particularities. Further, German academics have embraced Europeanisation and even developed a specific subfield of procedural law dealing with

31 Hau in this volume, section 2.2.2.

32 Després in this volume, section 1.

33 Krans [n 9].

34 See Nylund in this volume, section 4.1.

35 See Wallerman in this volume, sections 1, 3 and 4. This seems also to be a common approach in England, see Andrews in this volume, section 4.

Europeanisation. There are numerous textbooks and monographs on the topic.[36] A similar development can be traced in the Netherlands, where courts and lawyers alike are increasingly aware of the European dimension of civil procedure and willing to make use of it in their daily work. The Dutch Supreme Court has dealt with the question of *ex officio* application of EU law in a number of cases, and academics have debated that and other topics.[37]

Academics may also influence Europeanisation of national civil procedure. In Germany, European civil procedure has emerged as a sub-discipline of its own including a body of literature consisting of textbooks, commentaries and scholarly publications. In other countries, academic interest has been more limited, sometimes focused on a few particular topics, and still in others almost absent. Academics may contribute by raising awareness of relevant European law and by making information more readily available.

6. Methods of Implementation

Member states choose different methods for absorption of EU procedural law. Depending on the methods for implementation, the willingness and ability of courts and lawyers to recognise questions related to EU law, and the interplay between these and other factors, EU procedural law may either become an appendix, a satellite orbiting national civil procedure, or an integrated part of national civil procedure with potentially transformative, though not always unproblematic, capabilities. In some countries, European civil procedure seems to have become an appendix rather than an integrated part of civil procedure. Therefore, lawyers may consider EU law to be relevant for cross-border cases only.

When implementing EU law, legislators in some countries tend to be open about the European origin of the new legislation, while others are tacit. If the legislator does not express the source of the legislation, interpretation and application of the law can be more difficult. The underlying EU law – be it a directive or soft law – serves as a source for interpretation of the national legislation. Although Poland has implemented collective redress for consumers, the Polish legislator did not disclose on a national level that the background for the measure was a recommendation from the EU.[38] Euroscepticism may be a reason for choosing 'hidden' implementation and approximation of European law. In France, EU procedural law has been implemented in sectorial laws, rather than the Code of Civil Procedure. However, mediation has been introduced by adding a new book to the Code.[39]

The regulations creating European cross-border proceedings, such as the European order for payment procedure[40], are not freestanding and independent of the national civil justice system. On the contrary, national procedural rules govern part of the

36 See Hau in this volume, sections 1 and 2.2.2; and Krans in this volume, section 1.

37 See Krans in this volume, sections 1 and 2.

38 See Piszcz in this volume, section 2.

39 Després in this volume, section 4.

40 Regulation (EC) 1896/2006 creating a European order for payment procedure [2006] OJ L399/1.

procedure and the national legislator should fill gaps and build bridges between the European proceedings and national proceedings.[41] Slovenia has chosen a 'minimalistic' approach for implementation, with no additional measures to implementing regulations, and a 'copy paste' method of implementing some directives. The result has been uncertainty.[42] In Hungary, the legislator has chosen to implement EU law by amending the Hungarian Code of Civil Procedure in a fragmented manner. Changes are made in different parts of the Code, which has resulted in a weakened and less user-friendly structure of the Code.[43] Germany, on the other hand, has chosen to add an eleventh book to the Civil Procedure Code, where rules implementing European procedural law are collected.[44]

European rules on cross-border proceedings and special proceedings for consumer, collective redress and IP cases can serve as model laws for developing national law. However, several authors in this volume point at missed opportunities for advancement of national law. Aligning European procedures, or proceedings induced by European law, with existing national procedures is often rational, as the structure will be more navigable and streamlined. There are nevertheless several examples where Europeanisation result in overlapping procedures and institutions. For example in Belgium, the existing ADR-platform, Belmed, was not included in the implementation of the Consumer ODR Regulation.[45] Neither has the Belgian summary order for payment been amended to mirror the European order for payment procedure, although the Belgian system is according to Taelman in need of amelioration.[46] Similar observations are made in several other papers.[47]

Sometimes EU law function as an argument for specific reforms. Proponents of certain changes can use European law to impel their conceptions. Case law from the European Court of Human Rights was a central argument for the advocates of a strict separation of power in the English debate on constitutional reform and the role of the Lord Chancellor and House of Lords.[48]

7. Enforcement, Coherence and Fragmentation

Member States and the EU have different attitudes towards the second and third pillars of European influences on national civil procedure. From a European point of view, the second and third pillars enhance enforcement of EU law both in a national and cross-

41 If the debtor opposes the European order for payment, proceedings continue before the national courts according to national procedural rules (see article 17 of the regulation). By introducing national rules governing the transition from the European order for payment procedure to national civil proceedings, the legislator can enhance legal certainty of both parties.

42 See Galič in this volume, section 2.1.

43 See Harsági this volume, section 4.

44 For a list of sections of ZPO, see Hau in this volume, section 2.2.2.

45 Regulation (EU) 524/2013 on online resolution for consumer disputes [2013] OJ L165/1.

46 See Taelman in this volume, section 2.

47 See Piszcz in this volume, section 3; Galič in this volume, section 2.2; Wallerman in this volume n, section 1. For criticism towards the approach of 'model laws' see Andrews in this volume, section 5.

48 See Andrews in this volume, section 6.

border perspective. The emphasis is on more efficient enforcement. From a national perspective, the second and third pillar threaten the coherence of the national civil procedure law by introducing special rules for certain types of cases or for cross-border cases.[49] Although special measures in intellectual property right cases increases access to court and efficient remedies, one may ask why a party owning a patent or licence for production should have far better opportunities to secure evidence through disclosure and a better chance to recover legal expenses from the opposing party, than for instance a person injured in a car accident. Why should consumer law be applied *ex officio* to protect the weaker party, when labour law does not even though the employee is in a comparably weak position vis-à-vis the employer? National law becomes inevitably more fragmented.

The aim of the second and third pillar – increased and equivalent enforcement – may paradoxically lead to external fragmentation instead of harmonisation.[50] The regulations creating European cross-border proceedings have to be implemented as they are 'torsos' relying partly on national law. The proper functioning of the regulation is then dependent on the existence and the quality of the 'bridge' between the EU law cross-border proceeding and national proceedings. Implementation of directives always require transposing EU law to national law, which in turn inevitably creates some differences between the countries. Sometimes a change in the conduct of proceedings, the role and duties of the judge, and non-codified principles of evidence is required to bring national civil procedure in conformity with EU law. The underlying legal culture will naturally have a significant influence on the outcome. The result is far from full harmonisation. Full harmonisation is, however, not a *sine qua non* for efficient and equivalent enforcement of EU law and smooth cross-border proceedings.

The underlying legal system and method of implementation may also be part of the explanation of the limited success of the regulations creating special European proceedings for cross-border cases. As the proceedings are party dependent on existing national proceedings, problems with the existing national proceedings will rub off on the European proceedings. Lack of bridges between European proceedings and national proceedings will also decrease the appeal of European proceedings. Where the national proceedings are attractive, the need for European proceedings will be perceived as significantly lower.

8. Outlooks

Our outlook can be short: this project has revealed many aspects on EU law and national civil procedure law. It has also revealed several unanswered questions. It is advisable that academics do not turn away from this topic, but embrace it. Further research might serve as an academic foundation for developing ideas and understanding ongoing processes, but also – and perhaps even foremost – judicial practice, both in domestic cases as in cross border cases.

49 See also Petersen in this volume, section 4; and Krans in this volume, section 5.

50 For more details, see Krans [n 9], 582–585.

There are several options for questions for further research. All or some of the countries in this book can be studied more in detail, or research could be expanded to other Member States. Countries with a similar underlying legal culture and length of membership can be studied to try to reduce the impact of these two factors and to concentrate on other factors, such as the strategies chosen for implementation, or how the interest of legal academics influence Europeanisation. What if the scope is narrowed to take a close look at one specific Directive or topic? A more detailed look at specific types of EU-legislation (Regulations, Directives or the Treaties itself) is another option. Does the level and way of impact of EU law somehow related to legal culture? One can also consider in particular each of the different pillars. There is an interesting road ahead.

INDEX

IUS COMMUNE EUROPAEUM

A peer-reviewed book series in which the common foundations of the legal systems of the Member States of the European Union are the central focus.

The *Ius Commune Europaeum* series includes horizontal comparative legal studies as well as studies on the effect of treaties within the national legal systems. All the classic fields of law are covered. The books are published in various European languages under the auspices of METRO, the Institute for Transnational Legal Research at Maastricht University.

Recently published:
Volume 138: *The Nature of Mutual Recognition in European Law.* W. van Ballegooij
Volume 139: *Evidence in Contemporary Civil Procedure. Fundamental Issues in a Comparative Perspective*, C.H. van Rhee and A. Uzelac (eds.)
Volume 140: *The effect of D&O insurance on managerial risk taking*, Max Gaber
Volume 141: *Information and Notification Duties*, Ilse Samoy and Marco B. Loos
Volume 142: *The Application of the Theory of Efficient Breach in Contract Law. A Comparative Law and Economics Perspective*, Wenqing Liao
Volume 143: *A European Legal Framework for Nuclear Liability. Rethinking Current Approaches*, Tobias Heldt
Volume 144: *The Development of European Private Law in a Multilevel Legal Order*, E.A.G. Van Schagen
Volume 145: *Property Law Perspectives IV*, D. Gruyaert, E. Ramaekers and L. Rostill (eds.)
Volume 146: *The Citizen in European Private Law: Norm-setting, Enforcement and Choice*, C. Cauff man and J. Smits (eds.)
Volume 147: *Legal Certainty in Real Estate Transactions: A Comparison of England and France*, B. Du Marais and D. Marrani (eds.)
Volume 148: *Scarcity and the State I. The Allocation of Limited Rights by the Administration*, P. Adriaanse, F. Van Ommeren, W. Den Ouden and J. Wolswinkel (eds.)
Volume 149: *Optional Instruments of the European Union. A Definitional, Normative and Explanatory Study*, W.A. Bull

www.ingramcontent.com/pod-product-compliance
Ingram Content Group UK Ltd.
Pitfield, Milton Keynes, MK11 3LW, UK
UKHW051927100926
8556IPUK00022B/1423

9 781780 683805